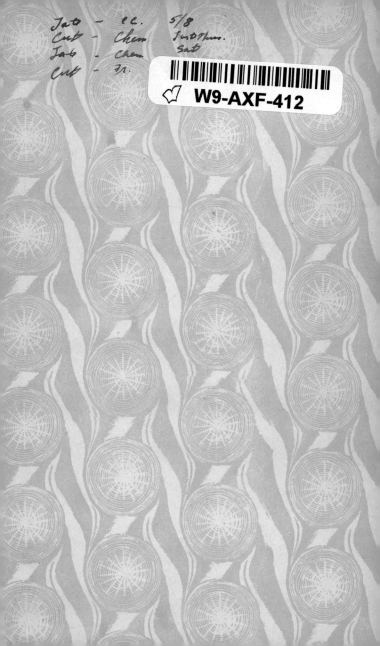

W9-AXF-412

Everyman, I will go with thee, and be thy guide,
In thy most need to go by thy side.

This is No. 843 of Everyman's Library. A
list of authors and their works in this series
will be found at the end of this volume. The
publishers will be pleased to send freely to all
applicants a separate, annotated list of the
Library.

J. M. DENT & SONS LIMITED
10–13 BEDFORD STREET LONDON W.C.2

E. P. DUTTON & CO. INC.
286–302 FOURTH AVENUE
NEW YORK

EVERYMAN'S LIBRARY
EDITED BY ERNEST RHYS

POETRY & THE DRAMA

LAOCOÖN, NATHAN THE WISE
and MINNA VON BARNHELM
BY GOTTHOLD EPHRAIM LESSING
TRANSLATED WITH AN INTRO-
DUCTION BY WILLIAM A. STEEL

GOTTHOLD EPHRAIM LESSING, born in
1729 in Upper Lusatia. Educated at Leipzig
University. Visited England, and afterwards
lived in Berlin and Leipzig. Travelled to
Italy, 1772. Died in 1781.

LAOCOÖN

NATHAN THE WISE

MINNA VON BARNHELM

LESSING

LONDON: J. M. DENT & SONS LTD.
NEW YORK: E. P. DUTTON & CO. INC.

All rights reserved
Made in Great Britain
at The Temple Press Letchworth
and decorated by Eric Ravilious
for
J. M. Dent & Sons Ltd.
Aldine House Bedford St. London
Toronto   .   Vancouver
Melbourne . Wellington
First Published in this Edition 1930

INTRODUCTION

A feature in the story of German literature which all its critics have remarked is the rapidity of its development in the course of the eighteenth century, and the astonishing contrast between the opening and the closing decades of the period. The second half of the century witnessed the outburst of splendour in Goethe and Schiller and Kant, and showed Germany keeping step with England and France. The fertilising influences of the Renaissance had reached Germany late, for in England the Elizabethan age had come, and flourished in full luxuriance, and Milton had followed his greater predecessor, whilst in Germany poetry, drama and literature generally still remained a poverty-stricken and almost negligible product.

There were special reasons for this retardation. Early in the seventeenth century the curse of war had brooded heavily over Europe, with particular darkness over Germany—for thirty years the cock-pit where was fought out the fateful struggle between the Catholic South and the Protestant North. On both sides the armies were mercenaries, and their marches to and fro were marches of military locusts, devouring and destroying everywhere. Nor was it merely material desolation that resulted; the springs of intellectual and spiritual activity also were choked in the universal debacle. The war was over by 1648, but a prolonged period was required for complete recovery.

Another hindrance to the advance of German letters was the absence of national unity, the want of an acknowledged centre of the national life. Berlin, Leipzig, Hamburg, all contended for the central place, at least in the production of books and in theatrical enterprise; and thus an advantage was lost which England and France enjoyed by their great capitals. It is also worth remarking that whatever furtherance for intellectual activities can be looked for from men in the high places of society was conspicuously wanting. The King himself, the great Frederick, besides being almost exclusively absorbed by the interests of his army, was cold not only to German literature but even to the German language. He liked to speak French and to have Frenchmen about him. There is nothing blameworthy in Frederick's preference. Who is there that does not prefer lightness, clarity and grace to heaviness and clumsiness? If we criticise the mistaken notions of French dramatists of those days, their bondage to ancient rules and examples, let us at the same time freely acknowledge their merits. Lessing himself confesses that he owed much to them, acknowledging a particular obligation to Diderot, as " the man who has taken so great a share in forming his taste. Be this what it may," he writes, " I know that without Diderot's example and doctrines it would have taken a quite different direction." Frederick's preference for French writers, then, can be easily understood, yet the natural consequence of his attitude was undoubtedly to chill and discourage German authors and to undermine their efforts. Frederick's real service was in a different field; he brought to Germany a national self-consciousness and self-confidence which it had hitherto lacked.

When, moreover, German literature began once more to show signs of vitality and renewal, the leaders who undertook its superintendence were unfortunately unequal to the task. They wanted the natural genius which the great business demanded, and they followed mistaken paths. For some time before Lessing's birth in 1729, the outstanding literary figure was Gottsched, dictator for a generation in German letters, implicitly obeyed by all who wrote. The praise cannot be withheld from him of labouring indefatigably to stir up amongst aspiring men the ambition to write well; but by all accounts we have of him his place was distinctly in the second class, a man pedantical and essentially prosaic, without the gift of critical discernment. This was characteristically shown in the book he issued for the guidance of poets—*Kritische Dichtkunst für die Deutschen*, a volume of precepts and rules from which none must deviate. Lessing quietly laughs at Gottsched's classification of a collection of poems he published—1st class, poems addressed to Royal personages; 2nd, those addressed to counts, noble people, and such-like; 3rd, friendly lyrics! It was idle to look for inspiration to Gottsched : rules and precepts may furnish useful warnings against grave blunders, but they also can easily become bonds and fetters. The worst of his counsel was that he directed his disciples to wrong models and false ideals; they were instructed to imitate the French in their artificial and pseudo-classic drama, in short, to imitate what was itself an imitation. There could be only one result—originality and independence were discountenanced, and the denial of freedom led to lifeless and uninspired performances. To rely on a code of rules, or even on patterns drawn from Greek perfection, was a mistake. A wiser counsel by far is embodied in the old poet's words—" *Look in thy heart, and write !* "

No wonder, then, that under tuition like Gottsched's the field of German poetry and drama took on the aspect of Ezekiel's vision, a valley of dry bones. It had, however, now not long to wait for an inspiring breath to restore it to life and vigour, to bring flesh again on the dry bones, and set it on its feet, standing up boldly in freedom and self-reliance. After a faint dawn of day in Klopstock's poem *Der Messias*, a rather ineffectual echo of Milton's *Paradise Lost*, the full sunlight broke on the desolate scene from the genius of Lessing. His was the life-giving spirit. No qualifications were lacking to him for the task. From his early boyhood he was a student and lover of books, and he speedily acquired a knowledge of Greek and Roman literature that was extraordinarily wide and exact, as a thousand passages in *Laocoön* bear witness. His faultless taste was early formed, and his native gifts, a keen analytic intellect and instinctive justness of judgment, made him the perfect critic. No better plan of education could have been framed for him than to be permitted to browse in the library at home, and to be taught the rudiments of learning by his father, who did this work so thoroughly that young Lessing, entering at the age of twelve the " Prince's School " in Meissen, immediately took a foremost place among his fellows. " Tasks which others find too hard," wrote the rector to the father, " are child's play to him."

The design of Lessing's parents was that he should follow his father's profession. This was entirely contrary to his own inclinations. It was only after years of painful struggle, in which he had to endure much misunderstanding and censure of the bitterest kind, that he could enter upon his chosen career as a dramatist and journalist. His father and mother were puritans of the straitest sect, with a fanatical fear and hatred of the stage, an attitude which even now is not unknown amongst ourselves, especially in provincial places. Indirectly, no doubt, the narrow-mindedness and persecution of which he was so intimate a witness were a stimulus to Lessing in the frequent controversies of his career, in which he was always a champion of freedom and tolerance. With his characteristic tenacity he held to his own choice.

Parenthetically, it may be remarked how great a part of Lessing's energy was expended in controversy : not only on dramatic or purely literary questions, though these drew volume after volume from him, but on theology and philosophy, which largely engaged his pen for years together. It was labour he delighted in, for he was a born controversialist. His keen wit, his stores of exact and many-sided knowledge, gave him a peculiar advantage in these contests, and he enjoyed the still greater advantage that he contended only for truth, when his opponents were more concerned for orthodoxy. The enemies he chiefly loved to assail were bigotry, narrow-mindedness and pretension. When Lessing began in earnest his efforts to raise German literature and drama to a higher level, he followed his favourite method of controversy and chose for an object of attack, Gottsched, the literary dictator, as the embodiment of the principles and practice that were hindering the advance.

" Our tragedies were full of nonsense, bombast, filth, and the wit of the mob. Our comedies consisted of disguises and enchantments, and blows were their wittiest ideas. To see this corruption it was not necessary to be the finest and greatest spirit. And Herr Gottsched was not the first who saw it ; he was only the first who had confidence in his own power to remove it. And how did he set to work ? He understood a little French, and began to translate ; everyone who could rhyme and understand ' Oui, monsieur,' he encouraged also to translate. . . . If the masterpieces of Shakespeare, with some modest changes, had been translated, I am convinced that better consequences would have followed than could follow from acquaintance with Corneille and Racine. . . .

For genius can only be kindled by genius; and most easily by a genius which seems to have to thank nature for everything and does not frighten us away by the tedious perfections of art." [1]

We have here one out of many proofs of Lessing's acquaintance with and sympathetic appreciation of the English dramatic writers. The drama is, of course, his chief interest, but his knowledge of other departments of our literature extended beyond it. In an article contributed to a quarterly magazine projected in Berlin he has the following on an effort by some of his friends to imitate the essays of the English *Spectator* :—
" You know who were the first authors in this kind of literature—men wanting neither in wit, thought, scholarship nor knowledge of the world—Englishmen who, in the greatest calm, and in easy circumstances, could study with attention whatever influences the spirit and manners of the nation. But who are their imitators among us? For the most part, young witlings, who had scarce mastered the German language." [2]

The first really notable dramatic work of Lessing was a prose tragedy, *Miss Sara Sampson*, in which the influence of English models was immediately traced, and which was forthwith pronounced a novel type—a " *bürgerliches Trauerspiel* " it was styled, or " tragedy of common life." This piece had, therefore, an importance in the history of the German theatre beyond its intrinsic literary or theatrical value; it marked the beginning of an epoch, and became the favourite type on the German stage. From the day of its production the regard of German playwrights was turned not to France but to England. Lessing had written successful comedies when scarcely out of his boyhood, but *Miss Sara Sampson* made him known to the nation and to foreign critics. It also confirmed Lessing in the choice of dramatic writing as his proper sphere. More triumphant successes were soon to follow. It was in the three well-known dramas—*Emilia Galotti, Minna von Barnhelm* and *Nathan der Weise*—that Lessing reached his highest level.

It is perhaps the last-named that is best known, but each of the three is worthy of his genius. *Emilia Galotti* is a tragedy on the lines of the story of Roman Virginia, most poignantly

[1] Sime's *Lessing*, Vol. I. p. 181.   [2] *Ibid.*, p. 127.

affecting, well-constructed for stage purposes (eminently *bühnen-fähig* as the Germans say), but almost too painful for popular acceptance. *Minna von Barnhelm* is the best of German comedies, all critics agree; it is a story of military life in the Frederician time, full of humour and good-humour, touched here and there, but only slightly, with the German weakness of over-sentimentality, and having the great merit of being as enjoyable to-day as when it was first produced. This in itself is a testimony to the human quality of it. The characterisation is superbly worked out, every figure an unmistakable personality. It is still frequently staged. A few months ago a representation was given in London, under the auspices of the British Drama League, and was heartily received although the actors were but young pupils, boys and girls, of a municipal school in a German town. *Nathan der Weise* is more properly a dramatic poem than a stage play, an eloquent plea for *tolerance*, and embodying much of the earnest thought of Lessing upon subjects lying nearest to his heart. These two plays, along with the famous essay in literary criticism, *Laocoön*, are the fragments of Lessing's immense production presented in this little volume of translations. The *Laocoön* is too large and too multifarious for any attempt at detailed description in this brief preface. In its own department of literary criticism it is authoritative, and one of the acknowledged classics of the world.

Before closing these introductory words something should be said of the personal fortunes of Lessing. He was born in 1729 in Kamenz, a small town in the kingdom of Saxony, where his father was Pastor Primarius, or chief pastor, of the place. His short life of fifty-two years, ending in 1781 in Brunswick, was a record of incessant and ill-rewarded labour, vexed perpetually by care and poverty. He quickly gained his wide reputation as a critic and dramatist, and his work, especially his excellent dramatic pieces, ought to have brought him at least the means of comfortable living, if not a fortune. So far from this was his experience that, at the close, what he possessed did not suffice to cover the expenses of his funeral. One secret of his troubles was the constant demands upon him for help made by the poor pastor's large family at home, whose members thought that a man so distinguished as their famous brother must have an income corresponding, whereas

he was frequently himself in the most desperate straits. Until
1776, when he was forty-seven, he was not in a position to
marry. His wife, Eva König, to whom he had been greatly
attached for many years, was the widow of a manufacturer in
Vienna. It was the happiest of unions, but even here ill-luck
pursued him, for his wife lived only one year after marriage,
dying in childbirth.

Lessing's days were few and full of trouble; they were full
also of most fruitful labour. After two centuries his fame
continues, based firmly on his dramatic poems, and even more
securely on his critical writings, which the world will not
willingly let die.

W. A. S.

BIBLIOGRAPHY OF
GOTTHOLD EPHRAIM LESSING
(1729–1781)

COLLECTED WORKS : The most important of these is edited by
K. Lachmann, the Sämmtliche Schriften appearing in 13 vols. in
Berlin, 1838–40; in 12 vols. in Leipzig, 1853–57; reissued by F.
Muncker in 23 vols., 1886–1924.

PLAYS : Die Alte Jungfer, a comedy in 3 acts, 1749; Philotas, a
tragedy in 1 act, 1759; Der Misogyne, a comedy in 2 acts, 1762;
Der Junge Gelehrte in der Einbildung, a comedy in 1 act, 1764;
Minna von Barnhelm, a comedy in 5 acts, 1767; trans. into English
by J. J. Johnstone, as The Disbanded Officer, 1786; anonymously
as The School for Honour, 1799; by Fanny Holcroft, 1806; by
W. E. Wrankmore, 1858; by Major-General P. Maxwell, 1899; by
E. U. Ouless as The Way of Honour, 1929. Emilia Galotti, a tragedy
in 5 acts, 1772, trans. into Eng. by B. Thompson 1801; by Fanny
Holcroft, 1805; by C. L. Lewes, 1867. Miss Sara Sampson, first
bourgeois tragedy of the German stage, in 5 acts, 1772; Nathan der
Weise, dramatic poem, in 5 acts, 1779; the most widely translated
of all Lessing's works, trans. into English by R. E. Raspe, 1781;
by Wm. Taylor of Norwich, 1791; by A. Reid, 1860; by E. Frothingham, 2nd ed., 1868; by Andrew Wood, 1877; by E. K. Corbett,
1883; by R. D. Boylan, 1888; by W. Jacks, 1894; by Major-
General P. Maxwell, 1895. Faust, 1836; Der Schatz, comedy in
1 act, 1877.

MISCELLANEOUS WORKS : Ein Vade Mecum für den Herrn Samuel
Gotthold Lange, a criticism of Lange's trans. of Horace, etc., 1754;
Pope ein Metaphysiker, in collaboration with Moses Mendelssohn,
1755; Fabeln, 1759; trans. by J. Richardson, 1773; anonymously
in 1825, 1829, 1845, 1860. Selected Fables ed. by Carl Heath, 1907;
Laokoon, 1766, followed by numerous other editions in Germany;
trans. by W. Ross, 1836; by E. C. Beasley, 1853, revised edition,
1888; by Sir R. Phillimore, 1874, other editions, 1905, 1910; by

E. Frothingham, 1874. Briefe Antiquarischen Inhalts, 1768; Hamburgische Dramaturgie, theatrical criticisms, 1769; Selections edited by G. Waterhouse, 1926; Kleinigkeiten, a volume of poems, 1769; Wie die Alten den Tod gebildet, an important essay, 1769; Berengarius Turonensis, 1770; Zur Geschichte und Litteratur, 3 vols., 1773–81; Eine Parabel, a reply to the criticisms of Pastor Goetze, 1778; Ernst und Falk, 1778–1870; trans. as Lessing's Masonic Dialogues, by the Rev. A. Cohen, 1927. Die Erziehung des Menschengeschlechts, 1780; trans. as The Education of the Human Race, by F. W. Robertson, 1858; latest edition, 1927. Fragmente des Wolfenbuttel'schen ungenannten, a rationalistic attack on Christianity, 1784; Leben des Sophokles, 1790.

LETTERS: Freundschaftlicher Briefwechsel zwischen G. E Lessing und seiner Frau, 1789; Gelehrter Briefwechsel zwischen ihm, J. J. Reisse und Moses Mendelssohn, 1789 and 1820; Briefwechsel mit seinen Bruder K. G. Lessing, 1795; Briefwechsel mit Frau W. Gleim, 1757–79, 1795; Briefwechsel zwischen Lessing und seiner Frau, 1870.

BIOGRAPHIES: In German the most important are those by C. G Lessing, 1793; by T. W. Danzel, 1850–54, 2nd ed., 1880; by A Stahr, 1859; trans. into English by E. P. Evans, 1866; by J. H. J Dünster, 1882; by Erich Schmidt, 1884, 3rd ed., 1909; by A. W Ernst, 1903.

In English there are Lives by James Sime, New York, 1877; by Helen Zimmern, 1878; by T. W. H. Rolleston, with a bibliography by J. P. Anderson, 1889. See also Wilhelm Todt: Lessing in England, 1767–1850, 1912.

CONTENTS

LAOCOÖN

OR

THE LIMITS OF PAINTING AND POETRY:

WITH INCIDENTAL ILLUSTRATIONS ON VARIOUS POINTS IN THE HISTORY OF ANCIENT ART

"Ὕλη καὶ τρόποις μιμήσεως διαφέρουσι
(Πλουτ. ποτ. Ἀθ. κατὰ Π. ἢ κατὰ Σ. ἐνδ.)

B

LAOCOÖN

PREFACE

THE first who likened painting and poetry to each other must have been a man of delicate perception, who found that both arts affected him in a similar manner. Both, he realised, present to us appearance as reality, absent things as present; both deceive, and the deceit of either is pleasing.

A second sought to penetrate to the essence of the pleasure, and discovered that in both it flows from one source. Beauty, the conception of which we at first derive from bodily objects, has general rules which can be applied to various things : to actions, to thoughts, as well as to forms.

A third, who reflected on the value and the application of these general rules, observed that some of them were predominant rather in painting, others rather in poetry; that, therefore, in the latter poetry could help out painting, in the former painting help out poetry, with illustrations and examples.

The first was the amateur; the second the philosopher; the third the critic.

The two former could not easily make a false use either of their feeling or of their conclusions. But in the remarks of the critic, on the other hand, almost everything depends on the justice of their application to the individual case; and, where there have been fifty witty to one clear-eyed critic, it would have been a miracle if this application had at all times been made with the circumspection needful to hold the balance true between the two arts.

Supposing that Apelles and Protogenes in their lost treatises upon painting confirmed and illustrated the rules of the same by the already settled rules of poetry, then one can certainly believe it must have been done with the moderation and exactitude with which we still find Aristotle, Cicero, Horace, Quintilian, in their writings, applying the principles and practice of painting to eloquence and poetry. It is the prerogative of the ancients, in everything to do neither too much nor too little.

But we moderns in several things have considered ourselves

their betters, when we transformed their pleasant little bye-
ways to highroads, even if the shorter and safer highroads
shrink again to footpaths as they lead us through the wilds.

The startling antithesis of the Greek Voltaire, that painting
is a dumb poetry, and poetry a vocal painting, certainly was
not to be found in any manual. It was a sudden inspiration,
such as Simonides had more than once; the true element in it
is so illuminating that we are inclined to ignore what in it is
false or doubtful.

Nevertheless, the ancients did not ignore it. Rather, whilst
they confined the claim of Simonides solely to the effect of the
two arts, they did not omit to point out that, notwithstanding
the complete similarity of this effect, they were yet distinct,
both in their subjects and in the manner of their imitation
(ὕλη καὶ τρόποις μιμήσεως).

But entirely as if no such difference existed, many of our
most recent critics have drawn from that correspondence
between painting and poetry the crudest conclusions in the
world. Now they force poetry into the narrower bounds of
painting; and again, they propose to painting to fill the whole
wide sphere of poetry. Everything that is right for the one is
to be granted to the other also; everything which in the one
pleases or displeases is necessarily to please or displease in the
other; and, obsessed by this notion, they utter in the most
confident tone the shallowest judgments; and we see them,
in dealing with the works of poets and painters beyond reproach,
making it a fault if they deviate from one another, and casting
blame now on this side and now on that, according as they
themselves have a taste for poetry or for painting.

Indeed, this newer criticism has in part seduced the virtuosos
themselves. It has engendered in poetry the rage for description, and in painting the rage for allegorising, in the effort to
turn the former into a speaking picture without really knowing
what she can and should paint, and to turn the latter into a
silent poem without considering in what measure she can
express general concepts and not at the same time depart from
her vocation and become a freakish kind of writing.

To counteract this false taste and these ill-founded judgments is the primary object of the pages that follow. They
have come together incidentally, according to the order of my
reading, instead of being built up by a methodical development
of general principles. They are, therefore, rather unordered
collectanea for a book than themselves a book.

Yet I flatter myself that even as such they are not wholly to be despised. Of systematic books there is no lack amongst us Germans. Out of a few assumed definitions to deduce most logically whatever we will—this we can manage as well as any nation in the world.

Baumgarten confessed that for a great part of the examples in his *Æsthetics* he was indebted to Gesner's Dictionary. If my argument is not as conclusive as Baumgarten's, at all events my examples will taste more of the original sources.

As I started, as it were, from Laocoön and return to him several times, I have desired to give him a share in the superscription. Some other little digressions concerning various points in the history of ancient art contribute less to my purpose, and they only stand here because I cannot hope ever to find for them a more suitable place.

I would further remind the reader that under the name of Painting I include the plastic arts in general, and am not prepared to maintain that under the name of Poetry I may not have had some regard also to the other arts whose method of imitation is progressive.

I

THE general distinguishing excellence of the Greek master-pieces in painting and sculpture Herr Winckelmann places in a noble simplicity and quiet greatness, both in arrangement and in expression. "Just as the depths of the sea," he says, "always remain quiet, however the surface may rage, in like manner the expression in the figures of the Greek artists shows under all passions a great and steadfast soul.

"This soul is depicted in the countenance of the Laocoön, and not in the countenance alone, under the most violent sufferings. The pain which discovers itself in every muscle and sinew of the body, and which, without regarding the face and other parts, one seems almost oneself to feel from the painfully contracted abdomen alone—this pain, I say, yet expresses itself in the countenance and in the entire attitude without passion. He raises no agonising cry, as Virgil sings of his Laocoön; the opening of the mouth does not permit it: much rather is it an oppressed and weary sigh, as Sadolet describes it. The pain of the body and the greatness of the soul are by the whole build of the figure distributed and, as it were, weighed out in equal parts. Laocoön suffers, but he suffers like the Philoctetes of Sophocles: his misery touches us to the soul; but we should like to be able to endure misery as this great man endures it.

"The expression of so great a soul goes far beyond the fashioning which beautiful Nature gives. The artist must have felt in himself the strength of spirit which he impressed upon the marble. Greece had artist and philosopher in one person, and more than one Metrodorus. Wisdom stretched out her hand to Art and breathed more than common souls into the figures that she wrought," etc., etc.

The remark which is fundamental here—that the pain does not show itself in the countenance of Laocoön with the passion which one would expect from its violence—is perfectly just. This, too, is incontestable, that even in this very point in which a sciolist might judge the artist to have come short of Nature

6

and not to have reached the true pathos of the pain : that just here, I say, his wisdom has shone out with especial brightness.

Only in the reason which Winckelmann gives for this wisdom, and in the universality of the rule which he deduces from this reason, I venture to be of a different opinion.

I confess that the disapproving side-glance which he casts on Virgil at first took me rather aback; and, next to that, the comparison with Philoctetes. I will make this my starting-point, and write down my thoughts just in the order in which they come.

"Laocoön suffers like the Philoctetes of Sophocles." How, then, does the latter suffer? It is singular that his suffering has left with us such different impressions—the complaints, the outcry, the wild curses, with which his pain filled the camp and disturbed the sacrifices and all the sacred functions, resounded no less terribly through the desert island, as it was in part they that banished him thither. What sounds of anger, of lamentation, of despair, by which even the poet in his imitation made the theatre resound! People have found the third act of this drama disproportionately short compared with the rest. From this one gathers, say the critics, that the ancient dramatists considered an equal length of acts as of small consequence. That, indeed, I believe; but in this question I should prefer to base myself upon another example than this. The piteous outcries, the whimpering, the broken ἆ, ἆ, φεῦ, ἀτταταῖ, ὤμοι, μοι! the whole long lines full of παπα, παπα, of which this act consists and which must have been declaimed with quite other hesitations and drawings-out of utterance than are needful in a connected speech, doubtless made this act last pretty well as long in the presentation as the others. On paper it appears to the reader far shorter than it would to the listeners.

To cry out is the natural expression of bodily pain. Homer's wounded warriors not seldom fall to the ground with cries. Venus scratched screams loudly; not in order that she may be shown as the soft goddess of pleasure, but rather that suffering Nature may have her rights. For even the iron Mars, when he feels the spear of Diomede, screams so horribly, like ten thousand raging warriors at once, that both hosts are terrified.

However high in other respects Homer raises his heroes above Nature, they yet ever remain faithful to her when it comes to the point of feeling pain and injury, and to the utterance of this feeling by cries, or tears, or abusive language.

By their deeds they are creatures of a superior order, by their sensibilities mere men.

I am well aware that we Europeans of a wiser posterity know better how to control our mouth and our eyes. Politeness and dignity forbid cries and tears. The active fortitude of the first rude ages has with us been transformed into the fortitude of endurance. Yet even our own ancestors were greater in the latter than in the former. Our ancestors, however, were barbarians. To conceal all pains, to face the stroke of death with unaltered eye, to die smiling under the teeth of vipers, to bewail neither his sin nor the loss of his dearest friend, are the marks of the ancient Northern hero. Palnatoko gave his Jomsburgers the command to fear nothing nor once to utter the word fear.

Not so the Greek ! He both felt and feared ; he uttered his pain and his trouble ; he was ashamed of no human weaknesses ; but none must hold him back on the way to honour or from the fulfilment of duty. What with the barbarian sprang from savagery and hardness, was wrought in him by principle. With him heroism was like the hidden sparks in the flint, which sleep quietly so long as no outward force awakes them, and take from the stone neither its clearness nor its coldness. With the barbarian, heroism was a bright devouring flame, which raged continually and consumed, or at least darkened, every other good quality in him. When Homer leads out the Trojans to battle with wild outcries, and the Greeks, on the other hand, in resolute silence, the commentators remark with justice that the poet in this wishes to depict those as barbarians and these as civilised people. I am surprised that they have not remarked in another passage a similar characteristic contrast. The opposing hosts have concluded a truce ; they are busy with the burning of their dead, which on neither side takes place without hot tears : δάκρυα θερμὰ χέοντες. But Priam forbids his Trojans to weep ; οὐδ' εἴα κλαίειν Πρίαμος μέγας. He forbids them to weep, says the Dacier, because he dreads that they will weaken themselves too much and return to battle on the morrow with less courage. Good ! But I ask, Why must Priam dread this ? Why does not Agamemnon, too, give his Greeks the same command ? The sense of the poet goes deeper. He would teach us that only the civilised Greek can at the same time weep and be brave, whilst the uncivilised Trojan in order to be so must first stifle all human feeling. Νεμεσσῶμαί γε μὲν οὐδὲν κλαίειν, in another place, he puts in the mouth of the understanding son of wise Nestor.

It is worthy of remark that amongst the few tragedies that have come down to us from antiquity two pieces are to be found in which bodily pain is not the smallest part of the calamity that befalls the suffering hero : there is, besides the Philoctetes, the dying Hercules. And even the latter Sophocles represents complaining, whining, weeping and crying aloud. Thanks to our polite neighbours, those masters of the becoming, to-day a whimpering Philoctetes, a screaming Hercules, would be the most laughable, the most unendurable persons on the stage. It is true one of their latest dramatists has ventured on Philoctetes. But would he venture to show them the true Philoctetes?

Amongst the lost dramas of Sophocles is numbered even a " Laocoön." Would that Fate had only granted us this Laocoön also! From the slight references made to it by some ancient grammarians it is not easy to gather how the theme was handled. Of one thing I feel sure : that the poet will not have depicted Laocoön as more of a stoic than Philoctetes and Hercules. All stoicism is untheatrical, and our pity is always proportionate to the suffering which the interesting subject expresses. If we see him bear his misery with greatness of soul, then indeed this greatness of soul will excite our admiration, but admiration is a cold emotion, whose passive wonder excludes every other warmer passion as well as every other more significant representation.

And now I come to the inference I wish to draw. If it is true that outcries on the feeling of bodily pain, especially according to the ancient Greek way of thinking, can quite well consist with a great soul; then the expression of such a soul cannot be the reason why, nevertheless, the artist in his marble refuses to imitate this crying : there must be other grounds why he deviates here from his rival, the poet, who expresses this crying with obvious intention.

II

Whether it be fable or history that Love prompted the first attempt in the plastic arts, it is at least certain that she was never weary of lending her guiding hand to the ancient masters. For if painting, as the art which imitates bodies on plane surfaces, is now generally practised with an unlimited range of subject, certainly the wise Greek set her much straiter bounds, and confined her solely to the imitation of beautiful bodies. His artist portrayed nothing but the beautiful; even the ordinary beautiful, beauty of inferior kinds, was for him only an occasional theme, an exercise, a recreation. In his work the perfection of the subject itself must give delight; he was too great to demand of those who beheld it that they should content themselves with the bare, cold pleasure arising from a well-caught likeness or from the daring of a clever effort; in his art nothing was dearer to him, and to his thinking nothing nobler, than the ultimate purpose of art.

"Who will wish to paint you, when no one wishes to see you?" says an old epigrammatist concerning an extremely misshapen man. Many a more modern artist would say, "Be you as misshapen as is possible, I will paint you nevertheless. Though, indeed, no one may wish to see you, people will still wish to see my picture; not in so far as it represents you, but in so far as it is a demonstration of my art, which knows how to make so good a likeness of such a monster."

To be sure, with pitiful dexterities that are not ennobled by the worth of their subjects, the propensity to such rank boasting is too natural for the Greeks to have escaped without their Pauson, their Pyreicus. They had them; but they did strict justice upon them. Pauson, who confined himself entirely to the beauty of vulgar things and whose lower taste delighted most in the faulty and ugly in human shape, lived in the most sordid poverty. And Pyreicus, who painted, with all the diligence of a Dutch artist, nothing but barbers' shops, filthy factories, donkeys and cabbages, as if that kind of thing had so much charm in Nature and were so rarely to be seen, got the nickname of the rhyparograph, the dirt-painter, although the luxurious rich weighed his works against gold, to help out their merit by this imaginary value.

The magistrates themselves considered it not unworthy of their attention to keep the artist by force in his proper sphere. The law of the Thebans, which commanded him in his imitation to add to beauty, and forbade under penalties the exaggeration of the ugly, is well known. It was no law against the bungler, as it is usually, and even by Junius, considered. It condemned the Greek "Ghezzi"; the unworthy artifice of achieving likeness by exaggeration of the uglier parts of the original: in a word, caricature.

Indeed, it was direct from the spirit of the Beautiful that the law of the Hellanodiken proceeded. Every Olympian victor received a statue; but only to the three-times victor was an Iconian statue awarded. Of mediocre portraits there ought not to be too many amongst works of art. For although even a portrait admits of an ideal, still the likeness must be the first consideration; it is the ideal of a certain man, not the ideal of a man.

We laugh when we hear that with the ancients even the arts were subject to municipal laws. But we are not always right when we laugh. Unquestionably the laws must not usurp power over the sciences, for the ultimate purpose of the sciences is truth. Truth is a necessity of the soul; and it is nothing but tyranny to offer her the slightest violence in satisfying this essential need. The ultimate purpose of the arts, on the other hand, is pleasure, and pleasure can be dispensed with. So, of course, it may depend on the law-giver what kind of pleasure, and in what measure any kind of it, he will permit. The plastic arts in particular, beyond the unfailing influence they exert on the character of a nation, are capable of an effect that demands the close supervision of the law. When beautiful men fashioned beautiful statues, these in their turn affected them, and the State had beautiful statues in part to thank for beautiful citizens. With us the tender, imaginative power of mothers appears to express itself only in monsters.

From this point of view I believe that in certain ancient legends, which men cast aside without hesitation as lies, something of truth may be recognised. The mothers of Aristomenes, of Aristodamas, of Alexander the Great, of Scipio, of Augustus, of Galerius, all dreamed in their pregnancy that they had to do with a serpent. The serpent was a symbol of deity, and the beautiful statues and pictures of a Bacchus, an Apollo, a Mercury and a Hercules were seldom without a serpent. The honest women had by day feasted their eyes on the god, and the bewildering dream called up the image of the reptile. Thus I save the dream, and surrender the interpretation which the pride of their sons and the shamelessness of flatterers gave it. For there must certainly be a reason why the adulterous phantasy was never anything but a serpent.

Here, however, I am going off the line. I merely wished to establish the fact that with the ancients beauty was the supreme law of the plastic arts. And this being established, it necessarily follows that all else after which also the plastic arts might strive, if it were inconsistent with beauty must wholly yield to her, and if it were consistent with beauty must at least be subordinate.

I will dwell a little longer on *expression*. There are passions and degrees of passion which express themselves in the countenance by the most hideous grimaces, and put the whole frame into such violent postures that all the beautiful lines are lost which define it in a quieter condition. From these, therefore, the ancient artists either abstained wholly or reduced them to lower degrees in which they were capable of a measure of beauty. Rage and despair disfigured none of their works. I dare maintain that they never depicted a Fury.

Wrath they reduced to sternness : with the poet it was an angry Jupiter who sent forth his lightnings ; with the artist the god was calmly grave.

Lamentation was toned down to sadness. And where this softening could not take place, where lamentation would have been just as deforming as belittling—what then did Timanthes ? His picture of Iphigenia's sacrifice, in which he imparted to all the company the peculiar degree of sadness befitting them individually, but veiled the father's face, which should have shown the supreme degree, is well known, and many nice things have been said about it. He had, says one, so exhausted himself in sorrowful countenances that he despaired of being able to give the father one yet more grief-stricken. He confessed thereby, says another, that the pain of a father in such events is beyond all expression. I, for my part, see here neither the impotence of the artist nor the impotence of art. With the degree of emotion the traces of it are correspondingly heightened in the countenance ; the highest degree is accompanied by the most decided traces of all, and nothing is easier for the artist than to exhibit them. But Timanthes knew the limits which the Graces set to his art. He knew that such misery as fell to Agamemnon's lot as a father expresses itself by distortions which are at all times ugly. So far as beauty and dignity could be united with the expression of sorrow, so far he carried it. He might have been willing to omit the ugliness had he been willing to mitigate the sorrow ; but as his composition did not admit of both, what else remained to him but to veil it ? What he dared not paint he left to be guessed. In a word, this veiling was a sacrifice which the artist offered to Beauty. It is an example, not how one should force expression beyond the bounds of art, but rather how one must subject it to the first law of art, the law of Beauty.

And if we now refer this to the Laocoön, the motive for which I am looking becomes evident. The master was striving after the highest beauty, under the given circumstances of bodily pain. This, in its full deforming violence, it was not possible to unite with that. He was obliged, therefore, to abate, to lower it, to tone down cries to sighing; not because cries betrayed an ignoble soul, but because they disfigure the face in an unpleasing manner. Let one only, in imagination, open wide the mouth in Laocoön, and judge! Let him shriek, and see! It was a form that inspired pity because it showed beauty and pain together; now it has become an ugly, a loathsome form, from which one gladly turns away one's face, because the aspect of pain excites discomfort without the beauty of the suffering subject changing this discomfort into the sweet feeling of compassion.

The mere wide opening of the mouth—apart from the fact that the other parts of the face are thereby violently and unpleasantly distorted—is a blot in painting and a fault in sculpture which has the most untoward effect possible. Montfaucon showed little taste when he passed off an old, bearded head with widespread mouth for an oracle-pronouncing Jupiter. Must a god shriek when he unveils the future? Would a pleasing contour of the mouth make his speech suspicious? I do not even believe Valerius, that Ajax in the imaginary picture of Timanthes should have cried aloud. Far inferior artists, in times when art was already degraded, never once allow the wildest barbarians, when, under the victor's sword, terror and mortal anguish seize them, to open the mouth to shrieking-point.

Certain it is that this reduction of extremest physical pain to a lower degree of feeling is apparent in several works of ancient art. The suffering Hercules in the poisoned garment, from the hand of an unknown ancient master, was not the Sophoclean who shrieked so horribly that the Locrian cliffs and the Euboean headlands resounded. It was more sad than wild. The Philoctetes of Pythagoras Leontinus appeared to impart his pain to the beholder, an effect which the slightest trace of the horrible would have prevented. Some may ask where I have learnt that this master made a statue of Philoctetes? From a passage of Pliny which ought not to have awaited my emendation, so manifestly forged or garbled is it.

III

But, as we have already seen, Art in these later days has been assigned far wider boundaries. Let her imitative hand, folks say, stretch out to the whole of visible Nature, of which the Beautiful is only a small part. Let fidelity and truth of expression be her first law, and as Nature herself at all times sacrifices beauty to higher purposes, so also must the artist subordinate it to his general aim and yield to it no further than fidelity of expression permits. Enough, if by truth and faithful expression an ugliness of Nature be transformed into a beauty of Art.

Granted that one would willingly, to begin with, leave these conceptions uncontested in their worth or worthlessness, ought not other considerations quite independent of them to be examined—namely, why the artist is obliged to set bounds to expression and never to choose for it the supreme moment of an action?

The fact that the material limits of Art confine her imitative effort to one single moment will, I believe, lead us to similar conclusions.

If the artist can never, in presence of ever-changing Nature, choose and use more than one single moment, and the painter in particular can use this single moment only from one point of vision; if, again, their works are made not merely to be seen, but to be considered, to be long and repeatedly contemplated, then it is certain that that single moment, and the single viewpoint of that moment, can never be chosen too significantly. Now that alone is significant and fruitful which gives free play to the imagination. The more we see, the more must we be able to add by thinking. The more we add thereto by thinking, so much the more can we believe ourselves to see. In the whole gamut of an emotion, however, there is no moment less advantageous than its topmost note. Beyond it there is nothing further, and to show us the uttermost is to tie the wings of fancy and oblige her, as she cannot rise above the sensuous impression, to busy herself with weaker pictures below it, the visible fullness of expression acting as a frontier which she dare not transgress. When, therefore, Laocoön sighs, the imagination can hear him shriek; but if he shrieks, then she cannot mount a step higher from this representation, nor, again, descend a step lower without seeing him in a more tolerable and consequently more uninteresting condition. She hears him only groan, or she sees him already dead.

Further. As this single moment receives from Art an unchangeable continuance, it must not express anything which thought is obliged to consider transitory. All phenomena of whose very essence, according to our conceptions, it is that they break out suddenly and as suddenly vanish, that what they are they can be only for a moment—all such phenomena, whether agreeable or terrible, do, by the permanence which Art bestows, put on an aspect so abhorrent to Nature that at every repeated view of them the impression becomes weaker, until at last the whole thing inspires us with horror or loathing. La Mettrie, who had himself painted and engraved as a second Democritus, laughs only the first time that one sees him. View him often, and from a philosopher he becomes a fool, and the laugh becomes a grin. So, too, with cries. The violent pain which presses out the cry either speedily relaxes or it destroys the sufferer. If, again, the most patient and resolute man cries aloud, still he does not cry out without intermission. And just this unintermitting aspect in the material imitations of Art it is which would make his cries an effeminate or a childish weakness. This at least the artist of the Laocoön had to avoid, if cries had not been themselves damaging to beauty, and if even it had been permitted to his art to depict suffering without beauty.

Among the ancient painters Timomachus seems to have chosen by preference themes of the extremest emotion. His frenzied Ajax, his Medea the child-murderess, were famous pictures. But from the descriptions we have of them it clearly appears that he understood excellently well, and knew how to combine, that point where the beholder does not so much see the uttermost as reach it by added thought, and that appearance with which we do not join the idea of the transitory so necessarily that the prolongation of the same in Art must displease us. Medea he had not taken at the moment in which she actually murders the children, but some moments earlier, when motherly love still battles with jealousy. We foresee the end of the fight. We tremble beforehand, about to see Medea at her cruel deed, and our imagination goes out far beyond everything that the painter could show us in this terrible moment. But for this very reason we are so little troubled by the continued indecision of Medea, as Art presents it, that rather we devoutly wish it had so continued in Nature

itself, that the struggle of passions had never been decided, or
had at least endured long enough for time and reflection to
weaken rage and assure the victory to motherly feeling.   To
Timomachus, moreover, this wisdom of his brought great and
manifold tributes, and raised him far above another unknown
painter who had been misguided enough to represent Medea
in the height of her rage, and thus to give to this transient
extreme of frenzy a permanence that revolts all Nature.   The
poet who blames him on this account remarks, very sensibly,
addressing the picture itself : " Dost thou, then, thirst perpetually for the blood of thy children?   Is there constantly a
new Jason, always a new Creusa here, to embitter thee for
evermore?   To the devil with thee, even in picture ! " he adds,
with angry disgust.

Of the Frenzied Ajax of Timomachus we can judge by Philos-
tratus' account.   Ajax appeared not as he rages amongst the
herds and binds and slays oxen and goats for his enemies.
Rather, the master showed him when, after these mad-heroic
deeds, he sits exhausted and is meditating self-destruction.
And that is actually the Frenzied Ajax; not because just then
he rages, but because one sees that he has raged, because one
perceives the greatness of his frenzy most vividly by the despair
and shame which he himself now feels over it.   One sees the
storm in the wreckage and corpses it has cast upon the shore.

IV

Glancing at the reasons adduced why the artist of the Laocoön
was obliged to observe restraint in the expression of physical
pain, I find that they are entirely drawn from the peculiar
nature of Art and its necessary limits and requirements.   Hardly,
therefore, could any one of them be made applicable to poetry.

Without inquiring here how far the poet can succeed in
depicting physical beauty, so much at least is undeniable, that,
as the whole immeasurable realm of perfection lies open to his
imitative skill, this visible veil, under which perfection becomes
beauty, can be only one of the smallest means by which he
undertakes to interest us in his subject.   Often he neglects this
means entirely, being assured that if his hero has won our good-
will, then his nobler qualities either so engage us that we do
not think at all of the bodily form, or, if we think of it, so pre-
possess us that we do, on their very account, attribute to him,

if not a beautiful one, yet at any rate one that is not uncomely. At least, with every single line which is not expressly intended for the eye he will still take this sense into consideration. When Virgil's Laocoön cries aloud, to whom does it occur then that a wide mouth is needful for a cry, and that this must be ugly? Enough, that *clamores horrendos ad sidera tollit* is an excellent feature for the hearing, whatever it might be for the vision. Whosoever demands here a beautiful picture, for him the poet has entirely failed of his intention.

In the next place, nothing requires the poet to concentrate his picture on one single moment. He takes up each of his actions, as he likes, from its very origin and conducts it through all possible modifications to its final close. Every one of these modifications, which would cost the artist an entire separate canvas or marble-block, costs the poet a single line; and if this line, taken in itself, would have misled the hearer's imagination, it was either so prepared for by what preceded, or so modified and supplemented by what followed, that it loses its separate impression, and in its proper connection produces the most admirable effect in the world. Were it therefore actually unbecoming to a man to cry out in the extremity of pain, what damage can this trifling and transient impropriety do in our eyes to one whose other virtues have already taken us captive? Virgil's Laocoön shrieks aloud, but this shrieking Laocoön we already know and love as the wisest of patriots and the most affectionate of fathers. We refer his cries not to his character but purely to his unendurable suffering. It is this alone we hear in his cries, and the poet could make it sensible to us only through them. Who shall blame him then, and not much rather confess that, if the artist does well not to permit Laocoön to cry aloud, the poet does equally well in permitting him?

But Virgil here is merely a narrative poet. Can the dramatic poet be included with him in this justification? It is a different impression which is made by the narration of any man's cries from that which is made by the cries themselves. The drama, which is intended for the living artistry of the actor, might on this very ground be held more strictly to the laws of material painting. In him we do not merely suppose that we see and hear a shrieking Philoctetes; we hear and see him actually shriek. The closer the actor comes to Nature in this, the more sensibly must our eyes and ears be offended; for it is undeniable that they are so in Nature when we hear such loud and violent utterances of pain. Besides, physical pain does not generally

c

excite that degree of sympathy which other evils awaken. Our imagination is not able to distinguish enough in it for the mere sight of it to call out something like an equivalent feeling in ourselves. Sophocles could, therefore, easily have overstepped a propriety not merely capricious, but founded in the very essence of our feelings, if he allowed Philoctetes and Hercules thus to whine and weep, thus to shriek and bellow. The by-standers could not possibly take so much share in their suffering as these unmeasured outbursts seem to demand. They will appear to us spectators comparatively cold, and yet we cannot well regard their sympathy otherwise than as the measure of our own. Let us add that the actor can only with difficulty, if at all, carry the representation of physical pain to the point of illusion; and who knows whether the later dramatic poets are not rather to be commended than to be blamed, in that they have either avoided this rock entirely or only sailed round it with the lightest of skiffs?

How many a thing would appear irrefragable in theory if genius had not succeeded in proving the contrary by actual achievement! None of these considerations is unfounded, and yet Philoctetes remains one of the masterpieces of the stage. For some of them do not really touch Sophocles, and by treating the rest with contempt he has attained beauties of which the timid critic without this example would never dream. The following notes deal with this point in fuller detail.

1. How wonderfully has the poet known how to strengthen and enlarge the idea of the physical pain! He chose a wound —(for even the circumstances of the story one can contemplate as if they had depended on choice, in so far, that is to say, as he chose the whole story just because of the advantages the circumstances of it afforded him)—he chose, I say, a wound and not an inward malady, because a more vivid representation can be made of the former than of the latter, however painful this may be. The mysterious inward burning which consumed Meleager when his mother sacrificed him in mortal fire to her sisterly rage would therefore be less theatrical than a wound. And this wound was a divine judgment. A supernatural venom raged within without ceasing, and only an unusually severe attack of pain had its set time, after which the unhappy man fell ever into a narcotic sleep in which his exhausted nature must recover itself to be able to enter anew on the selfsame way of suffering. Chateaubrun represents him merely as wounded

by the poisoned arrow of a Trojan. What of extraordinary can so commonplace an accident promise? To such every warrior in the ancient battles was exposed; how did it come about that only with Philoctetes had it such terrible consequences? A natural poison that works nine whole years without killing is, besides, more improbable by far than all the mythical miraculous with which the Greek has furnished it.

2. But however great and terrible he made the bodily pains of his hero, he yet was in no doubt that they were insufficient in themselves to excite any notable degree of sympathy. He combined them, therefore, with other evils, which likewise, regarded in themselves, could not particularly move us, but which by this combination received just as melancholy a tinge as in their turn they imparted to the bodily pains. These evils were—a total deprivation of human society, hunger, and all the inconveniences of life to which in such deprivations one is exposed under an inclement sky. Let us conceive of a man in these circumstances, but give him health, and capacities, and industry, and we have a Robinson Crusoe who makes little demand upon our compassion, although otherwise his fate is not exactly a matter of indifference. For we are rarely so satisfied with human society that the repose which we enjoy when wanting it might not appear very charming, particularly under the representation which flatters every individual, that he can learn gradually to dispense with outside assistance. On the other hand, give a man the most painful, incurable malady, but at the same time conceive him surrounded by agreeable friends who let him want for nothing, who soften his affliction as far as lies in their power, and to whom he may unreservedly wail and lament; unquestionably we shall have pity for him, but this pity does not last, in the end we shrug our shoulders and recommend him patience. Only when both cases come together, when the lonely man has an enfeebled body, when others help the sick man just as little as he can help himself, and his complainings fly away in the desert air; then, indeed, we behold all the misery that can afflict human nature close over the unfortunate one, and every fleeting thought in which we conceive ourselves in his place awakens shuddering and horror. We perceive nothing before us but despair in its most dreadful form, and no pity is stronger, none more melts the whole soul than that which is mingled with representations of despair. Of this kind is the pity which we feel for Philoctetes, and feel most strongly at that moment when we see him deprived

of his bow, the one thing that might preserve him his wretched life. Oh, the Frenchman, who had neither the understanding to reflect on this nor the heart to feel it! Or, if he had, was small enough to sacrifice all this to the pitiful taste of his country-men. Chateaubrun gives Philoctetes society. He lets a young Princess come to him in the desert island. Nor is she alone, for she has her governess with her; a thing of which I know not whether the Princess or the poet had the greater need. The whole excellent play with the bow he set quite aside. Instead of it he gives us the play of beautiful eyes. Certainly to young French heroes bow and arrow would have appeared a great joke. On the other hand, nothing is more serious than the anger of beautiful eyes. The Greek torments us with the dreadful apprehension that poor Philoctetes must remain on the desert island without his bow, and perish miserably. The Frenchman knows a surer way to our hearts : he makes us fear the son of Achilles must retire without his Princess. At the time the Parisian critics proclaimed this a triumphing over the ancients, and one of them proposed to call Chateaubrun's piece " La Difficulté vaincue."

3. After the general effect let us consider the individual scenes, in which Philoctetes is no longer the forsaken invalid ; in which he has hope of speedily leaving the comfortless wilder-ness behind and of once more reaching his own kingdom; in which, therefore, the painful wound is his sole calamity. He whimpers, he cries aloud, he goes through the most frightful convulsions. To this behaviour it is that the reproach of offended propriety is particularly addressed. It is an English-man who utters this reproach; a man, therefore, whom we should not easily suspect of a false delicacy. As we have already hinted, he gives a very good reason for the reproach. All feelings and passions, he says, with which others can only slightly sympathise, are offensive when they are expressed too violently. " For this reason there is nothing more unbecoming and more unworthy of a man than when he cannot bear pain, even the most violent, with patience, but weeps and cries aloud. Of course we may feel sympathy with bodily pain. When we see that any one is about to get a blow on the arm or the shin-bone, and when the blow actually falls, in a certain measure we feel it as truly as he whom it strikes. At the same time, however, it is certain that the trouble we thus experience amounts to very little; if the person struck, therefore, sets up a violent outcry, we do not fail to despise him, because we are

not at all in the mind to cry out with so much violence." (Adam Smith, *Theory of the Moral Sentiments*, Part I, sect. 2, chap. i, p. 41, London, 1761.) Nothing is more fallacious than general laws for human feelings. The web of them is so fine-spun and so intricate that it is hardly possible for the most careful speculation to take up a single thread by itself and follow it through all the threads that cross it. And supposing it possible, what is the use of it? There does not exist in Nature a single unmixed feeling; along with every one of them there arise a thousand others simultaneously, the very smallest of which completely alters the first, so that exceptions on exceptions spring up which reduce at last the supposed general law itself to the mere experience of a few individual cases. We despise him, says the Englishman, whom we hear shriek aloud under bodily pain. No; not always, nor at first; not when we see that the sufferer makes every effort to suppress it; not when we know him otherwise as a man of fortitude; still less when we see him even in his suffering give proof of his fortitude, when we see that the pain can indeed force cries from him, but can compel him to nothing further—that he will rather submit to the longer endurance of this pain than change his opinions or his resolves in the slightest, even if he might hope by such a change to end his agony. And all this we find in Philoctetes. With the ancient Greeks moral greatness consisted in just as unchanging a love to friends as an unalterable hatred to enemies. This greatness Philoctetes maintains in all his torments. His pain has not so dried his eyes that they can spare no tears for the fate of his old friends. His pain has not made him so pliable that, to be rid of it, he will forgive his enemies and allow himself willingly to be used for their selfish purposes. And this rock of a man ought the Athenians to have despised because the surges that could not shake him made him give forth a cry? I confess that in the philosophy of Cicero, generally speaking, I find little taste; and least of all in that second book of his Tusculan Disputations, where he pours out his notions about the endurance of bodily pain. One might almost think he wanted to train a gladiator, he declaims so passionately against the outward expression of pain. In this alone does he seem to find a want of fortitude, without considering that it is frequently anything but voluntary, whilst true bravery can only be shown in voluntary actions. In Sophocles he hears Philoctetes merely complain and cry aloud, and overlooks utterly his otherwise steadfast bearing. Where save here could he have found the opportunity for his rhetorical outburst against the poets? "They would make us weaklings, showing us as they do the bravest of men lamenting and bewailing themselves." They must bewail themselves, for a theatre is not an arena. The condemned or venal gladiator it behoved to do and suffer everything with decorum. No complaining word must be heard from him, nor painful grimace be seen. For as his wounds and his death were to delight the spectators, Art must learn to conceal all feeling. The least utterance of it would have aroused compassion, and compassion often excited would have speedily brought an end to these icily gruesome spectacles. But what here it was not desired to excite is the one object of the tragic stage, and demands therefore an exactly opposite demeanour. Its heroes must show feeling, must utter their pain, and let Nature work in them undisguisedly. If they betray restraint and training, they leave our hearts cold, and pugilists in the cothurnus could at best only excite astonishment. This designation would befit all the persons of the so-called Seneca tragedies, and I firmly believe that the gladiatorial plays were the principal reason why the Romans in tragedy remained so far below the mediocre. To disown human nature was the lesson the spectators learned in the bloody amphitheatre, where certainly a Ctesias might study his art, but never a Sophocles. The tragic genius, accustomed to these artistic death scenes, necessarily sank into bombast and rodomontade. But just as little as such rodomontade could inspire true heroism, could the laments of Philoctetes make men weak. The complaints are those of a man, but the actions those of a hero. Both together make the human hero, who is neither soft nor hardened, but appears now the one and now the other, according as Nature at one time, and duty and principle at another, demand. He is the highest that Wisdom can produce and Art imitate.

4. It is not enough that Sophocles has secured his sensitive Philoctetes against contempt; he has also wisely taken precautions against all else that might, according to the Englishman's remark, be urged against him. For if we certainly do not always despise him who cries aloud in bodily pain, still it is indisputable that we do not feel so much sympathy for him as these outcries seem to demand. How, then, shall all those comport themselves who have to do with the shrieking Philoctetes? Shall they affect to be deeply moved? That is against nature. Shall they show themselves as cold and as

disconcerted as we are really accustomed to be in such cases? That would produce for the spectator the most unpleasant dissonance. But, as we have said, against this Sophocles has taken precautions. In this way, namely, that the secondary persons have an interest of their own; that the impression which the cries of Philoctetes make on them is not the one thing that occupies them, and the spectator's attention is not so much drawn to the disproportion of their sympathy with these cries, but rather to the change which arises or should arise in their disposition and attitude from sympathy, be it as weak or as strong as it may. Neoptolemus and his company have deceived the unhappy Philoctetes; they recognise into what despair their betrayal will plunge him; and now, before their eyes, a terrible accident befalls him. If this accident is not enough to arouse any particular feeling of sympathy within them, it still will move them to repent, to have regard to a misery so great, and indispose them to add to it by treachery. This is what the spectator expects, and his expectations are not disappointed by the noble-minded Neoptolemus. Philoctetes mastering his pain would have maintained Neoptolemus in his dissimulation. Philoctetes, whom his pain renders incapable of dissimulation, however imperatively necessary it may seem to him, so that his future fellow-travellers may not too soon regret their promise to take him with them; Philoctetes, who is nature itself, brings Neoptolemus, too, back to his own nature. This conversion is admirable, and so much the more touching as it is entirely wrought by humane feeling. With the Frenchman, on the contrary, beautiful eyes have their share in it. But I will say no more of this burlesque. Of the same artifice—namely, to join to the pity which bodily pain should arouse another emotion in the onlookers—Sophocles availed himself on another occasion : in the *Trachiniae*. The agony of Hercules is no enfeebling agony, it drives him to frenzy in which he pants for nothing but revenge. He had already, in his rage, seized Lichas and dashed him to pieces upon the rocks. The chorus is of women; so much the more naturally must fear and horror overwhelm them. This, and the expectant doubt whether yet a god will hasten to the help of Hercules, or Hercules succumb to the calamity, form here the real general interest, mingled merely with a slight tinge of sympathy. As soon as the issue is determined by the oracle, Hercules becomes quiet, and admiration of his final steadfast resolution takes the place of all other feelings. But in comparing the suffering Hercules with the suffering Philoctetes, one must never forget that the former is a demigod and the latter only a man. The man is not for a moment ashamed of his lamentations; but the demigod is ashamed that his mortal part has prevailed so far over the immortal that he must weep and whimper like a girl. We moderns do not believe in demigods, but our smallest hero we expect to feel and act as a demigod.

Whether an actor can bring the cries and grimaces of pain to the point of illusion I will not venture either to assert or to deny. If I found that our actors could not, then I should first like to know whether it would be impossible also to a Garrick; and if even he did not succeed, I should still be able to suppose a perfection in the stage-business and declamation of the ancients of which we to-day have no conception.

V

There are some learned students of antiquity who regard the Laocoön group as indeed a work of Greek masters, but of the time of the Emperors, because they believe that the Laocoön of Virgil served as its model. Of the older scholars who are of this opinion I will name only Bartholomew Marliani, and of the modern, Montfaucon. They doubtless found so close an agreement between the work of art and the poet's description that they thought it impossible that the two should have lighted by chance upon identical details such as are far from offering themselves unsought. At the same time their presumption is that if it be a question of the honour of the invention and first conception, the probability is incomparably greater that it belongs rather to the poet than to the artist.

Only they appear to have forgotten that a third case is possible. For it may be that the poet has as little imitated the artist as the artist has the poet, and that both have drawn from an identical source older than either. According to Macrobius, this more ancient source might have been Pisander. For when the works of this Greek poet were still extant, it was a matter of common knowledge, *pueris decantatum*, that the Roman had not so much imitated as faithfully translated from him the whole of the Capture and Destruction of Ilium, his entire Second Book. Now, therefore, if Pisander had been Virgil's predecessor also in the story of Laocoön, then the

Greek artists needed not to learn their lesson from a Latin poet, and the surmise as to their era is based upon nothing.

All the same, were I obliged to maintain the opinion of Marliani and Montfaucon, I should suggest to them the following way out. Pisander's poems are lost; how the story of Laocoön was told by him no one can say with certainty; but it is probable that it was with the same details of which we still find traces in the Greek writers. Now, these do not agree in the least with Virgil's narrative, and the Roman poet must have recast the Greek legend as he thought best. His manner of telling the tale of Laocoön is his own invention; consequently, if the artists in their representation are in harmony with him, it is almost a certainty that they followed him and wrought according to his pattern.

In Quintus Calaber, indeed, Laocoön displays a similar suspicion of the Wooden Horse as in Virgil; but the wrath of Minerva which he thereby draws upon himself expresses itself quite differently. The earth trembles under the warning Trojan; horror and dread seize him; a burning pain rages in his eyes; his brain reels; he raves; he goes blind. Only when, though blind, he ceases not to urge the burning of the Wooden Horse, does Minerva send two terrible dragons, and these attack only the children of Laocoön. In vain they stretch out their hands to their father; the poor blind man cannot help them; they are torn in pieces, and the serpent glides away into the earth. To Laocoön himself they do nothing; and that this account was not peculiar to Quintus, but must rather have been universally accepted, is proved by a passage in Lycophron, where these serpents bear the epithet " child-eaters."

If, however, this account had been universally received amongst the Greeks, the Greek artists in that case would hardly have been bold enough to deviate from it, and it would hardly have happened that they should deviate from it in precisely the same way as a Roman poet did if they had not known this poet, if perhaps they had not actually had the express commission to follow his lead. On this point, I think, we must insist if we would defend Marliani and Montfaucon. Virgil is the first and only one who describes the father as well as the children destroyed by the serpents; the sculptors do this likewise, while yet as Greeks they ought not : therefore it is probable that they did it at the prompting of Virgil.

I quite understand how far this probability falls short of

historical certainty. But as I do not intend to draw any historical conclusions from it, I yet believe at least that it can stand as a hypothesis which the critic in forming his views may take into account. Proven or not proven, that the sculptors followed Virgil in their works, I will assume it merely to see how in that case they did follow him. Concerning the outcries, I have already explained my opinion. Perhaps a further comparison may lead us to observations not less instructive.

The idea of binding the father with his two sons into one group by the deadly serpents is unquestionably a very happy one, evincing an uncommonly graphic fancy. To whom is it to be assigned? The poet, or the artist? Montfaucon refuses to find it in the poet. But Montfaucon, as I think, has not read him with sufficient attention.

> . . . *Illi agmine certo*
> *Laocoönta petunt, et primum parva duorum*
> *Corpora natorum serpens amplexus uterque*
> *Implicat et miseros morsu depascitur artus.*
> *Post ipsum, auxilio subeuntem ac tela ferentem,*
> *Corripiunt, spirisque ligant ingentibus.* . . .

The poet has depicted the serpents as of a marvellous length. They have enfolded the boys, and when the father comes to their aid, seize him also (*corripiunt*). From their size they could not at once uncoil themselves from the boys; there must therefore be a moment in which they had attacked the father with their heads and foreparts, while they still with their other parts enveloped the children. This moment is required in the development of the poetic picture; the poet makes it sufficiently felt; only the time had not yet been reached for finishing the picture. That the ancient commentators actually realised this appears to be shown by a passage in Dentatus. How much less would it escape the artists in whose understanding eyes everything that can advantage them stands out so quickly and so plainly.

In the coils themselves with which the poet's fancy sees the serpents entwine Laocoön, he very carefully avoids the arms, in order to leave the hands their freedom.

> *Ille simul manibus tendit divellere nodos.*

In this the artists must necessarily follow him. Nothing gives more life and expression than the movement of the hands; in emotion especially the most speaking countenance without it is insignificant. Arms fast bound to the body by the coils of the serpents would have spread frost and death over the whole group. For this reason we see them, in the chief figure as well as in the secondary figures, in full activity, and busiest there where for the moment there is the most violent anguish.

Further, too, the artists, in view of the convolutions of the serpents, found nothing that could be more advantageously borrowed from the poet than this movement of the arms. Virgil makes the serpents wind themselves doubly about the body and doubly about the neck of Laocoön, with their heads elevated above him.

> *Bis medium amplexi, bis collo squamea circum*
> *Terga dati, superant capite et cervicibus altis.*

This picture satisfies the imagination completely; the noblest parts are compressed to suffocation, and the poison goes straight to the face. Nevertheless, it was not a picture for artists, who want to exhibit the effects of the pain and the poison in the bodily frame. For in order to make these visible the chief parts must be as free as possible, and no external pressure whatever must be exercised upon them which could alter and weaken the play of the suffering nerves and straining muscles. The double coil of the serpents would have concealed the whole body, so that the painful contraction of the abdomen, which is so expressive, would have remained invisible. What one would still have perceived of the body, over, or under, or between the coils would have appeared under pressures and swellings caused not by the inward pain, but by the external burden. The neck so many times encircled would have spoiled completely the pyramidal tapering of the group which is so agreeable to the eye; and the pointed serpent heads standing out into the air from this swollen bulk would have made so abrupt a break in proportion that the form of the whole would have been repulsive in the extreme. There are doubtless draughtsmen who would nevertheless have been unintelligent enough to follow the poet slavishly. But what would have come of that, we can, to name no other instances, understand from a drawing of Francis Cleyn, which can be looked on only with disgust. (This occurs in the splendid edition of Dryden's English Virgil.) The ancient sculptors perceived at a glance that their art demanded an entire modification. They removed all the serpent coils from neck and body to thighs and feet. Here these coils, without injuring the expression, could cover and press as much as was needful. Here they aroused at once the idea of retarded flight and of a kind of immobility which is exceedingly advantageous to the artistic permanence of a single posture.

I know not how it has come about that the critics have passed over in perfect silence this distinction, which is exhibited so plainly in the coilings of the serpents, between the work of art and the poet's description. It exalts the artistic wisdom of the work just as much as the other which they mention, which, however, they do not venture to praise, but rather seek to excuse. I mean the difference in the draping of the subject. Virgil's Laocoön is in his priestly vestments, but in the group appears, with both his sons, completely naked. I am told there are people who find something preposterous in representing a prince, a priest, unclothed, at the altar of sacrifice. And to these people connoisseurs of art reply, in all seriousness, that certainly it is an offence against custom, but that the artists were compelled to it, because they could not give their figures any suitable attire. Sculpture, say they, cannot imitate any kind of cloth; thick folds would make a bad effect. Of two embarrassments, therefore, they had chosen the smaller, and were willing rather to offend against truth than to incur the risk of blame for their draperies. If the ancient artists would laugh at the objection, I really cannot tell what they would have said about the answer. One cannot degrade Art further than by such a defence. For, granted that sculpture could imitate the different materials just as well as painting, should then Laocoön necessarily have been clothed? Should we lose nothing by this draping? Has a costume, the work of slavish hands, just as much beauty as the work of the Eternal Wisdom, an organised body? Does it demand the same faculties, is it equally meritorious, does it bring the same honour, to imitate the former as to imitate the latter? Do our eyes only wish to be deceived, and is it all the same to them with what they are deceived?

With the poet a dress is no dress; it conceals nothing; our imagination sees through it at all times. Let Laocoön in Virgil have it or lack it, his suffering in every part of his body is, to the imagination, an evil equally visible. The brow is bound about for her with the priestly fillet, but it is not veiled. Indeed, it does not only not hinder, this fillet, it even strengthens yet more the conception that we form of the sufferer's misfortunes.

Perfusus sanie vittas atroque veneno.

His priestly dignity helps him not a whit; the very symbol which secures him everywhere respect and veneration is soaked and defiled by the deadly venom.

But this accessory idea the artist had to sacrifice if the main work were not to suffer damage. Besides, had he left to Laocoön only this fillet, the expression would in consequence have been much weakened. The brow would have been partly covered, and the brow is the seat of expression. So, just as in that other particular, the shriek, he sacrificed expression to beauty, in the same way here he sacrificed custom to expression. Generally speaking, custom, in the view of the ancients, was a matter of little consequence. They felt that the highest aim of Art pointed to dispensing with the customary altogether. Beauty is this highest aim; necessity invented clothing, and what has Art to do with necessity? I grant you there is also a beauty of drapery; but what is it compared with the beauty of the human form? And will he who is able to reach the higher content himself with the lower? I am much afraid that the most finished master in draperies shows by that very dexterity in what it is he is lacking.

VI

My hypothesis—that the artists imitated the poet—does not redound to their disparagement. On the contrary, this imitation sets their wisdom in the fairest light. They followed the poet without allowing themselves to be misled by him in the slightest. They had a pattern, but as they had to transpose this pattern from one art into another, they found opportunity enough to think for themselves. And these thoughts of theirs, which are manifest in their deviation from their model, prove that they were just as great in their art as he in his own.

And now I will reverse the hypothesis and suppose the poet to have imitated the artists. There are scholars who maintain this supposition to be the truth. Whether they had historical grounds for that, I do not know. But when they found the work of art so superlatively beautiful, they could not persuade themselves that it might belong to a late period. It must be of the age when Art was in its perfect flower, because it deserved to be of that age.

It has been shown that, admirable as Virgil's picture is, there are yet various features of it which the artists could not use. The statement thus admits of being reduced to this, that a good poetic description must also yield a good actual painting, and that the poet has only so far described well when the artist can follow him in every feature. One is inclined to presume this restricted sense, even before seeing it confirmed by examples; merely from consideration of the wider sphere of poetry, from the boundless field of our imagination, and from the spiritual nature of the pictures, which can stand side by side in the greatest multitude and variety without one obscuring or damaging another, just as the things themselves would do or the natural signs of the same within the narrow bounds of space and time.

But if the less cannot include the greater, the greater can contain the less. This is my point—if not, every feature which the descriptive poet uses can be used with like effect on the canvas or in the marble. Might perhaps every feature of which the artist avails himself prove equally effective in the work of the poet? Unquestionably; for what we find beautiful in a work of art is not found beautiful by the eye, but by our imagination through the eye. The picture in question may therefore be called up again in our imagination by arbitrary or natural signs, and thus also may arise at any time the corresponding pleasure, although not in corresponding degree.

This, however, being admitted, I must confess that to my mind the hypothesis that Virgil imitated the artists is far less conceivable than the contrary supposition. If the artists followed the poet, I can account for their deviations. They were obliged to deviate, because the selfsame features as the poet delineated would have occasioned them difficulties such as do not embarrass the poet. But what should make the poet deviate? If he had followed the group in every detail would he not, all the same, have presented to us an admirable picture? I can conceive quite well how his fancy, working on its own account, might suggest one feature and another; but the reasons why his imagination should think that beautiful features, already before his eyes, ought to be transformed into those other features—such reasons, I confess, never dawn upon me.

It even seems to me that if Virgil had had the group as his pattern he could scarcely have refrained from permitting the union together, as it were in a knot, of the three bodies to be at least conjectured. It was too vivid not to catch his eye, and he would have appreciated its excellent effect too keenly not to give it yet more prominence in his description. As I have said, the time was not yet arrived to finish this picture of the entwined group. No; but a single word more would perhaps have given to it, in the shadow where the poet had to leave it, a very obvious impression. What the artist was able to discover without this word, the poet, if he had seen it in the artist's work, would not have left unspoken.

The artist had the most compelling reasons not to let the suffering of Laocoön break out into a cry. But if the poet had had before him the so touching union of pain and beauty in the work of art, what could have so imperatively obliged him to leave completely unsuggested the idea of manly dignity and great-hearted endurance which arises from this union of pain and beauty, and all at once to shock us with the terrible outcries of Laocoön? Richardson says, " Virgil's Laocoön must shriek, because the poet desires to arouse not so much pity for him as terror and horror in the ranks of the Trojans." I grant, although Richardson seems not to have considered it, that the poet does not make the description in his own person, but lets Æneas make it, and this, too, in the presence of Dido, to whose compassion Æneas could never enough appeal. It is not, however, the shriek that surprises me, but the absence of any gradation leading up to the cry, a gradation that the work of art would naturally have shown the poet to be needful, if, as we have supposed, he had had it for a pattern. Richardson adds, " The story of Laocoön should lead up merely to the pathetic description of the final ruin; the poet, therefore, has not thought fit to make it more interesting, in order not to waste upon the misfortune of a single citizen the attention which should be wholly fixed on Troy's last dreadful night." Only, this sets out the affair as one to be regarded from a painter's point of view, from which it cannot be contemplated at all. The calamity of Laocoön and the Destruction of the City are not with the poet pictures set side by side; the two together do not make a great whole which the eye either should or could take in at a glance; and only in such a case would it be needful to arrange that our eyes should fall rather upon Laocoön than upon the burning city. The two descriptions follow each other successively, and I do not see what disadvantage it could bring to the second, how greatly soever the preceding one had moved us. That could only be, if the second in itself were not sufficiently touching.

Still less reason would the poet have had to alter the coiling of the serpents. In the work of art they leave the hands busy and bind the feet. This disposition pleases the eye, and it is

a living picture that is left by it in the imagination. It is so
clear and pure that it can be presented almost as effectively by
words as by actual material means.

> . . . *Micat alter, et ipsum*
> *Laocoönta petit, totumque infraque supraque*
> *Implicat et rabido tandem ferit ilia morsu*
>
> *At serpens lapsu crebro redeunte subintrat*
> *Lubricus, intortoque ligat genua infima nodo.*

These are the lines of Sadolet, which would, no doubt, have
come from Virgil with a more picturesque power if a visible
pattern had fired his fancy, and which would in that case
certainly have been better than what he now gives us in their
place :—

> *Bis medium amplexi, bis collo squamea circum*
> *Terga dati, superant capite et cervicibus altis.*

These details, certainly, fill the imagination ; but she must
not rest in them, she must not endeavour to make an end here ;
she must see now only the serpents and now only Laocoön,
she must try to represent to herself what kind of figure is made
by the two together. As soon as she sinks to this the Virgilian
picture begins to dissatisfy, and she finds it in the highest
degree unpictorial.

If, however, the changes which Virgil had made in the pattern
set before him had not been unsuccessful, they would yet be
merely arbitrary. One imitates in order to resemble. Can
resemblance be preserved when alterations are made needlessly ?
Rather, when this is done, the design obviously is—not to be
like, and therefore not to imitate.

Not the whole, some may object, but perhaps this part and
that. Good ! But what, then, are these single parts that
agree in the description and in the work of art so exactly that
the poet might seem to have borrowed them from the latter ?
The father, the children, the serpents—all these the story
furnished to the poet as well as to the artists. Excepting the
story itself, they agree in nothing beyond the one point that
they bind father and children in a single serpent-knot. But
the suggestion of this arose from the altered detail, that the
selfsame calamity overtook the father and the children. This
alteration, as has already been pointed out, Virgil appears to
have introduced ; for the Greek legend says something quite
different. Consequently, when, in view of that common bind-

ing by the serpent coils, there certainly was imitation on one
side or the other, it is easier to suppose it on the artist's side
than on that of the poet.   In all else the one deviates from
the other; only with the distinction that, if it is the artist who
has made these deviations, the design of imitating the poet
can still persist, the aim and the limitations of his art obliging
him thereto; if, on the other hand, it is the poet who is supposed to have imitated the artist, then all the deviations referred
to are an evidence against the supposed imitation, and those
who, notwithstanding, maintain it, can mean nothing further
by it than that the work of art is older than the poetic description.

VII

When one says that the artist imitates the poet, or that the
poet imitates the artist, this is capable of two interpretations.
Either the one makes the work of the other the actual subject
of his imitation, or they have both the same subject and the
one borrows from the other the style and fashion of the imitation. When Virgil describes the shield of Æneas, it is in the
first of these senses that he imitates the artist who made it.
The work of art itself, not that which is represented upon it,
is the subject of his imitation, and although certainly he describes
at the same time what one sees represented thereon, yet he
describes it only as a part of the shield, and not the thing itself.
If Virgil, on the other hand, had imitated the Laocoön group,
this would be an imitation of the second kind. For he would
not have imitated the group, but what the group represents,
and only the characteristics of his imitation would have been
borrowed from it. In the first imitation the poet is original,
in the second he is a copyist. The former is a part of the general
imitation which constitutes the essence of his art, and he works
as genius, whether his subject be a work of other arts or of
Nature. The latter, on the contrary, degrades him wholly
from his dignity; instead of the things themselves, he imitates
the imitations of them, and gives us cold recollections of features
from another's genius in place of original features of his own.

When, however, poet and artist, as not seldom happens,
view the subjects that they have in common from an identical
standpoint, it can hardly fail that there should be agreement in
many particulars without implying the slightest degree of
imitation or common aim between them. These agreements
D

in contemporaneous artists and poets, concerning things that are no longer extant, may contribute to reciprocal illustration ; but to attempt to establish such illustration by finding design in what was mere accident, and especially to attribute to the poet in every trifle a reference to this statue or that painting, is to render him a very equivocal service. And not to him alone, but to the reader also, for whom the most beautiful passage is thereby made, if God will, very intelligible, but at the same time admirably frigid.

This is the purpose, and the error, of a famous English work. Spence wrote his *Polymetis* with much classical erudition and a very intimate acquaintance with the surviving works of ancient art. His design of explaining by these the Roman poets, and, on the other hand, of deriving from the poets elucidations for ancient works of art hitherto unexplained, he often accomplished very happily. But nevertheless I contend that his book is altogether intolerable to any reader of taste.

It is natural that, when Valerius Flaccus describes the Winged Lightning upon the Roman shields—

> *Nec primus radios, miles Romane, corusci*
> *Fulminis et rutilas scutis diffuderis alas,*

this description becomes to me far clearer when I perceive the representation of such a shield upon an ancient monument. It may be that Mars, hovering exactly as Addison fancied he saw him hovering, over the head of Rhea upon a coin, was also represented by the ancient armourers on shields and helmets and that Juvenal had such a shield or helmet in mind when he alluded to it in a single word which, until Addison, remained a riddle for all the commentators. For my part, I think that the passage of Ovid where the exhausted Cephalus calls to the cooling breezes :

> *Aura . . . venias. . . .*
> *Meque juves, intresque sinus, gratissima, nostros !*

and his Procris takes this Aura for the name of a rival—that to me, I say, this passage appears more natural when I gather from the works of ancient artists that they actually personified the soft breezes and worshipped a kind of female sylphs under the name of Aurae. I grant you, that when Juvenal styles a distinguished good-for-nothing a Hermes-statue, one could hardly find the likeness in the comparison without seeing such a statue, without knowing that it is a miserable pillar, which bears merely the head, or at most the torso, of the god, and, because we perceive thereon neither hands nor feet, awakens the conception of slothfulness. Illustrations of this sort are not to be despised, although, in fact, they are neither always necessary nor always adequate. The poet had the work of art in view as a thing existing for itself, and not as an imitation; or with both artist and poet certain conceptions of an identical kind were taken for granted, in consequence of which a further agreement in their representations must appear, from which, again, we can reason back to the generally accepted nature of these conceptions.

But when Tibullus describes the form of Apollo, as he appeared to him in a dream—the most beautiful of youths, his temples bound about with the modest laurel; Syrian odours exhaling from the golden hair that flows about his neck; a gleaming white and rosy red mingled on the whole body, as on the tender cheek of the bride as she is led to her beloved—why must these features be borrowed from famous old pictures? Echion's *nova nupta verecundia notabilis* may have been seen in Rome, may have been copied a thousand times. Had then the bridal blush itself vanished from the world? Since the painter had seen it, was it no larger to be seen by a poet save in the painter's imitation? Or if another poet speaks of the exhausted Vulcan, or calls his face heated before the forge a red and fiery countenance, must he needs learn first from the work of a painter that labour wearies and heat reddens? Or when Lucretius describes the changes of the seasons and causes them to pass before us in their natural order with the entire succession of their effects in earth and sky, was Lucretius an ephemeron? Had he not lived through a whole year himself to witness all these transformations, but must depict them after a procession in which their statues were carried around? Must he first learn from these statues the old poetic artifice whereby abstract notions are turned into actual beings? Or Virgil's *pontem indignatus Araxes*, that splendid poetic picture of a stream overflowing its banks and tearing down the bridge thrown over it, does it not lose all its beauty if the poet is there alluding merely to a work of art in which this river-god is represented as actually breaking down a bridge? What do we want with these commentaries which in the clearest passages supplant the poet in order to let the suggestion of an artist glimmer through?

I lament that so useful a look as *Polymetis* might otherwise have been has, by reason of this tasteless crotchet of foisting upon the ancient poets in place of their own proper fancy an acquaintance with another's, been made so offensive and so much more damaging to the classic authors than the watery expositions of the shallowest philologist could ever have been. I regret yet more that in this matter Spence should have been preceded by Addison himself, who, from a passionate desire to exalt the works of ancient art into a means of interpretation, has just as little distinguished between the cases in which it is becoming in a poet to imitate the artist and those in which it is disparaging.

VIII

Of the likeness which poetry and painting bear to each other Spence has the most singular conceptions possible. He believes the two arts in ancient times to have been so closely united that they always went hand in hand, that the poet constantly kept the painter in view, and the painter the poet. That poetry is the more comprehensive art, that beauties are at her command which painting can never attain, that she may frequently have reason to prefer unpicturesque beauties to picturesque—of this he does not appear to have a notion, and therefore the smallest difference which he detects between poets and artists of the old world puts him in a difficulty, and he resorts to the most extraordinary subterfuges to escape from his embarrassment.

The ancient poets generally endow Bacchus with horns. It is quite wonderful, then, says Spence, that we find these horns so seldom on his statues. He lights on this explanation and on that : on the uncertainty of the antiquaries, on the smallness of the horns themselves, which might have crept into conceal- ment under the grapes and ivy-leaves, the unfailing head covering of the god. He winds about and about the true reason without ever suspecting it. The horns of Bacchus were not natural horns, such as we see on the fauns and satyrs. They were but a garnishment of the brow, which he could assume and lay aside at will.

> *Tibi, cum sine cornibus adstas,*
> *Virgineum caput est—*

so runs the solemn invocation of Bacchus in Ovid. He could thus show himself also without horns, and did so when he would appear in his virginal beauty. The artists certainly would also wish so to represent him, and would therefore avoid every less pleasing adjunct. Such an adjunct the horns would have been if attached to the diadem, as we may see them on a head in the royal cabinet at Berlin. Such an adjunct was the diadem itself, hiding the beautiful brow, and for this reason it occurs on the statues of Bacchus just as rarely as the horns, although indeed it was dispensed with just as often by the poets, both in the representations of Bacchus and in those of his great progenitor. The horns and the diadem prompted the poet's allusions to the deeds and the character of the god; to the artist, on the contrary, they were hindrances to the exhibition of greater beauties, and if Bacchus, as I believe, for that very reason had the surname *Biformis*, Δίμορφος, because he could show himself in a fair and in a terrible aspect, then it was quite natural for the artists greatly to prefer that one of his forms which best answered the purpose of their art.

Minerva and Juno in the Roman poets often dart forth lightning. " Then why not also in their images? " asks Spence. He replies, " It was an especial privilege of these two goddesses, the grounds of which were perhaps only to be learned in the Samothracian mysteries; artists, moreover, were regarded by the ancient Romans as common people, were therefore seldom admitted to those mysteries, and so doubtless knew nothing of them, and what they did not know they could not depict." I might in return ask Spence, Did these common people work out their own notions, or work at the command of more distinguished persons who might have been instructed in the mysteries? Were artists among the Greeks regarded with a like contempt? Were the Roman artists not for the greater part born Greeks? And so on.

Statius and Valerius Flaccus depict an angry Venus, and with features so terrible that at the moment we should rather take her for one of the Furies than for the Goddess of Love. Spence looks round in vain amongst the works of ancient art for such a Venus. And what is his conclusion? That more is permitted to the poet than to the sculptor or the painter? That is the conclusion he ought to have drawn, but he has accepted the principle once for all, that in a poetic description nothing is good which would be unsuitable to be represented in a painting or a statue. Consequently, the poets must have erred. " Statius and Valerius belong to an age when Roman poetry was in its decline. They show in this particular also their corrupt taste and their faulty judgment. With the poets of a better time one will not find these offences against graphic expression."

To speak in this way betrays a very poor faculty of discrimination. All the same, I do not intend to take up the cudgels for either Statius or Valerius, but will confine myself to but one general observation. The gods and sacred persons, as the artist represents them, are not entirely the same beings which the poet knows. With the artist they are personified abstractions which must constantly retain the selfsame characterisation, if they are to be recognisable. With the poet, on the other hand, they are actual persons who live and act, who possess beyond their general character other qualities and emotions, which will stand out above it according to occasion and circumstance. Venus to the sculptor is nothing but Love; he must therefore endow her with the modest, blushful beauty and all the gracious charms that delight us in beloved objects and that we therefore combine in the abstract conception of Love. Deviate however slightly from this ideal, and we shall fail to recognise the picture. Beauty, but with more majesty than modesty, is at once no Venus, but a Juno. Charms, but commanding, masculine, rather than gracious charms, give us a Minerva in place of a Venus. In reality, an angry Venus, a Venus moved by revenge and rage, is to the sculptor a contradiction in terms; for Love as Love is never angry, never revengeful. To the poet, on the other hand, Venus certainly is Love, but she is more : she is the Goddess of Love, who beyond this character has an individuality of her own, and consequently must be just as capable of the impulse of aversion as of inclination. What wonder, then, that to him she blazes in rage or anger, especially when it is injured love that so transforms her?
Certainly it is true that the artist also in composition may just as well as the poet introduce Venus or any other divinity, out of her character, as a being actually living and acting. But in that case her actions must at least not contradict her character, even if they are not direct consequences of it. Venus commits to her son's charge her divine weapons; this action the artist can represent as well as the poet. Here nothing hinders him from giving to Venus all the grace and beauty that appertain to her as the Goddess of Love; rather, indeed, will she thereby be so much the more recognisable in his work. But when Venus would avenge herself on her contemners, the men of Lemnos; when in magnified and savage form, with stained cheeks and disordered hair, she seizes the torch, throws around her a black vesture and stormily plunges down on a gloomy cloud; surely that is not a moment for the artist, because in

such a moment he cannot by any means make her distinguishable. It is purely a moment for the poet, since to him the privilege is granted of so closely and exactly uniting with it another aspect, in which the goddess is wholly Venus, that we do not lose sight of her even in the Fury. This Flaccus does :

> *Neque enim alma videri*
> *Jam timet, aut tereti crinem subnectitur auro*
> *Sidereos diffusa sinus.   Eadem effera et ingens*
> *Et maculis suffecta genas, primumque sonantem*
> *Virginibus Stygiis nigramque simillima pallam.*

Statius does just the same :

> *Illa Paphon veterem centumque altaria linquens,*
> *Nec vultu nec crine prior, solvisse jugalem*
> *Ceston et Idalias procul ablegasse volucres*
> *Fertur.   Erant certe, media qui noctis in umbra*
> *Divam alios ignes majoraque tela gerentem*
> *Tartarias inter thalamis volitasse sorores*
> *Vulgarent : utque implicitis arcana domorum*
> *Anguibus et sacra formidine cuncta replevit*
> *Limina.—*

Or we might say, to the poet alone belongs the art of depicting with negative traits, and by mixing them with positive to bring two images into one. No longer the gracious Venus, no longer the hair fastened with golden clasps, floated about by no azure vesture, but without her girdle, armed with other flames, with greater arrows, companioned by like Furies. But because the artist is obliged to dispense with such an artifice, must the poet too in his turn abstain from using it ? If painting will be the sister of poesy, let not the younger forbid to the elder all the garniture and bravery which she herself cannot put on.

IX

If in individual cases we wish to compare the painter and the poet with one another, the first and most important point is to observe whether both of them have had complete freedom, whether they have, in the absence of any outward compulsion, been able to aim at the highest effect of their art.

Religion was often an outward compulsion of this kind for the ancient artist. His work, designed for reverence and worship, could not always be as perfect as if he had had a single eye to the pleasure of the beholder. Superstition overloaded the gods with symbols, and the most beautiful of them were not everywhere worshipped for their beauty. In his temple at Lemnos, from which the pious Hypsipyle rescued her father under the shape of the god, Bacchus stood horned, and so doubtless he appeared in all his temples, for the horns were a symbol that indicated his essential nature. Only the free artist who wrought his Bacchus for no holy shrine left this symbol out; and if amongst the statues of him still extant we find all without horns, this is perhaps a proof that they are not of the consecrated forms in which he was actually worshipped. Apart from this, it is highly probable that it was upon these last that the rage of the pious iconoclasts in the first centuries of Christianity chiefly fell, their fury sparing only here and there a work of art which had not been defiled by idolatrous worship.

As, however, works of both kinds are still found amongst antiquities in excavation, I should like the name of " works of art " to be reserved for those alone in which the artist could show himself actually as artist, in which beauty has been his first and last object. All the rest, in which too evident traces of religious ritual appear, are unworthy of the name, because Art here has not wrought on her own account, but has been an auxiliary of religion, looking in the material representations which she made of it more to the significant than to the beautiful; although I do not mean by this that she did not often put great significance into the beauty, or, out of indulgence to the art and finer taste of the age, remitted her attention to the former so much that the latter alone might appear to predominate.

If we make no such distinction, then the connoisseur and the antiquary will be constantly at strife because they do not understand each other. If the former, with his insight into the aims of art, contends that this or that work was never made by the ancient artist—that is to say, not as artist, not voluntarily— then the latter will assert that neither religion nor any other cause lying outside the region of art has caused the artist to make it—the artist, that is to say, as workman. He will suppose that he can refute the connoisseur with the first figure that comes to hand, which the other without scruple, but to the great annoyance of the learned world, will condemn to the rubbish-heap once more from which it has been drawn.

Yet, on the other hand, it is possible to exaggerate the influence of religion upon art. Spence affords a singular example of that tendency. He found that Vesta was not worshipped in her temple under any personal image, and this he

deemed enough to warrant the conclusion that no statues of
this goddess ever existed, and that every one so considered
really represented not Vesta, but a vestal. Strange inference !
Did the artist, then, lose his right to personify a being to whom
the poets give a distinct personality, whom they make the
daughter of Saturnus and Ops, whom they expose to the danger
of ill-usage at the hands of Priapus, and all else they relate of
her—did he lose his right, I ask, to personify this being in his
own way, because she was worshipped in one temple merely
under the symbol of fire? For Spence here falls into this
further error : that what Ovid says only of a certain temple of
Vesta—namely, of that at Rome—he extends to all temples of
the goddess without distinction and to her worship in general.
She was not everywhere worshipped as she was worshipped in
this temple at Rome, nor even in Italy itself before Numa
built it. Numa desired to see no divinity represented in human
or animal form; and without doubt the reform which he introduced in the service of Vesta consisted in this, that he banished
from it all personal representation. Ovid himself teaches us
that before Numa's time there were statues of Vesta in her
temple, which when her priestess Sylvia became a mother
raised their maiden hands in shame before their eyes. That
even in the temples which the goddess had in the Roman
provinces outside the city her worship was not wholly of the
kind which Numa prescribed, various ancient inscriptions appear
to prove, where mention is made of a " Pontificus Vestae."
At Corinth also there was a temple of Vesta without any statues,
with a mere altar whereon offerings were made to the goddess.
But had the Greeks therefore no statues of Vesta? At Athens
there was one in the Prytaneum, beside the statue of Peace.
The people of Iasos boasted of one, which stood in their city
under the open sky, that neither snow nor rain fell upon it.
Pliny mentions a sitting figure from the hand of Scopas which
in his time was to be seen in the Servilian Gardens at Rome.
Granted that it is difficult for us now to distinguish a mere
vestal from Vesta herself, does this prove that the ancients
could not distinguish them, or indeed did not wish to distinguish them? Notoriously, certain characteristics indicate
rather the one than the other. Only in the hands of the goddess can we expect to find the sceptre, the torch, the palladium.
The tympanum which Codinus associates with her belongs to
her perhaps only as the Earth, or Codinus did not recognise
very well what he saw.

X

I notice another expression of surprise in Spence which shows plainly how little he can have reflected on the limits of Poetry and Painting. " As for what concerns the Muses in general," he says, " it is certainly singular that the poets are so sparing in the description of them—more sparing by far than we should expect with goddesses to whom they owe such great obligations."

What is this, but to wonder that when the poets speak of them they do not use the dumb language of the painter ? Urania is for the poets the Muse of Astronomy; from her name, from her functions, we recognise her office. The artist in order to make it distinguishable must exhibit her with a pointer and a celestial globe; this wand, this celestial globe, this attitude of hers are his alphabet from which he helps us to put together the name Urania. But when the poet would say that Urania had long ago foretold his death by the stars :

Ipsa diu positis letum praedixerat astris Urania.—

why should he, thinking of the painter, add thereto, Urania, the pointer in her hand, the celestial globe before her ? Would it not be as if a man who can and may speak aloud should at the same time still make use of the signs which the mutes in the Turk's seraglio have invented for lack of utterance ?

The very same surprise Spence again expresses concerning the personified moralities, or those divinities whom the ancients set over the virtues and the conduct of human life. " It is worthy of remark," says he, " that the Roman poets say far less of the best of these personified moralities than we should expect. The artists in this respect are much richer, and he who would learn the particular aspect and attire of each need only consult the coins of the Roman Emperors : the poets speak of these beings frequently, indeed, as of persons; in general, however, they say very little of their attributes, their attire and the rest of their outward appearance."

When the poet personifies abstract qualities, these are sufficiently characterised by their names and by what they do. To the artist these means are wanting. He must therefore attach symbols to his personifications by which they can be distinguished. By these symbols, because they are something different and mean something different, they become allegorical figures. A woman with a bridle in her hand : another leaning

on a pillar, are in art allegorical beings. But Temperance and
Steadfastness are to the poet allegorical beings, and merely
personified abstractions. The symbols, in the artist's representation, necessity has invented. For in no other way can he
make plain what this or that figure signifies. But what the
artist is driven to by necessity, why should the poet force on
himself when no such necessity is laid upon him?

What surprises Spence so much deserves to be prescribed to
the poets as a law. They must not make painting's indigence
the rule of their wealth. They must not regard the means
which Art has invented in order to follow poetry as if they were
perfections which they have reason to envy. When the artist
adorns a figure with symbols, he raises a mere figure to a superior
being. But when the poet makes use of these plastic bedizen-
ments, he makes of a superior being a mere lay-figure.

And just as this rule is authenticated by its observance
amongst the ancient poets, so is its deliberate violation a
favourite weakness amongst their successors. All their creatures
of imagination go in masquerade, and those who understand
this masquerade best generally understand least the chief thing
of all, which is to let their creatures act and to distinguish and
characterise them by their actions.

Yet amongst the attributes with which the artists distinguish
their abstract personalities there is one sort which is more
susceptible and more worthy of poetic employment. I mean
those which properly have nothing allegorical in their nature,
but are to be regarded as implements of which the beings to
whom they are assigned would or might make use when acting
as real persons. The bridle in the hand of Temperance, the
pillar on which Steadfastness leans, are purely allegorical, and
thus of no use to the poet. The scales in the hand of Justice
are certainly less purely allegorical, because the right use of
the scales is really a part of justice. But the lyre or flute in the
hand of a Muse, the spear in the hand of Mars, hammer
and tongs in the hands of Vulcan, are not symbols at all, but
mere instruments, without which these beings could not effect
the achievements we ascribe to them. Of this kind are the
attributes which the ancient poets did sometimes weave into
their descriptions, and which I on that ground, distinguishing
them from the allegorical, would call the poetic. The latter
signify the thing itself, the former only some likeness of it.

XI

Count Caylus, again, appears to require that the poet shall embellish the creatures of his imagination with allegorical attributes. The Count was more at home with painting than with poetry. In the work, nevertheless, where he expresses this requirement I have found the suggestion of more important considerations, the most essential of which, for the better judging of them, I will mention here.

The artist, according to the Count's view, should make himself very thoroughly acquainted with the greatest of descriptive poets, with Homer, with this " second Nature." He shows him what rich and still unused material for most admirable pictures is offered by the story handled by the Greek, and how much more perfect his delineations will prove the more closely he clings to the very smallest circumstances noticed by the poet.

Now in this proposition we see a mingling of the two kinds of imitation which we have separated above. The painter is not only to imitate what the poet has imitated, but he is further to imitate it with the self-same features; he is to use the poet not as narrator only, but as poet.

This second species of imitation, however, which detracts so much from the poet's merit, why is it not equally disparaging to the artist? If before Homer such a succession of pictures as Count Caylus cites from his pages had been extant, and we were aware that the poet had based his work on them, would he not lose unspeakably in our estimation? How comes it that we withdraw from the artist no whit of our esteem even though he does nothing more than translate the words of the poet into figures and colours?

The reason appears to be this. With the artist we deem the execution more difficult than the invention; with the poet, again, it is the contrary, and we deem the execution, as compared with the invention, the lighter task. Had Virgil taken from the sculptured group the entangling of Laocoön and his children, the merit in his picture which we consider the greater and the harder of attainment would be lost, and only the smaller would remain. For to shape this entangling by the power of imagination is far more important than to express it in words. Had, on the other hand, the artist borrowed this entangling from the poet, he would still, in our minds, retain sufficient merit, although the merit of invention is withdrawn. For expression in marble is more difficult by far than expression in words; and when we weigh invention and representation against each other we are always inclined to abate our demands on the artist for the one, in proportion to the excess we feel that we have received of the other.

There are two cases in which it is a greater merit for the artist to copy Nature through the medium of the poet's imitation than without it. The painter who represents a lovely landscape according to the description of a Thomson has done more than he who copies it direct from Nature. The latter has his model before him; the former must first of all strain his imagination to the point that enables him to see it before him. The one makes a thing of beauty out of lively sensuous impressions, the other from weak and wavering descriptions of arbitary signs.

But natural as the readiness may be to abate in our demands on the artist for the particular merit of invention, it is equally so on his part, for like reasons, to be indifferent to it. For when he sees that invention can never become his more shining merit, that his greatest praise depends on execution, it becomes all one to him whether the former is old or new, used once or times without number, and whether it belongs to himself or to another. He remains within the narrow range of a few designs, become familiar both to him and to everybody, and directs his inventive faculty merely to changes in the already known and to new combinations of old subjects. That, too, is actually the idea which the manuals of painting connect with the word *Invention*. For although certainly they divide into the pictorial and the poetic, yet the poetic is not made to consist in the production of the design itself, but purely in the arrangement or the expression. It is invention, but not invention of the whole, only of separate parts and their position in relation to each other. It is invention, but of that lower type which Horace recommended to his tragic poet :

> . . . *Tuque*
> *Rectius Iliacum carmen deducis in actus*
> *Quam si proferres ignota indictaque primus.*

Recommended, I say, but not commanded. Recommended, as easier for him, more fitting, more advantageous; but not commanded as better and nobler in itself.

In fact the poet has a great advantage who treats a well-known story and familiar characters. A hundred indifferent trifles which otherwise would be indispensable to the under-

standing of the whole he can pass by; and the more quickly
he becomes intelligible to his hearers, the more quickly he can
interest them. This advantage the painter also has if his theme
is not strange to us, if we make out at the first glance the purpose and meaning of his entire composition, if we at once not
merely see his characters speaking, but hear also what they
speak. It is on the first glance that the main effect depends,
and if this forces on us troublesome reflection and conjecture,
our inclination to be moved grows cold; in order to be avenged
on the unintelligible artist, we harden ourselves against the
expression, and woe betide him if he has sacrificed beauty to
expression ! We then find nothing whatever that can charm us
to tarry before his work; what we see does not please us; and
what we are to think concerning it we are left uninstructed.

Now let us consider these two things together; first, that the
invention or novelty of the theme is far from being the principal
thing that we desire of the painter; secondly, that a well-known
theme furthers and facilitates the effect of his art; and I judge
that the reason why he so seldom attempts new themes we
need not, with Count Caylus, seek in his convenience, his ignor-
ance, or the difficulty of the mechanical part of art, demanding
all his time and diligence; but we shall find it more deeply
founded, and it may be that what at first appears to be the
limitations of art and the spoiling of our pleasure we shall be
inclined to praise as a restraint wise in itself and useful to
ourselves. Nor am I afraid that experience will confute me.
The painters will thank the Count for his goodwill, but hardly
follow his counsels so generally as he expects. If they should,
in another hundred years a new Caylus would be wanted who
should bring again to remembrance the old themes and re-
conduct the artist into the field where others before him have
gathered immortal laurels. Or do we desire that the public
shall be as learned as the connoisseur with his books? That to
the public all scenes of history or fable which might suggest a
beautiful picture shall become known and familiar? I grant
that the artists would have done better if since Raphael's day
they had made Homer instead of Ovid their manual. But as
that in fact has not happened, let us leave the public in their
old rut, and not make their pleasure harder to attain than a
pleasure must be in order to be what it should.

Protogenes had painted the mother of Aristotle. I don't
know how much the philosopher paid him for the picture.
But, either instead of payment or in addition thereto, he gave

him counsel that was worth more than the payment. For I cannot imagine that his counsel was a mere flattery. But chiefly because he considered the need of art—to be intelligible— he advised him to paint the achievements of Alexander, achievements of which at that time all the world was speaking, and of which he could foresee that they would be memorable also to posterity. Yet Protogenes had not discernment enough to follow this counsel; *impetus animi*, says Pliny, *et quaedam artis libido*, a certain arrogance of art, a certain lust for the strange and the unknown, attracted him to quite other subjects. He preferred to paint the story of a Jalysus, of a Cydippe and the like, of which to-day one cannot even guess what they represented.

XII

Homer treats of a twofold order of beings and actions : visible and invisible. This distinction it is not possible for painting to suggest; with it all is visible, and visible in one particular way. When, therefore, Count Caylus lets the pictures of the invisible actions run on in unbroken sequence with the visible ; when in the pictures of mingled actions, in which visible and invisible things take part, he does not, and perhaps cannot, suggest how the latter, which only we who contemplate the picture should discover therein, are so to be introduced that the persons in the picture do not see them, or at least must appear not necessarily to see them; it is inevitable that the entire composition, as well as many a separate portion of it, becomes confused, inconceivable, and self-contradictory.

Yet, with the book in one's hand, there might be some remedy for this error. The worst of it is simply this, that by the abrogation of the difference between the visible and invisible things all the characteristic features are at once lost by which the higher are raised above the inferior species. For example, when at last the divided gods come to blows among themselves over the fate of the Trojans, the whole struggle passes with the poet invisibly, and this invisibility permits the imagination to enlarge the stage, and leaves it free play to conceive the persons of the gods and their actions as great, and elevated as far above common humanity as ever it pleases. But painting must assume a visible stage the various necessary parts of which become the scale for the persons acting on it, a scale which the eye has

immediately before it, and whose disproportion, as regards the
higher beings, turns these higher beings, who were so great in
the poet's delineation, into sheer monsters on the canvas of the
artist.

Minerva, on whom in this struggle Mars ventures the first
assault, steps back and snatches up from the ground with
powerful hand a black, rough, massive stone, which in ancient
days many hands of men together had rolled thither as a landmark—

> 'Η δ' ἀναχασσαμένη λίθον εἵλετο χειρὶ παχείη,
> Κείμενον ἐν πεδίῳ, μέλανατρηχύν τε μέγαν τε,
> Τὸν δ' ἄνδρες πρότεροι θέσαν ἔμμεναι οὖρον ἀρούρης.

In order to estimate adequately the size of this stone, let us bear
in mind that Homer makes his heroes as strong again as the
strongest men of his time, and represents these, too, as far
excelled in strength by the men whom Nestor had known in his
youth. Now, I ask, if Minerva flings a stone which not one
man, but several men of Nestor's youth had set for a landmark,
if Minerva flings such a stone at Mars, of what stature is the
goddess to be? If her stature is in proportion to the size of
the stone, the marvellous vanishes. A man who is three times
bigger than I must naturally also be able to fling a three-times
bigger stone. But if the stature of the goddess is not in keeping
with the size of the stone, there is imported into the picture an
obvious improbability, the offence of which is not removed by
the cold reflection that a goddess must have superhuman
strength. Where I see a greater effect I would also see a greater
instrument. And Mars, struck down by this mighty stone—

> 'Επτὰ δ' ἔπεσχε πέλεθρα . . .

covered three hides of land. It is impossible that the painter
can give the god this monstrous bulk. Yet if he does not, then
Mars does not lie upon the ground, not the Homeric Mars, but
only a common warrior.

Longinus remarks that it often appeared to him as if Homer
wished to elevate his men to gods and to degrade his gods to
men. Painting carries out this degradation. In painting everything vanishes completely which with the poet sets the gods
yet higher than godlike men. Stature, strength, swiftness—of
which Homer has in store a higher and more wonderful degree
for his gods than he bestows on his most pre-eminent heroes—

must in picture sink down to the common measure of humanity, and Jupiter and Agamemnon, Apollo and Achilles, Ajax and Mars, become the same kind of beings, to be recognised no otherwise than by stipulated outward signs.

The means of which painting makes use to indicate that in her compositions this or that must be regarded as invisible, is a thin cloud in which she covers it from the view of the persons concerned. This cloud seems to have been borrowed from Homer himself. For when in the tumult of the battle one of the greater heroes comes into danger from which only heavenly power can deliver him, the poet causes him to be enveloped by the tutelary deity in a thick cloud or in actual night, and thus to be withdrawn from the place; as Paris was by Venus, Idäus by Neptune, Hector by Apollo. And this mist, this cloud Caylus never forgets heartily to commend to the artist when he is sketching for him a picture of such events. But who does not perceive that with the poet the enveloping in mist and darkness is nothing but a poetical way of saying invisible? It has, on this account, always surprised me to find this poetical expression realised and an actual cloud introduced into the picture, behind which the hero, as behind a screen, stands hidden from his enemy. That was not the poet's intention. That is to transgress the limits of painting; for this cloud is here a true hieroglyph, a mere symbolic sign, that does not make the rescued hero invisible, but calls out to the beholder, "You must regard him as invisible to you." This is no better than the inscribed labels which issue from the mouths of the persons in ancient Gothic pictures.

It is true Homer makes Achilles, when Apollo snatches away Hector from him, strike yet three times at the thick vapour with his spear: τρὶς δ' ἠέρα τύψε βαθεῖαν. But even that, in the poet's language, means no more than that Achilles became so enraged that he struck yet thrice before he noticed that he no longer had his foe in front of him. An actual mist Achilles did not see, and the whole artifice by which the gods made things invisible consisted not at all in the cloud, but in the swift snatching. Only, in order to show at the same time that no human eye could follow the body thus snatched away, the poet first of all envelops it beforehand in vapour; not that instead of the body withdrawn a fog was seen, but that whatever is under fog we think of as not visible. Therefore at times he inverts the order of things, and, instead of making the object invisible, causes the subject to be struck with blindness. Thus

E

Neptune darkens the eyes of Achilles to save Æneas from his murderous hands, removing him in a moment from out the tumult of the rearguard. In fact, however, the eyes of Achilles are here just as little darkened as in the other case the withdrawn heroes were enveloped in fog; the poet merely adds the one thing and the other, in order thereby to make more perceptible the extreme swiftness of the withdrawal which we call the vanishing.

The Homeric mist, however, the painters have made their own not merely in the cases where Homer himself uses or would have used it—in actual invisibilities or vanishings—but everywhere when the beholder is to recognise something in the picture which the persons in it, either altogether or in part, do not recognise. Minerva became visible to Achilles alone when she held him back from assaulting Agamemnon. " To express this," says Caylus, " I know no other way than to veil her in a cloud from the rest of the council." This is quite contrary to the spirit of the poet. To be invisible is the natural condition of his gods : no blinding, no cutting-off of the light, was needed in order that they should not be seen, but an illumination, a heightening of mortal vision, was necessary if they were to be seen. It is not enough, therefore, that the cloud is an arbitrary and unnatural sign with the painters; this arbitrary sign has not at all the positive significance which it might have as such, for they use it as frequently to make the visible invisible as they do the reverse.

XIII

If Homer's works were entirely lost, and nothing was left of his *Iliad* and *Odyssey* save a succession of pictures such as Caylus has suggested might be drawn from them, should we from these pictures, even from the hand of the most perfect master, be able to form the conception we now have, I do not say of the poet's whole endowment, but even of his pictorial talent alone? Let us try the experiment with the first passage that occurs to us—the picture of the pestilence. What do we perceive on the canvas of the artist? Dead corpses, flaming funeral pyres, dying men busy with the dead, the angry god upon a cloud letting fly his arrows. The greatest riches of this picture is, compared with the poet, mere poverty. For if we were to replace Homer from the picture, what could we make

him say? " Then did Apollo become enraged and shot his
arrows amongst the Grecian host. Many Greeks died and their
corpses were burned." Now let us turn to Homer himself :—

Βῆ δὲ κατ' Οὐλύμποιο καρήνων | χωόμενος κῆρ,|
Τόξ' ὤμοισιν ἔχων | ἀμφηρεφέα τε φαρέτρην·
Ἔκλαγξαν δ' ἄρ' ὀϊστοὶ ἐπ' ὤμων χωομένοιο,
Αὐτοῦ κινηθέντος· ὁ δ' ἤϊε νυκτὶ ἐοικώς|.
Ἕζετ' ἔπειτ' ἀπάνευθε νεῶν, μετὰ | δ' ἰὸν ἔηκε·
Δεινὴ δὲ κλαγγὴ γένετ' ἀργυρέοιο βιοῖο·
Οὐρῆας μὲν πρῶτον ἐπῴχετο | καὶ κύνας ἀργούς,
Αὐτὰρ ἔπειτ' αὐτοῖσι | βέλος ἐχεπευκὲς ἐφιεὶς
Βάλλ'· αἰεὶ δὲ πυραὶ | νεκύων | καίοντο θαμειαί.

Just as far as life is above painting, the poet here is above the
painter. With his bow and quiver the enraged Apollo descends
from the rocky peak of Olympus. I do not merely see him
descend, I hear him. At every step the arrows rattle about
the shoulders of the wrathful god. He glides along like night.
And now he sits opposite the ships—fearfully twangs the silver
bow—he darts the first arrow at the mules and dogs. And
then, with a more poisonous shaft, he strikes the men themselves; and everywhere without cessation break into flame the
corpse-encumbered pyres. The musical painting which we hear
in the words of the poet it is not possible to translate into
another language. It is just as impossible to gather it from
the material picture, although it is only a very trivial advantage
which the poetic picture possesses. The chief advantage is that
what the material painting drawn from him exhibits the poet
leads us up to through a whole gallery of pictures.

But, then, perhaps the pestilence is not an advantageous
subject for painting. Here is another having more charms for
the eye—the gods taking counsel together over their wine. A
golden palace open to the sky, arbitrary groups of the most
beautiful and the most worshipful forms, their cups in their
hands, waited on by Hebe, the image of eternal youth. What
architecture, what masses of light and shade, what contrasts,
what manifold expression! Where can I begin, and where
leave off, to feast my eyes? If the painter so enchants me,
how much more will the poet! I turn to his pages, and find—
that I am deceived. Four simple lines only, such as might
serve for the inscription of a picture; the material for a picture
is there, but they themselves do not make a picture :—

Οἱ δὲ θεοὶ πὰρ Ζηνὶ καθήμενοι ἠγορόωντο
Χρυσέῳ ἐν δαπέδῳ, μετὰ δέ σφισι πότνια Ἥβη
Νέκταρ ἐῳνοχόει· τοὶ δὲ χρυσέοις δεπάεσσι
Δειδέχατ᾽ ἀλλήλους, Τρώων πόλιν εἰσορόωντες.

This an Apollonius or an even more mediocre poet would have said equally well; and Homer here stands just as far below the painter as in the former case the painter stood below him.

Yet more, Caylus finds in the whole of the Fourth Book of the *Iliad* no other picture, not one, than in these four lines. "However much," he remarks, "the Fourth Book is marked by manifold encouragements to the attempt, owing to the abundance of brilliant and contrasted characters and to the art with which the poet shows us the entire multitude whom he will set in action—yet it is perfectly unusable for painting." He might have added, Rich as it is otherwise in that which we call poetic picture. For truly these are for number and perfection as remarkable as in any other Book. Where is there a more finished or more striking picture than that of Pandarus, as, on the incitement of Minerva, he breaks the truce and lets fly his arrow at Menelaus? Or that of the approach of the Grecian host? Or that of the two-sided, simultaneous onset? Or that of Ulysses' deed by which he avenges the death of his Leucus?

What, then, follows from the fact that not a few of the finest descriptions in Homer afford no picture for the artist, and that the artist can draw pictures from him where he himself has none? That those which he has and the artist can use would be very poverty-stricken pictures if they did not show more than can be shown by the artist? What else do they, but give a negative to my former question? That from the material paintings for which the poems of Homer provide the subjects, however numerous they may be and however excellent, nothing can be concluded as to the pictorial talent of the poet.

XIV

But if it is so, and if one poem may yield very happy results for the painter yet itself be not pictorial; if, again, another in its turn may be very pictorial and yet offer nothing to the painter; this is enough to dispose of Count Caylus' notion, which would make this kind of utility the criterion or test of the poets and settle their rank by the number of pictures which they provide for the artist. Far be it from us, even if only by our silence, to allow this notion to gain the authority of a rule. Milton would fall the first innocent sacrifice to it. For it seems really that the contemptuous verdict which Caylus passes upon him was not mere national prejudice, but rather a consequence of his supposed principle. "The loss of sight," he says, "may well be the nearest resemblance Milton bore to Homer." True, Milton can fill no galleries. But if, so long as I had the bodily eye, its sphere must also be the sphere of my inward eye, then would I, in order to be free of this limitation, set a great value on the loss of the former. The *Paradise Lost* is not less the first epic poem since Homer on the ground of its providing few pictures, than the *Leidensgeschichte Christi* is a poem because we can hardly put the point of a needle into it without touching a passage that might have employed a multitude of the greatest artists. The Evangelists relate the facts with all the dry simplicity possible, and the artist uses the manifold parts of the story without their having shown on their side the smallest spark of pictorial genius. There are paintable and unpaintable facts, and the historian can relate the most paintable in just as unpictorial a fashion as the poet can represent the least paintable pictorially.

We are merely misled by the ambiguity of words if we take the matter otherwise. A poetic picture is not necessarily that which can be transmuted into a material painting; but every feature, every combination of features by means of which the poet makes his subject so perceptible that we are more clearly conscious of this subject than of his words is called pictorial, is styled a picture, because it brings us nearer to the degree of illusion of which the material painting is specially capable and which can most readily and most easily be drawn from the material painting.

XV

Now the poet, as experience shows, can raise to this degree of illusion the representations even of other than visible objects. Consequently the artist must necessarily be denied whole classes of pictures in which the poet has the advantage over him. Dryden's Ode on St. Cecilia's Day is full of musical pictures that cannot be touched by the paint-brush. But I will not lose myself in instances of the kind, from which in the end we learn nothing more than that colours are not tones and that eyes are not ears.

I will confine myself to the pictures of purely visible objects which are common to the poet and the painter. How comes it that many poetical pictures of this kind cannot be used by the painter, and, *vice versa*, many actual pictures lose the best part of their effect in the hands of the poet?

Examples may help us. I repeat it—the picture of Pandarus in the Fourth Book of the *Iliad* is one of the most finished and most striking in all Homer. From the seizing of the bow to the very flight of the arrow every moment is depicted, and all these moments are kept so close together, and yet so distinctly separate, that if we did not know how a bow was to be managed we might learn it from this picture alone. Pandarus draws forth his bow, fixes the bowstring, opens his quiver, chooses a yet unused, well-feathered shaft, sets the arrow on the string, draws back both string and arrow down to the notch, the string is brought near to his breast and the iron head of the arrow to the bow; back flies the great bent bow with a twang, the bowstring whirs, off springs the arrow flying eager for its mark.

This admirable picture Caylus cannot have overlooked. What, then, did he find in it to render it incapable of employing his artist? And for what reason did he consider fitter for this purpose the assembly of the carousing gods in council? In the one, as in the other, we find visible subjects, and what more does the poet want than visible subjects in order to fill his canvas? The solution of the problem must be this. Although both subjects, as being visible, are alike capable of actual painting, yet there exists the essential distinction between them, that the former is a visible continuous action, the different parts of which occur step by step in succession of time, the latter, on the other hand, is a visible arrested action, the different parts of which develop side by side in space. But now, if painting, in virtue of her signs or the methods of her imitation, which she can combine only in space, must wholly renounce time, then continuous actions as such cannot be reckoned amongst her subjects; but she must content herself with actions set side by side, or with mere bodies which by their attitudes can be supposed an action. Poetry, on the other hand——

XVI

But I will turn to the foundations and try to argue the matter from first principles.

My conclusion is this. If it is true that painting employs in its imitations quite other means or signs than poetry employs, the former—that is to say, figures and colours in space—but the latter articulate sounds in time; as, unquestionably, the signs used must have a definite relation to the thing signified, it follows that signs arranged together side by side can express only subjects which, or the various parts of which, exist thus side by side, whilst signs which succeed each other can express only subjects which, or the various parts of which, succeed each other.

Subjects which, or the various parts of which, exist side by side, may be called *bodies*. Consequently, bodies with their visible properties form the proper subjects of painting.

Subjects which or the various parts of which succeed each other may in general be called *actions*. Consequently, actions form the proper subjects of poetry.

Yet all bodies exist not in space alone, but also in time. They continue, and may appear differently at every moment and stand in different relations. Every one of these momentary appearances and combinations is the effect of one preceding and can be the cause of one following, and accordingly be likewise the central point of an action. Consequently, painting can also imitate actions, but only by way of suggestion through bodies.

On the other hand, actions cannot subsist for themselves, but must attach to certain things or persons. Now in so far as these things are bodies or are regarded as bodies, poetry too depicts bodies, but only by way of suggestion through actions.

Painting, in her co-existing compositions, can use only one single moment of the action, and must therefore choose the most pregnant, from which what precedes and follows will be most easily apprehended.

Just in the same manner poetry also can use, in her continuous imitations, only one single property of the bodies, and must therefore choose that one which calls up the most living picture of the body on that side from which she is regarding it. Here, indeed, we find the origin of the rule which insists on the unity and consistency of descriptive epithets, and on economy in the delineations of bodily subjects.

This is a dry chain of reasoning, and I should put less trust in it if I did not find it completely confirmed by Homer's practice, or if, rather, it were not Homer's practice itself which had led me to it. Only by these principles can the great manner of the Greeks be settled and explained, and its rightness established against the opposite manner of so many modern poets, who would emulate the painter in a department where they must necessarily be outdone by him.

Homer, I find, paints nothing but continuous actions, and all bodies, all single things, he paints only by their share in those actions, and in general only by one feature. What wonder, then, that the painter, where Homer himself paints, finds little or nothing for him to do, his harvest arising only there where the story brings together a multitude of beautiful bodies, in beautiful attitudes, in a place favourable to art, the poet himself painting these bodies, attitudes, places, just as little as he chooses? Let the reader run through the whole succession of pictures piece by piece, as Caylus suggests, and he will discover in every one of them evidence for our contention.

Here, then, I leave the Count, who wishes to make the painter's palette the touchstone of the poet, that I may expound in closer detail the manner of Homer.

For one thing, I say, Homer commonly names one feature only. A ship is to him now the black ship, now the hollow ship, now the swift ship, at most the well-rowed black ship. Beyond that he does not enter on a picture of the ship. But certainly of the navigating, the putting to sea, the disembarking of the ship, he makes a detailed picture, one from which the painter must make five or six separate pictures if he would get it in its entirety upon his canvas.

If indeed special circumstances compel Homer to fix our glance for a while on some single corporeal object, in spite of this no picture is made of it which the painter could follow with his brush; for Homer knows how, by innumerable artifices, to set this object in a succession of moments, at each of which it assumes a different appearance, and in the last of which the painter must await it in order to show us, fully arisen, what in the poet we see arising. For instance, if Homer wishes to let us see the chariot of Juno, then Hebe must put it together piece by piece before our eyes. We see the wheels, the axles, the seat, the pole and straps and traces, not so much as it is when complete, but as it comes together under the hands of Hebe. On the wheels alone does the poet expend more than one feature,

showing us the brazen spokes, the golden rims, the tires of
bronze, the silver hub, in fullest detail. We might suggest that
as there were more wheels than one, so in the description just
as much more time must be given to them as their separate
putting-on would actually itself require.

> Ἥβη δ' ἀμφ' ὀχέεσσι θοῶς βάλε καμπύλα κύκλα,
> Χάλκεα ὀκτάκνημα, σιδηρέῳ ἄξονι ἀμφίς.
> Τῶν ἦ τοι χρυσέη ἴτυς ἄφθιτος, αὐτὰρ ὕπερθε
> Χάλκε' ἐπίσσωτρα προσαρηρότα, θαῦμα ἰδέσθαι·
> Πλῆμναι δ' ἀργύρου εἰσὶ περίδρομοι ἀμφοτέρωθεν·
> Δίφρος δὲ χρυσέοισι καὶ ἀργυρέοισιν ἱμᾶσιν
> Ἐντέταται, δοιαὶ δὲ περίδρομοι ἄντυγές εἰσι.
> Τοῦ δ' ἐξ ἀργύρεος ῥυμὸς πέλεν· αὐτὰρ ἐπ' ἄκρῳ
> Δῆσε χρύσειον καλὸν ζυγόν, ἐν δὲ λέπαδνα
> Κάλ' ἔβαλε χρύσεια.

If Homer would show us how Agamemnon was dressed, then
the King must put on his whole attire piece by piece before our
eyes : the soft undervest, the great mantle, the fine laced boots,
the sword; and now he is ready and grasps the sceptre. We
see the attire as the poet paints the action of attiring; another
would have described the garments down to the smallest ribbon,
and we should have seen nothing of the action.

> Μαλακὸν δ' ἔνδυνε χιτῶνα,
> Καλὸν νηγάτεον, περὶ δὲ μέγα βάλλετο φᾶρος·
> Ποσσὶ δ' ὑπὸ λιπαροῖσιν ἐδήσατο καλὰ πέδιλα,
> Ἀμφὶ δ' ἄρ' ὤμοισιν βάλετο ξίφος ἀργυρόηλον·
> Εἵλετο δὲ σκῆπτρον πατρώιον, ἄφθιτον αἰεί.

And of this sceptre which here is called merely the paternal,
ancestral sceptre, as in another place he calls a similar one
merely χρυσείοις ἥλοισι πεπαρμένον—that is, the sceptre
mounted with studs of gold—if, I say, of this mighty sceptre
we are to have a fuller and exacter picture, what, then, does
Homer? Does he paint for us, besides the golden nails, the
wood also and the carved knob? Perhaps he might if the
description were intended for a book of heraldry, so that in
after times one like to it might be made precisely to pattern.
And yet I am certain that many a modern poet would have
made just such a heraldic description, with the naïve idea that
he has himself so painted it because the painter may possibly
follow him. But what does Homer care how far he leaves the

painter behind? Instead of an image he gives us the story of the sceptre : first, it is being wrought by Vulcan; then it gleams in the hands of Jupiter; again, it marks the office of Mercury; once more, it is the marshal's baton of the warlike Pelops, and yet again, the shepherd's crook of peace-loving Atreus.

Σκῆπτρον ἔχων, τὸ μὲν Ἥφαιστος κάμε τεύχων.
Ἥφαιστος μὲν δῶκε Διὶ Κρονίωνι ἄνακτι,
Αὐτὰρ ἄρα Ζεὺς δῶκε διακτόρῳ ἀργεϊφόντῃ·
Ἑρμείας δὲ ἄναξ δῶκεν Πέλοπι πληξίππῳ,
Αὐτὰρ ὁ αὖτε Πέλοψ δῶκ' Ἀτρεῖ, ποιμένι λαῶν·
Ἀτρεὺς δὲ θνῄσκων ἔλιπεν πολύαρνι Θυέστῃ,
Αὐτὰρ ὁ αὖτε Θυέστ' Ἀγαμέμνονι λεῖπε φορῆναι,
Πολλῇσιν νήσοισι καὶ Ἄργεϊ παντὶ ἀνάσσειν.

And so in the end I know this sceptre better than if a painter had laid it before my eyes or a second Vulcan delivered it into my hands. It would not surprise me if I found that one of the old commentators of Homer had admired this passage as the most perfect allegory of the origin, progress, establishment, and hereditary succession of the royal power amongst mankind. True, I should smile if I were to read that Vulcan, the maker of this sceptre, as fire, as the most indispensable thing for the preservation of mankind, represented in general the satisfaction of those wants which moved the first men to subject themselves to the rule of an individual monarch; that the first king, a son of Time (Ζεὺς Κρονίων), was an honest ancient who wished to share his power with, or wholly transfer it to, a wise and eloquent man, a Mercury (διακτόρῳ ἀργεϊφόντῃ); that the wily orator, at the time when the infant State was threatened by foreign foes, resigned his supreme power to the bravest warrior (Πέλοπι πληξίππῳ); that the brave warrior, when he had quelled the aggressors and made the realm secure, was able to hand it over to his son, who, as a peace-loving ruler, as a benevolent shepherd of his people (ποιμὴν λαῶν), made them acquainted with luxury and abundance, whereby after his death the wealthiest of his relations (πολύαρνι Θυέστῃ) had the way opened to him for attracting to himself by presents and bribes that which hitherto only confidence had conferred and which merit had considered more a burden than an honour, and to secure it to his family for the future as a kind of purchased estate. I should smile, but nevertheless should be confirmed in my esteem for the poet to whom so much meaning can be

attributed.—This, however, is a digression, and I am now
regarding the story of the sceptre merely as an artifice to make
us tarry over the one particular object without being drawn
into the tedious description of its parts. Even when Achilles
swears by his sceptre to avenge the contempt with which
Agamemnon has treated him, Homer gives us the history of
this sceptre. We see it growing green upon the mountains, the
axe cutting it from the trunk, stripping it of leaves and bark
and making it fit to serve the judges of the people for a symbol
of their godlike dignity.

> Ναὶ μὰ τόδε σκῆπτρον, τὸ μὲν οὔ ποτε φύλλα καὶ ὄζους
> Φύσει, ἐπεὶ δὴ πρῶτα τομὴν ἐν ὄρεσσι λέλοιπεν,
> Οὐδ' ἀναθηλήσει· περὶ γάρ ῥά ἑ χαλκὸς ἔλεψε
> Φύλλα τε καὶ φλοιόν· νῦν αὖτέ μιν υἷες 'Αχαιῶν
> 'Εν παλάμῃς φορέουσι δικασπόλοι, οἵ τε θέμιστας
> Πρὸς Διὸς εἰρύαται . . . .

It was not so much incumbent upon Homer to depict two
staves of different material and shape as to furnish us with a
symbol of the difference in the powers of which these staves
were the sign. The former a work of Vulcan, the latter carved
by an unknown hand in the mountains; the former the ancient
property of a noble house, the latter intended for any fist that
can grasp it; the former extended by a monarch over all Argos
and many an isle besides, the latter borne by any one out of the
midst of the Grecian hosts, one to whom with others the guarding
of the laws had been committed. Such was actually the distance that separated Agamemnon from Achilles, a distance
which Achilles himself, in all the blindness of his wrath, could
not help admitting.

Yet not in those cases alone where Homer combines with his
descriptions this kind of ulterior purpose, but even where he
has to do with nothing but the picture, he will distribute this
picture in a sort of story of the object, in order to let its parts,
which we see side by side in Nature, follow in his painting after
each other and as it were keep step with the flow of the narrative.
For instance, he would paint for us the bow of Pandarus—a
bow of horn, of such and such a length, well polished, and
mounted with gold plate at the extremities. How does he
manage it? Does he count out before us all these properties
dryly one after the other? Not at all; that would be to sketch,
to make a copy of such a bow, but not to paint it. He begins

with the chase of the deer, from the horns of which the bow
was made; Pandarus had waylaid and killed it amongst the
crags; the horns were of extraordinary length, and so he destined
them for a bow; they are wrought, the maker joins them,
mounts them, polishes them. And thus, as we have already
said, with the poet we see arising what with the painter we
can only see as already arisen.

Τόξον ἐΰξοον ἰξάλου αἰγὸς
'Αγρίου, ὅν ῥά ποτ' αὐτὸς ὑπὸ στέρνοιο τυχήσας
Πέτρης ἐκβαίνοντα δεδεγμένος ἐν προδοκῇσι,
Βεβλήκει πρὸς στῆθος· ὁ δ' ὕπτιος ἔμπεσε πέτρῃ.
Τοῦ κέρα ἐκ κεφαλῆς ἑκκαιδεκάδωρα πεφύκει·
Καὶ τὰ μὲν ἀσκήσας κεραοξόος ἤραρε τέκτων,
Πᾶν δ' ἐῢ λειήνας χρυσέην ἐπέθηκε κορώνην.

I should never have done, if I were to cite all the instances of
this kind. A multitude of them will occur to everyone who
knows his Homer.

XVII

But, some will object, the signs or characters which poetry
employs are not solely such as succeed each other ; they may be
also arbitrary; and, as arbitrary signs, they are certainly
capable of representing bodies just as they exist in space. We
find instances of this in Homer himself, for we have only to
remember his Shield of Achilles in order to have the most
decisive example in how detailed and yet poetical a manner
some single thing can be depicted, with its various parts side
by side.

I will reply to this twofold objection. I call it twofold,
because a just conclusion must prevail even without examples,
and, on the other hand, the example of Homer weighs with
me even if I know not how to justify it by any argument. It
is true, as the signs of speech are arbitrary, so it is perfectly
possible that by it we can make the parts of a body follow each
other just as truly as in actuality they are found existing side
by side. Only this is a property of speech and its signs in
general, but not in so far as it suits best the purposes of poetry.
The poet is not concerned merely to be intelligible, his representations should not merely be clear and plain, though this
may satisfy the prose writer. He desires rather to make the

ideas awakened by him within us living things, so that for the
moment we realise the true sensuous impressions of the objects
he describes, and cease in this moment of illusion to be conscious
of the means—namely, his words—which he employs for his
purpose. This is the substance of what we have already said
of the poetic picture. But the poet should always paint; and
now let us see how far bodies with their parts set side by side are
suitable for this kind of painting.

How do we arrive at the distinct representation of a thing in
space? First we regard its parts singly, then the combination
of these parts, and finally the whole. Our senses perform these
various operations with so astonishing a swiftness that they
seem to us but one, and this swiftness is imperatively necessary
if we are to arrive at a conception of the whole, which is nothing
more than the result of the conceptions of the parts and their
combination. Provided, then, the poet leads us in the most
beautiful order from one part of the object to another; provided he knows also how to make the combination of those
parts equally clear—how much time does he need for that?
What the eye sees at a glance, he counts out to us gradually,
with a perceptible slowness, and often it happens that when we
come to the last feature we have already forgotten the first.
Nevertheless, we have to frame a whole from those features;
to the eye the parts beheld remain constantly present, and it
can run over them again and again; for the ear, on the contrary,
the parts heard are lost if they do not abide in the memory.
And if they so abide, what trouble, what effort it costs to renew
their impressions, all of them in their due order, so vividly, to
think of them together with even a moderate swiftness, and thus
to arrive at an eventual conception of the whole. Let us try
it by an example which may be called a masterpiece of its
kind :—

> *Dort ragt das hohe Haupt vom edeln Enziane*
> *Weit übern niedern Chor der Pöbelkräuter hin,*
> *Ein ganzes Blumenvolk dient unter seiner Fahne,*
> *Sein blauer Bruder selbst dückt sich und ehret ihn.*
> *Der Blumen helles Gold, in Strahlen umgebogen,*
> *Thürmt sich am Stengel auf, und krönt sein grau Gewand,*
> *Der Blätter glattes Weiss, mit tiefem Grün durchzogen,*
> *Strahlt von dem bunten Blitz von feuchtem Diamant.*
> *Gerechtestes Gesetz ! dass Kraft sich Zier vermähle,*
> *In einem schönen Leib wohnt eine schöne Seele.*
> *Hier kriecht ein niedrig Kraut, gleich einem grauen Nebel,*
> *Dem die Natur sein Blatt im Kreuze hingelegt ;*

Die holde Blume zeigt die zwei vergöldten Schnäbel,
Die ein von Amethyst gebildter Vogel trägt.
Dort wirft ein glänzend Blatt, in Finger ausgekerbet,
Auf einen hellen Bach den grünen Wiederschein ;
Der Blumen zarten Schnee, den matter Purpur färbet,
Schliesst ein gestreifter Stern in weisse Strahlen ein.
Smaragd und Rosen blühn auch auf zertretner Heide,
Und Felsen decken sich mit einem Purpurkleide.

Here are weeds and flowers which the learned poet paints with much art and fidelity to Nature. Paints, but without any illusion whatever. I will not say that out of this picture he who has never seen these weeds and flowers can make no idea of them, or as good as none. It may be that all poetic pictures require some preliminary acquaintance with their subjects. Neither will I deny that for one who possesses such an acquaintance here the poet may not have awakened a more vivid idea of some parts. I only ask him, How does it stand with the conception of the whole? If this also is to be more vivid, then no single parts must stand out, but the higher light must appear divided equally amongst them all, our imagination must be able to run over them all with equal swiftness, in order to unite in one from them that which in Nature we see united in one. Is this the case here? And is not the case rather, as one has expressed it, " that the most perfect drawing of a painter must be entirely lifeless and dark compared with this poetic portrayal "? It remains infinitely below that which lines and colours on canvas can express, and the critic who bestows on it this exaggerated praise must have regarded it from an utterly false point of view : he must have looked rather at the ornaments which the poet has woven into it, at the heightening of the subject above the mere vegetative life, at the development of the inner perfection to which the outward beauty serves merely as a shell, than at the beauty itself and at the degree of life and resemblance in the picture which the painter and which the poet can assure to us from it. Nevertheless, it amounts here purely to the latter, and whoever says that the mere lines :—

Der Blumen helles Gold, in Strahlen umgebogen,
Thürmt sich am Stengel auf, und krönt sein grün Gewand,
Der Blätter glattes Weiss, mit tiefem Grün durchzogen,
Strahlt von dem bunten Blitz von feuchtem Diamant,

—that these lines in respect of their impression can compete with the imitation of a Huysum, can never have interrogated his feelings, or must be deliberately denying them. They may, indeed, if we have the flower itself in our hands, be recited concerning it with excellent effect; but in themselves alone they say little or nothing. I hear in every word the toiling poet, and am far enough from seeing the thing itself.

Once more, then; I do not deny to speech in general the power of portraying a bodily whole by its parts: speech can do so, because its signs or characters, although they follow one another consecutively, are nevertheless arbitrary signs; but I do deny it to speech as the medium of poetry, because such verbal delineations of bodies fail of the illusion on which poetry particularly depends, and this illusion, I contend, must fail them for the reason that the *co-existence* of the physical object comes into collision with the *consecutiveness* of speech, and the former being resolved into the latter, the dismemberment of the whole into its parts is certainly made easier, but the final reunion of those parts into a whole is made uncommonly difficult and not seldom impossible.

Wherever, then, illusion does not come into the question, where one has only to do with the understanding of one's readers and appeals only to plain and as far as possible complete conceptions, those delineations of bodies (which we have excluded from poetry) may quite well find their place, and not the prose-writer alone, but the dogmatic poet (for where he dogmatises he is not a poet) can employ them with much advantage. So Virgil, for instance, in his poem on agriculture, delineates a cow suitable for breeding from :—

> . . . Optima torvae
> Forma bovis, cui turpe caput, cui plurima cervix,
> Et crurum tenus a mento palearia pendent ;
> Tum longo nullus lateri modus : omnia magna,
> Pes etiam, et camuris hirtae sub cornibus aures.
> Nec mihi displiceat maculis insignis et albo,
> Aut juga detrectans interdumque aspera cornu
> Et faciem tauro propior, quaeque ardua tota,
> Et gradiens ima verrit vestigia cauda.

Or a beautiful foal :—

> . . . Illi ardua cervix
> Argutumque caput, brevis alvus, obesaque terga,
> Luxuriatque toris animosum pectus, etc.

For who does not see that here the poet is concerned rather with the setting forth of the parts than with the whole? He wants to reckon up for us the characteristics of a fine foal and of a well-formed cow, in order to enable us, when we have more or less taken note of these, to judge of the excellence of the one or the other; whether, however, all these characteristics can be easily gathered together into one living picture or not, that might be to him a matter of indifference.

Beyond such performances as these, the detailed pictures of physical objects, barring the above-mentioned Homeric artifice of changing the Co-existing into an actual Successive, has always been recognised by the best judges as a frigid kind of sport for which little or nothing of genius is demanded. " When the poetic dabbler," says Horace, " can do nothing more, he begins to paint a hedge, an altar, a brook winding through pleasant meads, a brawling stream, or a rainbow :—

> . . . *Lucus et ara Dianae*
> *Et properantis aquae per amoenos ambitus agros,*
> *Aut flumen Rhenum, aut pluvius describitur arcus.*"

Pope, who was a masculine man, looked back on the pictorial efforts of his poetic childhood with great contempt. He expressly required that whosoever would not unworthily bear the name of poet should as early as possible renounce the lust for description, and declared a merely descriptive poem to be a dinner of nothing but soup. Of Herr von Kleist I can avow that he was far from proud of his " Spring " : had he lived longer, he would have given it an entirely different shape. He thought of putting some design into it, and mused on means by which that multitude of pictures which he seemed to have snatched haphazard, now here, now there, from the limitless field of rejuvenated Nature, might be made to arise in a natural order before his eyes and follow each other in a natural succession. He would at the same time have done what Marmontel, doubtless on the occasion of his Eclogues, recommended to several German poets; from a series of pictures but sparingly interspersed with sensations he would have made a succession of sensations but sparingly interspersed with pictures.

XVIII

And yet may not Homer himself sometimes have lapsed into these frigid delineations of physical objects?

I will hope that there are only a few passages to which in this case appeal can be made; and I am assured that even these few are of such a kind as rather to confirm the rule from which they seem to be exceptions. It still holds good; succession in

time is the sphere of the poet, as space is that of the painter.
To bring two necessarily distant points of time into one and
the same picture, as Fr. Mazzuoli has done with the Rape of the
Sabine Women and their reconciling their husbands to their
kinsfolk, or as Titian with the whole story of the Prodigal Son,
his dissolute life, his misery, and his repentance, is nothing but
an invasion of the poet's sphere by the painter, which good
taste can never sanction. The several parts or things which
in Nature I must needs take in at a glance if they are to produce
a whole—to reckon these up one by one to the reader, in order
to form for him a picture of the whole, is nothing but an invasion
of the painter's sphere by the poet, who expends thereby a
great deal of imagination to no purpose. Still, as two friendly,
reasonable neighbours will not at all permit that one of them
shall make too free with the most intimate concerns of the
other, yet will exercise in things of less importance a mutual
forbearance and on either side condone trifling interferences
with one's strict rights to which circumstances may give occasion,
so it is with Painting and Poetry.

It is unnecessary here for my purpose to point out that in
great historical pictures the single moment is almost always
amplified to some extent, and that there is perhaps no single
composition very rich in figures where every figure has completely the movement and posture which at the moment of the
main action it ought to have; one is earlier, another later, than
historical truth would require. This is a liberty which the
master must make good by certain niceties of arrangement, by
the employment or the withdrawal of his *personæ*, such as will
permit them to take a greater or a smaller share in what is
passing at the moment. Let me here avail myself of but one
remark which Herr Mengs has made concerning the drapery of
Raphael. "All folds," he says, "have with him their reasons,
it may be from their own weight or by the pulling of the limbs.
We can often see from them how they have been at an earlier
moment; even in this Raphael seeks significance. One sees
from the folds whether a leg or an arm, before the moment
depicted, has stood in front or behind, whether the limb has
moved from curvature to extension, or after being stretched
out is now bending." It is undeniable that the artist in this
case brings two different moments into one. For as the foot
which has rested behind and now moves forward is immediately
followed by the part of the dress resting upon it, unless the dress
be of very stiff material and for that very reason is altogether

F

inconvenient to paint, so there is no moment in which the
dress makes a fold different in the slightest from that which the
present position of the limb demands; but if we permit it to
make another fold, then we have the previous moment of the
dress and the present moment of the limb. Nevertheless, who
will be so particular with the artist who finds his advantage in
showing us these two moments together? Who will not rather
praise him for having the intelligence and the courage to commit
a fault so trifling in order to attain a greater perfection of
expression?

The poet is entitled to equal indulgence. His progressive
imitation properly allows him to touch but one single side, one
single property of his physical subject at a time. But if the
happy construction of his language permits him to do this with
a single word, why should he not also venture now and then to
add a second such word? Why not even, if it is worth the
trouble, a third? Or, indeed, perhaps a fourth? I have said
that to Homer a ship was either the black ship, or the hollow
ship, or the swift ship, or at most the well-rowed black ship.
This is to be understood of his manner in general. Here and
there a passage occurs where he adds the third descriptive
epithet: Καμπύλα κύκλα, χάλκεα, ὀκτάκνημα, round, brazen,
eight-spoked wheels. Even the fourth: ἀσπίδα πάντοσε ἴσην,
καλήν, χαλκείην, ἐξήλατον, a completely polished, beautiful,
brazen, chased shield. Who will blame him for that? Who
will not rather owe him thanks for this little exuberance, when
he feels what an excellent effect it may have in a suitable place?

I am unwilling, however, to argue the poet's or the painter's
proper justification from the simile I have employed, of the
two friendly neighbours. A mere simile proves and justifies
nothing. But they must be justified in this way: just as in
the one case, with the painter, the two distinct moments touch
each other so closely and immediately that they may without
offence count as but one, so also in the other case, with the
poet, the several strokes for the different parts and properties
in space succeed each other so quickly, in such a crowded
moment, that we can believe we hear all of them at once.

And in this, I may remark, his splendid language served
Homer marvellously. It allowed him not merely all possible
freedom in the combining and heaping-up of epithets, but it
had, too, for their heaped-up epithets an order so happy as
quite to remedy the disadvantage arising from the suspension
of their application. In one or several of these facilities the

modern languages are universally lacking. Those, like the French, which, to give an example, for καμπύλα κύκλα, χάλκεα, ὀκτάκνημα, must use the circumlocution " the round wheels which were of brass and had eight spokes," express the sense, but destroy the picture. The sense, moreover, is here nothing, and the picture everything; and the former without the latter makes the most vivid poet the most tedious babbler— a fate that has frequently befallen our good Homer under the pen of the conscientious Madame Dacier. Our German tongue, again, can, it is true, generally translate the Homeric epithets by epithets equivalent and just as terse, but in the advantageous order of them it cannot match the Greek. We say, indeed, " *Die runden, ehernen, achtspeichigten* "; but " *Räder* " trails behind. Who does not feel that three different predicates, before we know the subject, can make but a vague and confused picture? The Greek joins the subject and the first predicate immediately, and lets the others follow after; he says, " *Runde Räder, eherne, achtspeichigte.*" So we know at once of what he is speaking, and are made acquainted, in consonance with the natural order of thought, first with the thing and then with its accidents. This advantage our language does not possess. Or, shall I say, possesses it and can only very seldom use it without ambiguity? The two things are one. For when we would place the epithets after, they must stand *in statu absoluto ;* we must say, " *Runde Räder, ehern und achtspeichigt.*" But in this *status* our adjectives are exactly like adverbs, and must, if we attach them as such to the next verb which is predicated of the thing, produce a meaning not seldom wholly false, and, at best, invariably ambiguous.

But here I am dwelling on trifles, and seem to have forgotten the Shield—Achilles' Shield, that famous picture in respect of which especially Homer was from of old regarded as a teacher of painting. A shield, people will say—that is surely a single physical object, the description of which and its parts ranged side by side is not permissible to a poet? And this particular shield, in its material, in its form, in all the figures that covered the vast surface of it, Homer has described in more than a hundred splendid verses, with such exactness and detail that it has been easy for modern artists to make a replica of it alike in every feature.

To this special objection I reply, that I have replied to it already. Homer, that is to say, paints the Shield not as a finished and complete thing, but as a thing in process. Here once more he has availed himself of the famous artifice, turning the *co-existing* of his design into a *consecutive*, and thereby making of the tedious painting of a physical object the living picture of an action. We see not the Shield, but the divine artificer at work upon it. He steps up with hammer and tongs to his anvil, and after he has forged the plates from the rough ore, the pictures which he has selected for its adornment stand out one after another before our eyes under his artistic chiseling. Nor do we lose sight of him again until all is finished. When it is complete, we are amazed at the work, but it is with the believing amazement of an eye-witness who has seen it in the making.

The same cannot be said of the Shield of Æneas in Virgil. The Roman poet either did not realise the subtlety of his mode here, or the things that he wanted to put upon his Shield appeared to him to be of a kind that could not well admit of being shown in execution. They were prophecies, which could not have been uttered by the god in our presence as plainly as the poet afterwards expounds them. Prophecies, as such, demand an obscurer language, in which the actual names of persons yet-to-be may not fitly be pronounced. Yet these veritable names, to all appearance, were the most important things of all to the poet and courtier. If, however, this excuse him, it does not remove the unhappy effect of his deviation from the Homeric way. Readers of any delicacy of taste will justify me here. The preparations which Vulcan makes for his labour are almost the same in Virgil as in Homer. But instead of what we see in Homer—that is to say, not merely the preparation for the work, but also the work itself—Virgil after he has given us a general view of the busy god with his Cyclops :—

> *Ingentem clypeum informant. . . .*
> *. . . Alii ventosis follibus auras*
> *Accipiunt redduntque, alii stridentia tingunt*
> *Aera lacu. Gemit impositis incudibus antrum.*
> *Illi inter sese multa vi brachia tollunt*
> *In numerum, versantque tenaci forcipe massam—*

drops the curtain at once and transports us to another scene, bringing us gradually into the valley where Venus arrives at Æneas' side with the armour that has meanwhile been completed. She leans the weapons against the trunk of an oak-tree, and when the hero has sufficiently gazed at, and admired, and touched and tested them, the description of the pictures on the Shield begins, and, with the everlasting : " Here is," " and

there is," " near by stands," and " not far off one sees," becomes
so frigid and tedious that all the poetic ornament which Virgil
could give it was needed to prevent us finding it unendurable.
Moreover, as this picture is not drawn by Æneas as one who
rejoices in the mere figures and knows nothing of their significance :—

> . . . *rerumque ignarus imagine gaudet ;*

nor even by Venus, although conceivably she must know just
as much of the future fortunes of her dear grandchildren as the
obliging goodman; but proceeds from the poet's own mouth,
the progress of the action meanwhile is obviously at a standstill.
No single one of his characters takes any share in it; nor does
anything represented on the Shield have any influence, even the
smallest, on what is to follow; the witty courtier shines out
everywhere, trimming up his matter with every kind of flattering
allusion, but not the great genius, depending on the proper
inner vitality of his work and despising all extraneous expedients
for lending it interest. The Shield of Æneas is consequently a
sheer interpolation, simply and only intended to flatter the
national pride of the Romans, a foreign tributary which the
poet leads into his main stream in order to give it a livelier
motion. The Shield of Achilles, on the other hand, is a rich
natural outgrowth of the fertile soil from which it springs; for
a Shield had to be made, and as the needful thing never comes
bare and without grace from the hands of the divinity, the
Shield had also to be embellished. But the art was, to treat
these embellishments merely as such, to inweave them into the
stuff, in order to show them to us only by means of the latter;
and this could only be done by Homer's method. Homer lets
Vulcan elaborate ornaments because he is to make a Shield
that is worthy of himself. Virgil, on the other hand, appears to
let him make the Shield for the sake of its ornaments, considering them important enough to be particularly described,
after the Shield itself has long been finished.

XIX

The objections which the elder Scaliger, Perrault, Terrasson,
and others make to the Shield in Homer are well known.
Equally well known is the reply which Dacier, Boivin, and
Pope made to them. In my judgment, however, the latter go
too far, and, relying on their good cause, introduce arguments

that are not only indefensible, but contribute little to the poet's justification.

In order to meet the main objection—that Homer has crowded the Shield with a multitude of figures such as could not possibly find room within its circumference—Boivin undertook to have it drawn, with a note of the necessary dimensions. His notion of the various concentric circles is very ingenious, although the words of the poet give not the slightest suggestion of it, whilst, furthermore, not a trace of proof is to be found that the ancients possessed shields divided off in this manner. Seeing that Homer himself calls it σάκος πάντοσε δεδαιδαλμένον—a shield artfully wrought upon all sides—I would rather, in order to reserve more room, have taken in aid the concave surface; for it is well known that the ancient artists did not leave this vacant, as the Shield of Minerva by Phidias proves. Yet it was not even enough for Boivin to decline availing himself of this advantage; he further increased without necessity the representations themselves for which he was obliged to provide room in the space thus diminished by half, separating into two or three distinct pictures what in the poet is obviously a single picture only. I know very well what moved him to do so, but it ought not to have moved him; instead of troubling himself to give satisfaction to the demands of his opponents, he should have shown them that their demands were illegitimate.

I shall be able to make my meaning clearer by an example. When Homer says of the one City :—

Λαοὶ δ' εἰν ἀγορῇ ἔσαν ἀθρόοι· ἔνθα δὲ νεῖκος
'Ωρώρει, δύο δ' ἄνδρες ἐνείκεον εἵνεκα ποινῆς
'Ανδρὸς ἀποφθιμένου· ὁ μὲν εὔχετο πάντ' ἀποδοῦναι
Δήμῳ πιφαύσκων, ὁ δ' ἀναίνετο μηδὲν ἑλέσθαι·
"Αμφω δ' ἱέσθην ἐπὶ ἵστορι πεῖραρ ἑλέσθαι.
Λαοὶ δ' ἀμφοτέροισιν ἐπήπυον, ἀμφὶς ἀρωγοί·
Κήρυκες δ' ἄρα λαὸν ἐρήτυον· οἱ δὲ γέροντες
"Ηατ' ἐπὶ ξεστοῖσι λίθοις ἱερῷ ἐνὶ κύκλῳ,
Σκῆπτρα δὲ κηρύκων ἐν χέρσ' ἔχον ἠεροφώνων·
Τοῖσιν ἔπειτ' ἤϊσσον, ἀμοιβηδὶς δὲ δίκαζον.
Κεῖτο δ' ἄρ' ἐν μέσσοισι δύω χρυσοῖο τάλαντα—

he is not then, in my view, trying to sketch more than a single picture—the picture of a public lawsuit on the questionable satisfaction of a heavy fine for the striking of a death-blow. The artist who would carry out this sketch cannot in any single effort avail himself of more than a single moment of the same; either the moment of the arraignment, or of the examination of witnesses, or of the sentence, or whatever other moment, before or after, he considers the most suitable. This single moment he makes as pregnant as possible, and endows it with all the illusions which art commands (art, rather than poetry) in the representation of visible objects. Surpassed so greatly on this side, what can the poet who is to paint this very design in words, and has no wish entirely to suffer shipwreck—what can he do but in like manner avail himself of his own peculiar advantages? And what are these? The liberty to enlarge on what has preceded and what follows the single moment of the work of art, and the power thus to show us not only that which the artist has shown, but also that which he can only leave us to guess. By this liberty and this power alone the poet draws level with the artist, and their works are then likest to each other when the effect of each is equally vivid; and not when the one conveys to the soul through the ear neither more nor less than the other can represent to the eye. This is the principle that should have guided Boivin in judging this passage in Homer; he would then not so much have made distinct pictures out of it as have observed in it distinct moments of time. True, he could not well have united in a single picture all that Homer tells us; the accusation and the defence, the production of witnesses, the acclamations of the divided people, the effort of the heralds to allay the tumult, and the decisions of the judge, are things which follow each other and cannot subsist side by side. Yet what, in the language of the schools, was not *actu* contained in the picture lay in it *virtute*, and the only true way of copying in words a material painting is this—to unite the latter with the actually visible, and refuse to be bound by the limits of art, within which the poet can indeed reckon up the *data* for a picture, but never produce the picture itself.

Just so is it when Boivin divides the picture of the besieged city into three different tableaux. He might just as well have divided it into twelve as into three. For as he did not at all grasp the spirit of the poet, and required him to be subject to the unities of the material painting, he might have found far more violations of these unities, so that it had almost been necessary to assign to every separate stroke of the poet a separate section of the Shield. But, in my opinion, Homer has not altogether more than ten distinct pictures upon the entire Shield, every one of which he introduces with the phrases ἐν μὲν ἔτευξε, *or* ἐν δὲ ποίησε, *or* ἐν δ' ἐτίθει, *or* ἐν δὲ ποίκιλλε 'Αμφιγυήεις. Where these introductory words do not occur one has no right to suppose a separate picture; on the contrary, all which they unite must be regarded as a single picture to which there is merely wanting the arbitrary concentration in a single point of time—a thing the poet was in nowise constrained to indicate. Much rather, had he indicated it, had he confined himself strictly to it, had he not admitted the smallest feature which in the actual execution could not be combined with it—in a word, had he managed the matter exactly as his critics demand, it is true that then these gentlemen would have found nothing to set down against him, but indeed neither would a man of taste have found anything to admire.

Pope was not only pleased with Boivin's plan of dividing and designing, but thought of doing something else of his own, by now further showing that each of these dismembered pictures was planned according to the strictest rules of painting as it is practised to-day. Contrast, perspective, the three unities—all these he found observed in the best manner possible. And this, although he certainly was well aware that, according to the testimony of quite trustworthy witnesses, painting in the time of the Trojan War was still in its cradle, so that either Homer must, by virtue of his god-like genius, not so much have adhered to what painting then or in his own time could perform, as, rather, to have divined what painting in general was capable of performing; or even those witnesses themselves cannot be so trustworthy that they should be preferred to the ocular demonstration of the artistic Shield itself. The former anyone may believe who will; of the latter at least no one can be persuaded who knows something more of the history of art than the mere data of historians. For, that painting in Homer's day was still in its infancy, he believes not merely because a Pliny or such another says so, but above all because he judges from the works of art which the ancients esteemed that many centuries later they had not got much further; he knows, for instance, that the paintings of Polygnotus are far from standing the test which Pope believes would be passed by the pictures on the Shield of Homer. The two great works at Delphi of the master just mentioned, of which Pausanias has left us so circumstantial a description, are obviously without any perspective. This division of the art was entirely unknown to the ancients, and what Pope adduces in order to prove that Homer had already some conception of it, proves nothing more than that Pope's own conception of it was extremely imperfect. "Homer," he says, "can have been no stranger to perspective, because he expressly mentions the distance of one object from another. He remarks, for instance, that the spies were set a little further off than the other figures, and that the oak-tree under which the meal was prepared for the reapers stood apart. What he says of the valley dotted over with flocks and cottages and stables is manifestly the description of a wide region seen in perspective. A general argument on the point may also certainly be drawn from the multitude of figures on the Shield, which could not all be represented in their full size; from which, therefore, we may unquestionably conclude that the art of reducing by perspective was in that age already well known." The mere observation of the optical experience that a thing appears smaller at a distance than close at hand, is far indeed from giving perspective to a picture. Perspective demands a single viewpoint, a definite natural field of vision, and it was this that was wanting in ancient paintings. The base in the pictures of Polygnotus was not horizontal, but towards the background raised so prodigiously that the figures which should appear to stand behind one another appeared to stand above one another. And if this arrangement of the different figures and their groups were general, as may be inferred from the ancient bas-reliefs, where the hindmost always stand higher than the foremost and look over their heads, then it is natural that we should take it for granted also in Homer's description, and not separate them unnecessarily from those of his pictures that can be combined in one picture. The twofold scene of the peaceful city through whose streets went the joyous crowd of a wedding-party, whilst in the market-place a great lawsuit was being decided, demands according to this no twofold picture, and Homer certainly was able to consider it a single one, representing to himself the entire city from so high a point of vision that it gave him a free and simultaneous prospect both of the streets and the market-place.

I am of opinion that the knowledge of true perspective in painting was only arrived at incidentally in the painting of scenery, and also that when this was already in its perfection, it yet cannot have been so easy to apply its rules to a single canvas, seeing that we still find in later paintings amongst the antiquities of Herculaneum many and diverse faults of perspective such as we should nowadays hardly forgive to a schoolboy.

But I absolve myself from the trouble of collecting my scattered notes concerning a point on which I may hope to receive the fullest satisfaction in Herr Winckelmann's promised history of art.

XX

I rather turn gladly to my own road, if a rambler can be said to have a road.

What I have said of physical objects in general is even more pertinent to beautiful physical objects. Physical beauty arises from the harmonious effect of manifold parts that can be taken in at one view. It demands also that these parts shall subsist side by side; and as things whose parts subsist side by side are the proper subject of painting, so it, and it alone, can imitate physical beauty. The poet, who can only show the elements of beauty one after another, in succession, does on that very account forbear altogether the description of physical beauty, as beauty. He recognises that those elements, arranged in succession, cannot possibly have the effect which they have when placed side by side; that the concentrating gaze which we would direct upon them immediately after their enumeration still affords us no harmonious picture; that it passes the human imagination to represent to itself what kind of effect this mouth, and this nose, and these eyes together have if one cannot recall from Nature or art a similar composition of such features.

Here, too, Homer is the pattern of all patterns. He says: "Nireus was beautiful; Achilles was more beautiful still; Helen possessed a divine beauty." But nowhere does he enter upon the more circumstantial delineation of those beauties. For all that, the poem is based on the beauty of Helen. How greatly would a modern poet have luxuriated in the theme !

True, a certain Constantinus Manasses tried to adorn his bald chronicle with a picture of Helen. I must thank him for the attempt. For really I should hardly know where else I could get hold of an example from which it might more obviously appear how foolish it is to venture something which Homer has so wisely forborne. When I read in him, for example :—

Ἦν ἡ γυνὴ περικαλλής, εὔοφρυς, εὐχρουστάτη,
Εὐπάρειος, εὐπρόσωπος, βοῶπις, χιονόχρους,
Ἑλικοβλέφαρος, ἁβρά, χαρίτων γέμον ἄλσος,
Λευκοβραχίων, τρυφερά, κάλλος ἄντικρυς ἔμπνουν,

Τὸ πρόσωπον κατάλευκον, ἡ παρειὰ ῥοδόχρους,
Τὸ πρόσωπον ἐπίχαρι, τὸ βλέφαρον ὡραῖον,
Κάλλος ἀνεπιτήδευτον, ἀβάπτιστον, αὐτόχρουν,
Ἔβαπτε τὴν λευκότητα ῥοδόχροια πυρίνη,
Ὡς εἴ τις τὸν ἐλέφαντα βάψει λαμπρᾷ πορφύρα.
Δειρὴ μακρά, κατάλευκος, ὅθεν ἐμυθουργήθη
Κυκνογενῆ τὴν εὔοπτον Ἑλένην χρηματίζειν—

then I imagine I see stones rolling up a mountain, from which
at the top a splendid picture is to be constructed, the stones,
however, all rolling down of themselves on the other side.
What kind of picture does it leave behind—this torrent of
words? What was Helen like, then? Will not, if a thousand
men read this, every man of the thousand make for himself his
own conception of her?

Still, it is certain the political verses of a monk are not poetry.
Let us therefore hear Ariosto, when he describes his enchanting
Alcina :—

> Di persona era tanto ben formata,
> Quanto mai finger san pittori industri :
> Con bionda chioma, lunga e annodata,
> Oro non è, che piu risplenda, e lustri,
> Spargeasi per la guancia delicata
> Misto color di rose e di ligustri
> Di terso avorio era la fronte lieta,
> Che lo spazio finia con giusta meta.
>
> Sotto due negri, e sottilissimi archi
> Son due negri occhi, anzi due chiari soli,
> Pietosi à riguardar, à mover parchi,
> Intorno à cui par ch' Amor scherzi, e voli,
> E ch' indi tutta la faretra scarchi,
> E che visibilmente i cori involi.
> Quindi il naso per mezo il viso scende
> Che non trova l'invidia ove l'emende.
>
> Sotto quel sta, quasi fra due valette,
> La bocca sparsa di natio cinabro,
> Quivi due filze son di perle elette,
> Che chiude, ed apre un bello e dolce labro ;
> Quindi escon le cortesi parolette,
> Da render molle ogni cor rozo e scabro ;
> Quivi si forma quel soave riso
> Ch' apre a sua posta in terra il paradiso.
>
> Bianca neve è il bel collo, e'l petto latte,
> Il collo è tondo, il petto colmo e largo ;
> Due pome acerbe, e pur d'avorio fatte,
> Vengono e van, come onda al primo margo,

Quando piacevole aura il mar combatte.
Non potria l'altre parti veder Argo,
Ben si può guidicar, che corrisponde,
A quel ch' appar di fuor, quel che s'asconde.

 Mostran le braccia sua misura giusta,
Et la candida man spesso si vede,
Lunghella alquanto, e di larghezza angusta,
Dove nè nodo appar, nè vena eccede.
Si vede al fin de la persona augusta
Il breve, asciutto e ritondetto piede.
Gli angelici sembianti nati in cielo
Non si ponno celar sotto alcun velo.

Milton says of the building of Pandemonium : " Some praised
the work, others the master of the work." The praise of the
one, then, is not always the praise of the other. A work of
art may deserve all applause while nothing very special redounds
from it to the credit of the artist. On the other hand, an artist
may justly claim our admiration even when his work does not
completely satisfy us. If we do not forget this, quite contra-
dictory verdicts may often be reconciled. The present case is
an instance. Dolce in his dialogue on Painting puts in Aretino's
mouth an extravagant eulogy of Ariosto on the strength of
these stanzas just cited ; and I, on the contrary, choose them
as an example of a picture that is no picture. We are both
right. Dolce admires in it the knowledge which the poet displays of physical beauty ; but I look merely to the effect which
this knowledge, expressed in words, produces on my imagination. Dolce argues, from that knowledge, that good poets are
also good painters ; and I, from the effect, that what painters
can by line and colour best express can only be badly expressed
by words. Dolce commends Ariosto's delineation to all painters
as the most perfect model of a beautiful woman ; and I commend it to all poets as the most instructive warning against
attempting even more unfortunately what failed in the hands
of an Ariosto. It may be that, when Ariosto says :—

 Di persona era tanto ben formata,
 Quanto mai finger san pittori industri—

he proves thereby that he perfectly understood the theory of
proportions as only the most diligent artist can gather it from
Nature and from antiquity. He may, who knows? in the
mere words :—

 Spargeasi per la guancia delicata
 Misto color di rose e di ligustri—

show himself the most perfect of colourists, a very Titian.
One might also, from the fact that he only compares Alcina's
hair with gold but does not call it golden hair, argue as cogently
that he disapproves the use of actual gold in laying on the
colour. One may even find in his " descending nose " :—

Quindi il naso per mezo il viso scende—

the profile of those ancient Greek noses, copied also by Roman
artists from the Greeks. What good is all this erudition and
insight to us his readers who want to have the picture of a
beautiful woman, who want to feel something of the soft excitement of the blood which accompanies the actual sight of beauty?
If the poet is aware what conditions constitute a beautiful
form, do we too, therefore, share his knowledge? And if we
did also know it, does he here make us aware of those conditions? Or does he in the least lighten for us the difficulty
of recalling them in a vividly perceptible manner? A brow in
its most graceful lines and limits :—

. . . la fronte
Che lo spazio finia con giusta meta ;

a rose in which envy itself can find nothing to improve :—

Che non trova l'invidia, ove l'emende ;

a hand somewhat long and rather slender :—

Lunghetta alquanto, e di larghezza angusta :

what kind of picture do we gather from these general formulas?
In the mouth of a drawing-master who is calling his pupils'
attention to the beauties of the school model they might perhaps be useful; for by a glance at the model they perceive the
pleasing lines of the delightful brow, the exquisite modelling
of the nose, the slenderness of the dainty hand. But in the
poet I see nothing, and feel with vexation how vain is my best
effort to see what he is describing.

In this particular, where Virgil can best imitate Homer by
forbearing action altogether, Virgil, too, has been rather happy.
His Dido also is to him nothing further than *pulcherrima Dido*.
If indeed he describes anything of her more circumstantially, it
is her rich jewelry, her splendid attire :—

Tandem progreditur . . .
Sidoniam picto chlamydem circumdata limbo :
Cui pharetra ex auro, crines nodantur in aurum,
Aurea purpuream subnectit fibula vestem.

If we on that account would apply to him what the ancient artist said to a pupil who had painted a Helen in elaborate finery—" As you are not able to paint her beautiful, you have painted her rich "—then Virgil would answer, " It is no fault of mine that I cannot paint her beautiful; the blame rests on the limits of my art; be mine the praise, to have remained within those limits."

I must not forget here the two songs of Anacreon in which he analyses for us the beauty of his beloved and of his Bathyllus. The turn he gives it there makes everything right. He imagines a painter before him, and sets him to work under his eye. So, he says, fashion me the hair, so the brow, so the eyes, so the mouth, so neck and bosom, so the hips and hands ! Of what the artist can put together only part by part the poet can only set a copy in the same way. His purpose is not that we shall recognise and feel in this verbal instruction of the painter the whole beauty of the beloved subject; he himself feels the insufficiency of the verbal expression, and for this very reason calls to his aid the expressive power of art, the illusion of which he so greatly heightens that the whole song appears to be more a hymn to Art than to his beloved. He does not see the image, he sees herself and believes that she is just about to open her lips in speech :—

> Ἀπέχει βλέπω γὰρ αὐτήν,
> Τάχα, κηρέ, καὶ λαλήσεις.

In the sketch, too, of Bathyllus the praise of the beautiful boy is so inwoven with praise of art and the artist that it is doubtful for whose honour Anacreon really intended the poem. He collects the most beautiful parts from various paintings in which the particular beauty of these parts was its characteristic feature; the neck he takes from an Adonis, breast and hands from a Mercury, the hips from a Pollux, the abdomen from a Bacchus; till he sees the whole Bathyllus in a perfect Apollo :—

> Μετὰ δὲ πρόσωπον ἔστω,
> Τὸν Ἀδώνιδος παρελθών,
> Ἐλεφάντινος τράχηλος·
> Μεταμάζιον δὲ ποίει
> Διδύμας τε χεῖρας Ἑρμοῦ,
> Πολυδεύκεος δὲ μηρούς,
> Διονυσίην δὲ νηδὺν . . .
> Τὸν Ἀπόλλωνα δὲ τοῦτον
> Καθελὼν ποίει Βάθυλλον.

Similarly also Lucian does not know how to give us a conception of the beauty of Panthea except by reference to the finest female statues of ancient artists. And what is this but to confess that language by itself is here powerless, that poetry stammers and eloquence is dumb where Art does not in some measure serve them as interpreter?

XXI

But does not Poetry lose too much if we take from her all pictures of physical beauty? Who wishes to do so? If we seek to close to her one single road, on which she hopes to achieve such pictures by following in the footsteps of a sister art, where she stumbles painfully without ever attaining the same goal, do we, then, at the same time close to her every other road, where Art in her turn can but follow at a distance?

Even Homer, who with evident intention refrains from all piecemeal delineation of physical beauties, from whom we can scarcely once learn in passing that Helen had white arms and beautiful hair—even he knows how, nevertheless, to give us such a conception of her beauty as far outpasses all that Art in this respect can offer. Let us recall the passage where Helen steps into the assembly of the Elders of the Trojan people. The venerable old men looked on her, and one said to the other :—

> Οὐ νέμεσις Τρῶας καὶ ἐϋκνήμιδας Ἀχαιοὺς
> Τοιῇδ' ἀμφὶ γυναικὶ πολὺν χρόνον ἄλγεα πάσχειν·
> Αἰνῶς ἀθανάτῃσι θεῆς εἰς ὦπα ἔοικεν.

What can convey a more vivid idea of Beauty than to have frigid age confessing her well worth the war that has cost so much blood and so many tears? What Homer could not describe in its component parts, he makes us feel in its working. Paint us, then, poet, the satisfaction, the affection, the love, the delight, which beauty produces, and you have painted beauty itself. Who can imagine as ill-favoured the beloved object of Sappho, the very sight of whom she confesses robbed her of her senses and her reason? Who does not fancy he beholds with his own eyes the fairest, most perfect form, as soon as he sympathises with the feeling which nothing but such a form can awaken? Not because Ovid shows us the beautiful body of his Lesbia part by part :—

Quos humeros, quales vidi tetigique lacertos !
Forma papillarum quam fuit apta premi !
Quam castigato planus sub pectore venter !
Quantum et quale latus ! quam juvenile femur !—

but because he does so with the voluptuous intoxication in
which it is so easy to awaken our longing, we imagine ourselves enjoying the same sight of exquisite beauty which he
enjoyed.

Another way in which poetry in its turn overtakes art in
delineation of physical beauty is by transmuting beauty into
charm. Charm is beauty in motion, and just for that reason
less suitable to the painter than to the poet. The painter can
only help us to guess the motion, but in fact his figures are
motionless. Consequently grace with him is turned into
grimace. But in poetry it remains what it is—a transitory
beauty which we want to see again and again. It comes and
goes ; and as we can generally recall a movement more easily
and more vividly than mere forms and colours, charm can in
such a case work more powerfully on us than beauty. All that
still pleases and touches us in the picture of Alcina is charm.
The impression her eyes make does not come from the fact
that they are dark and passionate, but rather that they :—

Pietosi à riguardar, à mover parchi—

look round her graciously and are gentle rather than flashing
in their glances ; that Love flutters about them and from them
empties all his quiver. Her mouth delights us, not because
lips tinted with cinnobar enclose two rows of choicest pearls ;
but because there the lovely smile is shaped which in itself
seems to open up an earthly paradise ; because from it the
friendly words come forth that soften the most savage breast.
Her bosom enchants us, less because milk and ivory and apples
typify its whiteness and delicate forms than because we see it
softly rise and fall, like the waves at the margin of the shore
when a playful zephyr contends with the ocean :—

Due pome acerbi, e pur d'avorio fatte
Vengono e van, come onda al primo margo,
Quando piacevole aura il mar combatte.

I am sure such features of charm by themselves, condensed
into one or two stanzas, will do more than all the five into
which Ariosto has spun them out, inweaving them with frigid
details of the fair form, far too erudite for our appreciation.
Even Anacreon himself would rather fall into the apparent

impropriety of demanding impossibilities from the painter than leave the picture of his beloved untouched with charm :—

Τρυφεροῦ δ' ἔσω γενείου,
Περὶ λυγδίνῳ τραχήλῳ
Χάριτες πέτοιντο πᾶσαι.

Her chin of softness, her neck of marble—let all the Graces hover round them, he bids the artist. And how? In the exact and literal sense? That is not capable of any pictorial realisation. The painter could give the chin the most exquisite curve, the prettiest dimple, *Amoris digitulo impressum* (for the ἔσω appears to me to signify a dimple); he could give the neck the most beautiful carnation; but he can do no more. The turning of this fair neck, the play of the muscles, by which that dimple is now more visible, now less, the peculiar charm, all are beyond his powers. The poet said the utmost by which his art could make beauty real to us, so that the painter also might strive for the utmost expression in his art. A fresh example of the principle already affirmed—that the poet even when he speaks of works of art is not bound in his descriptions to confine himself within the limits of art.

XXII

Zeuxis painted a Helen and had the courage to set under it those famous lines of Homer in which the enchanted Elders confess their emotions. Never were painting and poetry drawn into a more equal contest. The victory remained undecided, and both deserved to be crowned. For, just as the wise poet showed beauty merely in its effect, which he felt he could not delineate in its component parts, so did the no less wise painter show us beauty by nothing else than its component parts and hold it unbecoming to his art to resort to any other method. His picture consisted in the single figure of Helen, standing in naked beauty. For it is probable that it was the very Helen which he painted for her of Crotona.

Let us compare with this, for wonder's sake, the painting which Caylus sketches from Homer's lines for the benefit of a modern artist : " Helen, covered with a white veil, appears in the midst of an assemblage of old men, in whose ranks Priam also is to be found, recognisable by the signs of his royal dignity. It must be the artist's business to make evident to us the

G

triumph of beauty in the eager gaze and in the expression of
amazed admiration on the faces of the sober greybeards. The
scene is by one of the gates of the city. The background of
the painting thus can lose itself in the open sky or against the
city's lofty walls; the former were the bolder conception, but
one is as fitting as the other."

Let us imagine this picture carried out by the greatest master
of our time and place it against the work of Zeuxis. Which
will show the real triumph of beauty? That in which I myself
feel it, or this where I must argue it from the grimaces of the
susceptible greybeards? *Turpe senilis amor;* a lustful look
makes the most venerable countenance ridiculous; an old man
who betrays youthful passions is really a loathsome object.
This objection cannot be made to the Homeric elders; for the
emotion they feel is a momentary spark which their wisdom
extinguishes immediately; intended only to do honour to
Helen, but not to disgrace themselves. They confess their
feeling and forthwith add :—

> Ἀλλὰ καὶ ὥς, τοίη περ ἐοῦσ', ἐν νηυσὶ νεέσθω,
> Μηδ' ἡμῖν τεκέεσσί τ' ὀπίσσω πῆμα λίποιτο.

Without this resolution they would be old coxcombs, what,
indeed, they appear in the picture of Caylus. And on what,
then, do they direct their greedy glances? On a masked and
veiled figure ! That is Helen, is it? Inconceivable to me how
Caylus here can leave the veil. Homer, indeed, gives it her
expressly :—

> Αὐτίκα δ' ἀργεννῇσι καλυψαμένη ὀθόνῃσιν
> 'Ωρμᾶτ' ἐκ θαλάμοιο . . .

but it is to cross the streets in it; and if indeed with Homer
the elders already betray their admiration before she appears
to have again taken off or thrown back the veil, it was not then
the first time the old men saw her; their confession therefore
might not arise from the present momentary view: they may
have already often felt what on this occasion they first confessed themselves to feel. In the painting nothing like this
occurs. If I see here enchanted old men, I wish at the same
time to see what it is that charms them; and I am surprised
in the extreme when I perceive nothing further than, as we have
said, a masked and veiled figure on which they are passionately
gazing. What is here of Helen? Her white veil and something
of her well-proportioned outline so far as outline can become

visible beneath raiment. Yet perhaps it was not the Count's intention that her face should be covered, and he names the veil merely as a part of her attire. If this is so—his words, indeed, are hardly capable of such an interpretation : " *Hélène couverte d'un voile blanc* "—then another surprise awaits me ; he is so particular in commending to the artist the expression on the faces of the elders, but on the beauty of Helen's face he does not expend a syllable. This modest beauty, in her eyes the dewy shimmer of a remorseful tear, approaching timidly ! What ! Is supreme beauty something so familiar to our artists that they do not need to be reminded of it ? Or is expression more than beauty ? And are we in pictures, too, accustomed, as on the stage, to let the homeliest actress pass for a charming princess, if only her prince declares warmly enough the love he bears her ?

In truth, Caylus' picture would bear the same relation to that of Zeuxis as burlesque does to the loftiest poetry.

Homer was, without doubt, read in former times more diligently than to-day. Yet one finds ever so many pictures unmentioned which the ancient artists would have drawn from his pages. Only of the poet's hint at particular physical beauties they do appear to have made diligent use ; these they did paint, and in such subjects alone, they understood well enough, it was granted them to compete with the poet. Besides Helen, Zeuxis also painted Penelope, and the Diana of Apelles was the Homeric Diana in company of her nymphs. I may here call to mind that the passage of Pliny in which the latter is mentioned requires an emendation.* But to paint actions from Homer simply because they offer a rich composition, excellent contrasts, artistic lights, seemed to the ancient artists not to be their *métier*, nor could it be so long as art remained within the narrower limits of her own high vocation. Instead, they nourished themselves on the spirit of the poet ; they filled their imagination with his most exalted characteristics ; the fire of his enthusiasm kindled their own ; they saw and

---

* Pliny says of the Apelles : *Fecit et Dianam sacrificantium virginum choro mixtam : quibus vicisse Homeri versus videtur id ipsum describentis.* Nothing can be better deserved than this eulogy. Beautiful nymphs about a beautiful goddess who stands out above them with a brow of majesty make a sketch which is fitter for painting than for poetry. The *sacrificantium*, though, is to me very doubtful. What does the goddess amid sacrificial vestals ? And is this the occupation which Homer gives to the playmates of Diana ? Not at all ! they wander with her through the woods and hills, they hunt, they sport, they dance.

felt like him ; and so their works became copies of the Homeric,
not in the relation of a portrait to its original, but in that of a
son to his father—like, yet different. The resemblance often
lies only in a single feature, the rest having amongst them all
nothing alike except that they harmonise with the resembling
feature in the one case as well as in the other.

As, moreover, the Homeric masterpieces in poetry were
older than any masterpiece of art, as Homer had observed
Nature with a painter's eye earlier than a Phidias or an Apelles,
it is not to be wondered at that various observations of particular use to them the artists found already made in Homer
before they themselves had had the opportunity of making
them in Nature. These they eagerly seized on, in order to
imitate Nature through Homer. Phidias confessed that the
lines :—

ῌ, καὶ κυανέῃσιν ἐπ' ὀφρύσι νεῦσε Κρονίων·
'Αμβρόσιαι δ' ἄρα χαῖται ἐπερρώσαντο ἄνακτος
Κρατὸς ἀπ' ἀθανάτοιο· μέγαν δ' ἐλέλιξεν ῎Ολυμπον

served him as a model in his Olympian Jupiter, and that only
by their aid did he achieve a divine countenance, *propemodum
ex ipso cœlo petitum*. Whosoever considers this to mean nothing more than that the fancy of the artist was fired by the
poet's exalted picture, and thereby became capable of representations just as exalted—he, it seems to me, overlooks the
most essential point, and contents himself with something
quite general where, for a far more complete satisfaction, something very special is demanded. In my view Phidias confesses
here also that in this passage he first noticed how much expression lies in the eyebrows, *quanta pars animi* is shown in them.
Perhaps also it induced him to devote more attention to the
hair, in order to express in some measure what Homer means
by " ambrosial " locks. For it is certain that the ancient
artists before the days of Phidias little understood what was
significant and speaking in the countenance, and almost invariably neglected the hair. Even Myron was faulty in both these
particulars, as Pliny has remarked, and after him Pythagoras
Leontinus was the first who distinguished himself by the
elegance of coiffure. What Phidias learned from Homer, other
artists learned from the works of Phidias.

Another example of this kind I may specify which has always
very much pleased me. Let us recall what Hogarth has noted
concerning the Apollo Belvidere. " This Apollo," he says,

" and the Antinous are both to be seen in the same palace at Rome. If, however, the Antinous fills the spectator with admiration, the Apollo amazes him, and, indeed, as travellers have remarked, by an aspect above humanity which usually they are not capable of describing. And this effect, they say, is all the more wonderful because when one examines it, the disproportionate in it is obvious even to a common eye. One of the best sculptors we have in England, who recently went there on purpose to see this statue, corroborated what has just been said, and in particular that the feet and legs in relation to the upper part are too long and too broad. And Andreas Sacchi, one of the greatest Italian painters, seems to have been of the same opinion, otherwise he would hardly (in a famous picture now in England) have given to his Apollo, crowning the musician Pasquilini, exactly the proportions of Antinous, seeing that in other respects it appears to be actually a copy of the Apollo. Although we frequently see in very great works some small part handled carelessly, this cannot be the case here. For in a beautiful statue correct proportion is one of the most essential beauties. We must conclude, therefore, that these limbs must have been purposely lengthened, otherwise it would have been easy to avoid it. If we therefore examine the beauties of this figure thoroughly, we shall with reason conclude that what we have hitherto considered indescribably excellent in its general aspect has proceeded from that which appeared to be a fault in one of its parts " (Hogarth, *Analysis of Beauty*). All this is very illuminating, and I will add that in fact Homer has felt it and has pointed out that it gives a stately appearance, arising purely from this addition of size in the measurements of feet and legs. For when Antenor would compare the figure of Ulysses with that of Menelaus, he makes him say :—

Στάντων μὲν Μενέλαος ὑπείρεχεν εὐρέας ὤμους,
"Ἄμφω δ' ἑζομένω γεραρώτερος ἦεν 'Οδυσσεύς.

(" When both stood, then Menelaus stood the higher with his broad shoulders; but when both sat, Ulysses was the statelier.") As Ulysses therefore gained stateliness in sitting, which Menelaus in sitting lost, the proportion is easy to determine which the upper body had in each to feet and legs. Ulysses was the larger in the proportions of the former, Menelaus in the proportions of the latter.

XXIII

A single defective part can destroy the harmonious working of many parts towards beauty. Yet the object does not necessarily therefore become ugly. Even ugliness demands several defective parts which likewise must be seen at one view if we are to feel by it the contrary of that with which beauty inspires us.

Accordingly, ugliness also in its essential nature would not be a reproach to poetry; and yet Homer has depicted the extremest ugliness in Thersites, and depicted it, moreover, in its elements set side by side. Why was that permitted to him with ugliness which in the case of beauty he renounced with so fine a discernment? Is the effect of ugliness not just as much hindered by the successive enumeration of its elements as the effect of beauty is nullified by the like enumeration of its elements? To be sure it is, but herein lies also Homer's justification. Just because ugliness becomes in the poet's delineation a less repulsive vision of physical imperfection, and so far as effect is concerned ceases as it were to be ugliness, it becomes usable to the poet; and what he cannot use for its own sake, he uses as an ingredient in order to produce or intensify certain mixed states of feeling with which he must entertain us in default of feelings purely pleasurable.

These mixed feelings are awakened by the laughable and the terrible. Homer makes Thersites ugly in order to make him laughable. It is not, however, merely by his ugliness that he becomes so; for ugliness is imperfection and for the laughable a contrast is required of perfection and imperfection. This is the declaration of my friend Mendelssohn, to which I should like to add that this contrast must not be too sharp or too glaring, that the *opposita* (to continue in painter's language) must be of the kind that can melt into each other. The wise and honest Æsop, even if one assigns him the ugliness of Thersites, does not thereby become laughable. It was a ridiculous monastic whim to wish the τέλειον of his instructive tales transferred to his own person by the help of its deformity. For a misshapen body and a beautiful soul are like oil and vinegar, which, even when they are thoroughly mixed, still remain completely separated to the palate. They afford us no *tertium quid ;* the body excites disgust, the soul satisfaction, each its own for itself. Only when the misshapen body is at the same time frail and sickly, when it hinders the soul in her operations, when it becomes the source of hurtful prepossessions against her—then indeed disgust and satisfaction mingle and flow together, but the new apparition arising therefrom is not laughter, but pity, and the object which we otherwise should merely have esteemed becomes interesting. The misshapen and sickly Pope must have been far more interesting to his friends than the sound and handsome Wycherley.—But, however little would Thersites have been made laughable by mere ugliness, just as little would he have become laughable without it. The ugliness; the harmony of this ugliness with his character; the contradiction which both make to the idea he entertains of his own importance; the harmless effect of his malicious chatter, humiliating only to himself—all must work together to this end. The last-named particular is the οὐ φθαρτικόν which Aristotle makes indispensable to the laughable; just as also my friend makes it a necessary condition that such contrast must be of no moment and must interest us but little. For let us only suppose that Thersites' malicious belittling of Agamemnon had come to cost him dear, that instead of a couple of bloody weals he must pay for it with his life—then certainly we should cease to laugh at him. For this monster of a man is yet a man, whose destruction will always seem a greater evil than all his frailties and vices. This we can learn by experience if we read his end in Quintus Calaber. Achilles laments having killed Penthesilea; the beautiful woman in her blood, so bravely poured out, commands the esteem and pity of the hero, and esteem and pity turn to love. But the slanderous Thersites makes that love a crime. He declaims against the lewdness that betrays even the most valiant man to folly :—

> . . . Ἥτ' ἄφρονα φῶτα τίθησι
> Καὶ πινυτόν περ ἐόντα. . . .

Achilles gets into a rage, and without replying a word strikes him so roughly between cheek and ear that teeth and blood and soul together gush from his throat. Horrible unspeakably! The passionate, murderous Achilles becomes more hateful to me than the spiteful, snarling Thersites; the jubilant cry which the Greeks raise over the deed offends me. I take part with Diomede, who draws his sword forthwith to avenge his kinsman on the murderer : for I feel, too, that Thersites is my kinsman, a human being.

But grant only that Thersites' incitements had broken out in sedition, that the mutinous people had actually taken ship and traitorously forsaken their captains, that the captains had thus fallen into the hands of a revengeful enemy, and that a divine judgment had brought utter destruction to both fleet and people : in such a case how would the ugliness of Thersites appear? If harmless ugliness can be laughable, a mischievous ugliness is always terrible. I do not know how to illustrate this better than by a couple of excellent passages of Shakspeare. Edmund, the bastard son of Earl Gloucester in *King Lear*, is no less a villain than Richard, Duke of Gloucester, who paved his way by the most detestable crimes to the throne which he ascended under the name of Richard III. How comes it, then, that the former excites far less shuddering and horror than the latter? When I hear the Bastard say :—

> Thou, Nature, art my goddess, to thy law
> My services are bound; wherefore should I
> Stand in the plague of custom, and permit
> The curiosity of nations to deprive me,
> For that I am some twelve or fourteen moonshines
> Lag of a brother? Why bastard? Wherefore base?
> When my dimensions are as well compact,
> My mind as generous, and my shape as true
> As honest Madam's issue? Why brand they thus
> With base? with baseness? bastardy! base, base!
> Who in the lusty stealth of Nature take
> More composition and fierce quality
> Than doth, within a dull, stale, tired bed,
> Go to creating a whole tribe of fops
> Got 'tween asleep and wake?—

in this I hear a devil, but I see him in the form of an angel of light. When, on the other hand, I hear the Duke of Gloucester say :—

> But I, that am not shaped for sportive tricks
> Nor made to court an amorous looking-glass,
> I, that am rudely stamped and want Love's majesty,
> To strut before a wanton ambling nymph;
> I, that am curtailed of this fair proportion,
> Cheated of feature by dissembling Nature,
> Deformed, unfinished, sent before my time
> Into this breathing world scarce half made up,
> And that so lamely and unfashionably
> That dogs bark at me as I halt by them;
> Why, I (in this weak piping time of peace)
> Have no delight to pass away the time;
> Unless to spy my shadow in the sun
> And descant on my own deformity.

And therefore, since I cannot prove a lover
To entertain these fair, well-spoken days,
I am determined to prove a villain!

then I hear a devil and see a devil in a shape that only the
Devil should have.

XXIV

It is thus the poet uses the ugliness of forms; what use of
them is permitted to the painter? Painting, as imitative
dexterity, can express ugliness; but painting, as beautiful art,
will not express it. To her, as the former, all visible objects
belong; but, as the latter, she confines herself solely to those
visible objects which awaken agreeable sensations.

But do not even the disagreeable sensations please in the
imitation of them? Not all. A sagacious critic has already
made the remark concerning the sensation of disgust. "The
representations of fear," he says, "of sadness, of terror, of
pity and so on, can only excite discomfort in so far as we take
the evil to be actual. These, therefore, can be resolved into
pleasant sensations by the recollection that it is but an artistic
deceit. The unpleasant sensation of disgust, however, in
virtue of the laws of the imagination, ensues on the mere representation in the mind whether the subject be considered as
actual or not. Of what use is it, therefore, to the offended
soul if Art thus betrays herself by a surrender to imitation?
Her discomfort arose not from the foreboding that the evil was
actual but from the mere presentation of the same, and this *is*
actual. The sensations of disgust are therefore always nature,
never imitation."

The same principle holds good of the ugliness of forms. This
ugliness offends our sight, is repugnant to our taste for order
and harmony, and awakens aversion without respect to the
actual existence of the subject in which we perceive it. We
do not want to see Thersites, either in Nature or in picture,
and if in fact his picture displeases us less, this happens not for
the reason that the ugliness of his form ceases in the imitation
to be ugliness, but because we have the power of abstracting
our attention from this ugliness and satisfying ourselves merely
with the art of the painter. Yet even this satisfaction will
every moment be interrupted by the reflection how ill the art
has been bestowed, and this reflection will seldom fail to be
accompanied by contempt for the artist.

Aristotle suggests another reason why things on which we look in Nature with repugnance do yet afford us pleasure even in the most faithful copy—namely, the universal curiosity of mankind. We are glad if we either can learn from the copy τί ἕκαστον, what anything is, or if we can conclude from it ὅτι οὗτος ἐκεῖνος, that it is this or that. But even from this there follows no advantage to ugliness in imitation. The pleasure that arises from the satisfaction of our curiosity is momentary, and merely accidental to the subject from which it arises; the dissatisfaction, on the contrary, that accompanies the sight of ugliness is permanent, and essential to the subject that excites it. How, then, can the former balance the latter? Still less can the momentary agreeable amusement which the showing of a likeness gives us overcome the disagreeable effect of ugliness. The more closely I compare the ugly copy with the ugly original, the more do I expose myself to this effect, so that the pleasure of comparison vanishes very quickly, and there remains to me nothing more than the untoward impression of the twofold ugliness. To judge by the examples given by Aristotle, it appears as if he himself had been unwilling to reckon the ugliness of forms as amongst the unpleasing subjects which might yet please in imitation. These subjects are corpses and ravening beasts. Ravening wild beasts excite terror even though they are not ugly; and this terror, and not their ugliness, it is that is resolved into pleasant sensations by imitation. So, too, with corpses: the keener feeling of pity, the terrible reminder of our own annihilation it is that makes a corpse in Nature a repulsive subject to us; in the imitation, however, that pity loses its sharper edge by the conviction of the illusion, and from the fatal reminder an alloy of flattering circumstances can either entirely divert us, or unite so inseparably with it that we seem to find in it more of the desirable than the terrible.

As, therefore, the ugliness of forms cannot by and for itself be a theme of painting as fine art, because the feeling which it excites, while unpleasing, is not of that sort of unpleasing sensations which may be transformed into pleasing ones by imitation; yet the question might still be asked whether it could not to painting as well as to poetry be useful as an ingredient, for the intensifying of other sensations. May painting, then, avail itself of ugly forms for the arriving at the laughable and the terrible?

I will not venture to give this question a point-blank negative.

It is undeniable that harmless ugliness can even in painting be made laughable, especially when there is combined with it an affectation of charm and dignity. It is just as incontestable that mischievous ugliness does in painting, just as in Nature, excite horror, and that this laughable and this horrible element, which in themselves are mingled feelings, attain by imitation a new degree of offensiveness or of pleasure.

I must at the same time point out that, nevertheless, painting is not here completely in the same case with poetry. In poetry, as I have already remarked, the ugliness of forms does by the transmutation of their co-existing parts into successive parts lose its unpleasant effect almost entirely; from this point of view it ceases, as it were, to be ugliness, and can therefore ally itself more intimately with other appearances in order to produce a new and distinct effect. In painting, on the contrary, the ugliness has all its forces at hand, and works almost as strongly as in Nature itself. Consequently, harmless ugliness cannot well remain laughable for long; the unpleasant sensation gains the upper hand, and what was farcical to begin with becomes later merely disgusting. Nor is it otherwise with mischievous ugliness; the terrible is gradually lost and the monstrous remains alone and unchangeable.

Keeping this in view, Count Caylus was perfectly right to leave the episode of Thersites out of the list of his Homeric pictures. But are we therefore right, too, in wishing them cut out of Homer's own work? I am sorry to find that a scholar of otherwise just and fine taste is of this opinion. A fuller exposition of my own views on the matter I postpone to another opportunity.

XXV

The second distinction also, which the critic just named draws between disgust and other unpleasant emotions of the soul, is concerned with the aversion awakened within us by the ugliness of physical forms.

"Other unpleasant emotions," he says, "can often, apart from imitation and in Nature itself, gratify the mind, inasmuch as they never excite unmixed aversion, but in every case mingle their bitterness with pleasure. Our fear is seldom denuded of all hope; terror animates all our powers to evade the danger; anger is bound up with the desire to avenge ourselves, as sadness is with the agreeable representation of the happiness that

preceded it, whilst pity is inseparable from the tender feelings
of love and affection. The soul is permitted to dwell now on
the pleasurable, and now on the afflicting, parts of an emotion,
and to make for itself a mixture of pleasure and its opposite
which is more attractive than pleasure without admixture.
Only a very little attention to what goes on within is needed
to observe frequent instances of the kind ; what else would
account for the fact that to the angry man his anger, to the
melancholy man his dejection, is dearer than any pleasing
representations by which it is sought to quiet or cheer him ?
Quite otherwise is it in the case of disgust and the feelings
associated with it. In that the soul recognises no noticeable
admixture of pleasure. Distaste gains the upper hand, and
there is therefore no situation that we can imagine either in
Nature or in imitation in which the mind would not recoil
with repugnance from such representations.''

Perfectly true ! but as the critic himself recognises yet other
sensations akin to disgust which likewise produce nothing but
aversion, what can be nearer akin to it than the feeling of the
ugly in physical forms ? This sensation also is, in Nature, without the slightest admixture of delight, and as it is just as little
capable of it in imitation, so there is no situation in the latter
in which the mind would not recoil with repugnance from the
representation of it.

Indeed, this repugnance, if I have studied my feelings with
sufficient care, is wholly of the nature of disgust. The sensation
which accompanies ugliness of form is disgust, only somewhat
fainter in degree. This conflicts, indeed, with another note of
the critic, according to which he thinks that only the *blind*
senses—taste, smell, and touch—are sensitive to disgust. " The
two former," he says, " by an excessive sweetness and the third
by an excessive softness of bodies that do not sufficiently resist
the fibres that touch them. Such objects then become unendurable even to sight, but merely through the association of ideas
that recall to us the repugnance to which they give rise in the
taste, or smell, or touch. For, properly speaking, there are no
objects of disgust for the vision." Yet, in my opinion, things
of the kind can be named. A scar in the face, a hare-lip, a
flattened nose with prominent nostrils, an entire absence of
eyebrows, are uglinesses which are not offensive either to smell,
taste, or touch. At the same time it is certain that these
things produce a sensation that certainly comes much nearer to
disgust than what we feel at sight of other deformities of body

—a crooked foot, or a high shoulder; the more delicate our temperament, the more do they cause us those inward sensations that precede sickness. Only, these sensations very soon disappear, and actual sickness can scarcely result; the reason of which is certainly to be found in this fact, that they are objects of sight, which simultaneously perceives in them and with them a multitude of circumstances through the pleasant presentation of which those unpleasing things are so tempered and obscured that they can have no noticeable effect on the body. The blind senses, on the other hand—taste, smell, and touch—cannot, when they are affected by something unpleasant, likewise take cognisance of such other circumstances; the disagreeable, consequently, works by itself and in its whole energy, and cannot but be accompanied in the body by a far more violent shock.

Moreover, the disgusting is related to imitation in precisely the same way as the ugly. Indeed, as its unpleasant effect is more violent, it can even less than the ugly be made in and for itself a subject either of poetry or painting. Only because it also is greatly modified by verbal expression, I venture still to contend that the poet might be able to use at least some features of disgust as an ingredient for the mingled sensations of which we have spoken, which he intensifies so successfully by what is ugly.

The disgusting can add to the laughable; or representations of dignity and decorum, set in contrast with the disgusting, become laughable. Instances of this kind abound in Aristophanes. The weasel occurs to me which interrupted the good Socrates in his astronomical observations :—

ΜΑΘ. Πρώην δέ γε γνώμην μεγάλην ἀφηρέθη
    Ὑπ᾽ ἀσκαλαβώτου. ΣΤ. Τίνα τρόπον; κάτειπέ μοι.
ΜΑΘ. Ζητοῦντος αὐτοῦ τῆς σελήνης τὰς ὁδοὺς
    Καὶ τὰς περιφοράς, εἶτ᾽ ἄνω κεχηνότος
    Ἀπὸ τῆς ὀροφῆς νύκτωρ γαλεώτης κατέχεσεν.
ΣΤ. Ἥσθην γαλεώτῃ καταχέσαντι Σωκράτους.

Suppose that not to be disgusting which falls into his open mouth, and the laughable vanishes. The drollest strokes of this kind occur in the Hottentot tale, Tquassouw and Knoninquaiha in the *Connoisseur*, an English weekly magazine full of humour, ascribed to Lord Chesterfield. Everyone knows how filthy the Hottentots are and how many things they consider beautiful and elegant and sacred which with us awaken disgust and aversion. A flattened cartilage of a nose, flabby breasts hanging down to the navel, the whole body smeared with a cosmetic of goat's fat and soot gone rotten in the sun, the hair dripping with grease, arms and legs bound about with fresh entrails—let one think of this as the object of an ardent, reverent, tender love; let one hear this uttered in the exalted language of gravity and admiration and refrain from laughter!

With the terrible it seems possible for the disgusting to be still more intimately mingled. What we call the horrible is nothing but the disgusting and terrible in one. Longinus, it is true, is displeased with the τῆς ἐκ μὲν ῥινῶν μύξαι ῥέον in Hesiod's description of melancholy; but, in my opinion, not so much because it is a disgusting trait as because it is a merely disgusting trait contributing nothing to the terrible. For the long nails extending beyond the fingers (μακροὶ δ' ὄνυχες χείρεσσιν ὑπῆσαν) he does not appear to find fault with. Yet long nails are not less disgusting than a running nose. But the long nails are at the same time terrible, for it is they that lacerate the cheeks until the blood runs down upon the ground :—

> . . . Ἐκ δὲ παρειῶν
> Αἷμ' ἀπελείβετ' ἔραζε. . . .

A running nose, on the contrary, is nothing more than a running nose, and I only advise Melancholy to keep her mouth closed. Let one read in Sophocles the description of the vacant, barren den of the unhappy Philoctetes. There is nothing to be seen of the necessaries or the conveniences of life beyond a trodden matting of withered leaves, a misshapen bowl of wood, and a fireplace. The whole wealth of the sick, forsaken man! How does the poet complete the sad and fearful picture? With an addition of disgust. "Ha!" exclaims Neoptolemus, recoiling, —"torn rags drying in the wind, full of blood and matter!"

> NE. Ὁρῶ κενὴν οἴκησιν, ἀνθρώπων δίχα.
> ΟΔ. Οὐδ' ἔνδον οἰκοποιός ἐστί τις τροφή;
> NE. Στιπτή γε φυλλὰς ὡς ἐναυλίζοντί τῳ.
> ΟΔ. Τὰ δ' ἄλλ' ἔρημα, κοὐδέν ἐσθ' ὑπόστεγον;
> NE. Αὐτόξυλόν γ' ἔκπωμα, φλαυρουργοῦ τινος
> Τεχνήματ' ἀνδρός, καὶ πυρεῖ' ὁμοῦ τάδε.
> ΟΔ. Κείνου τὸ θησαύρισμα σημαίνεις τόδε.
> NE. Ἰοὺ ἰού· καὶ ταῦτά γ' ἄλλα θάλπεται
> Ῥάκη, ῥαρείας του νοσηλείας πλέα.

And, similarly, in Homer dead Hector, dragged along, his countenance disfigured with blood and dust and clotted hair :

Squalentem barbam et concretos sanguine crines

(as Virgil expresses it), a disgusting object, but all the more terrible on that account and all the more moving. Who can think of the torture of Marsyas in Ovid without a sensation of disgust ?

> *Clamanti cutis est summos derepta per artus,*
> *Nec quidquam nisi vulnus erat. Cruor undique manat,*
> *Detectique patent nervi, trepidaeque sine ulla*
> *Pelle micant venae : salientia viscera possis*
> *Et perlucentes numerare in pectore fibras.*

But who does not feel at the same time that the disgusting is here in place ? It makes the terrible horrible ; and the horrible itself in Nature, when our pity is engaged, is not wholly disagreeable ; how much less in the imitation ! I will not heap up instances. But one thing I must still note : that there is a variety of the terrible, the poet's way to which stands open simply and solely through the disgusting—this is the terrible of *hunger*. Even in common life it is impossible to express the extremity of hunger otherwise than by the narration of all the innutritious, unwholesome, and especially all the loathsome things, with which the appetite must be appeased. As the imitation can awaken in us nothing of the feeling of hunger itself, it resorts to another unpleasant feeling which in the case of the fiercest hunger we recognise as the smaller of two great evils. This feeling it seeks to excite within us in order that we may from the discomfort conclude how fearful must be that other discomfort under which this becomes of no account. Ovid says of the oread whom Ceres sent off to starve :—

> *Hanc (Famem) procul ut vidit. . . .*
> *. . . Refert mandata deae, paulumque morata,*
> *Quanquam aberat longe, quanquam modo venerat illuc,*
> *Visa tamen sensisse Famem. . . .*

An unnatural exaggeration ! The sight of one who hungers, were it even Hunger herself, has not this infectious power ; pity and horror and disgust it may make us feel, but not hunger. This horror Ovid has not spared us in his picture of famine, and in the hunger of Erysichthon, both in his description and that of Callimachus, the loathsome features are the strongest. After Erysichthon had devoured everything, not sparing even the beast which his mother had reared to be a burnt-offering for Vesta, Callimachus makes him fall upon horses and cats, and beg upon the streets for the crusts and filthy fragments from strange tables :—

> Καὶ τὰν βῶν ἔφαγεν, τὰν 'Εστία ἔτρεφε μάτηρ,
> Καὶ τὸν ἀεθλοφόρον καὶ τὸν πολεμήϊον ἵππον,
> Καὶ τὰν αἴλουρον, τὰν ἔτρεμε θηρία μικκά—
> Καὶ τόθ' ὁ τῶ βασιλῆος ἐνὶ τριόδοισι καθῆστο
> Αἰτίζων ἀκόλως τε καὶ ἔκβολα λύματα δαιτός—

And Ovid makes him finally put his teeth into his own limbs, to nourish his body with his own flesh :—

> *Vis tamen illa mali postquam consumpserat omnem*
> *Materiam. . . .*
> *Ipse suos artus lacero divellere morsu*
> *Coepit, et infelix minuendo corpus alebat.*

For that very reason were the repulsive Harpies made so noisome, so filthy, that the hunger which their snatching of the viands was to produce should be so much more terrible.   Listen to the lament of Phineus in Apollonius :—

> Τυτθὸν δ' ἦν ἄρα δή ποτ' ἐδητύος ἄμμι λίπωσι,
> Πνεῖ τόδε μυδαλέον τε καὶ οὐ τλητὸν μένος ὀδμῆς.
> Οὔ κέ τις οὐδὲ μίνυνθα βροτῶν ἄνσχοιτο πελάσσας
> Οὐδ' εἴ οἱ ἀδάμαντος ἐληλαμένον κέαρ εἴη.
> 'Αλλά με πικρὴ δῆτά κε δαιτὸς ἐπίσχει ἀνάγκη
> Μίμνειν, καὶ μίμνοντα κακῇ ἐν γαστέρι θέσθαι.

I would from this point of view gladly excuse the loathsome introduction of the Harpies in Virgil; but it is no actual present hunger which they cause, but only an impending one which they prophesy, and, furthermore, the whole prophecy is resolved in the end into a play upon words.   Dante, too, prepares us not only for the story of the starvation of Ugolino by the most loathsome and horrible situation in which he places him in hell with his aforetime persecutor; but the starvation itself also is not without elements of disgust, which more particularly over- comes us at the point where the sons offer themselves as food to their father.   There is in a drama of Beaumont and Fletcher a passage which I might cite here in place of all other examples were I not obliged to think it somewhat overdone.

I turn to the question of disgusting subjects in painting.   If it were quite incontestable that, properly speaking, there are no disgusting subjects whatever for sight, of which it might be

assumed that painting, as fine art, would refuse them : all the
same, she must avoid disgusting subjects in general, because
the association of ideas makes them disgusting to sight also.
Pardenone in a picture of Christ's burial makes one of the
onlookers hold his nose. Richardson condemns this on the
ground that Christ was not yet so long dead that His body
could have suffered corruption. In the Resurrection of Lazarus,
on the other hand, he thinks it might be permitted to the painter
to show by such an indication what the story expressly asserts—
that his body was already corrupt. In my view this representation is unendurable in this case also ; for not only the
actual stench, but the mere idea of it awakens disgust. We
flee offensive places even if we have actually a catarrh. Yet
painting accepts the disgusting not for disgust's sake : she
accepts it, as poetry does, in order to intensify by it the laughable and the terrible. But at her own risk ! What, however,
I have in this case noted of the ugly holds yet more certainly of
the disgusting. It loses in a *visible* imitation incomparably less
of its effect than in an *audible* one ; and therefore can mingle
less intimately with the laughable and terrible elements in the
former case than in the latter ; as soon as the first surprise is
past, as soon as the first eager glance is satisfied, it isolates
itself in its turn completely and lies there in all its crudeness.

XXVI

Herr Winckelmann's *History of Ancient Art* has been issued.
I will not venture a step further until I have read that work.
To reason too nicely about art from mere general conceptions
may lead to vagaries that sooner or later one will find confuted
in works of art. The ancients, too, knew the bonds that unite
poetry and painting, and they will not have drawn them tighter
than is advantageous to both. What their artists did will
teach me what artists in general ought to do ; and where such
a man carries before us the torch of history, speculation can
follow boldly.

We usually dip here and there in an important work before
we begin to read it seriously. My curiosity was above all things
to learn the author's opinion of the Laocoön—not, indeed, of the
art of the work, of which he has already spoken elsewhere, but
rather of its age. On that point to which party does he adhere ?
To those who believe Virgil to have had the group before his

H

eyes, or to those who think the artists followed the poet in
their work? It is very much to my liking that he is entirely
silent regarding a mutual imitation. Where is the absolute
necessity for that? It is not at all impossible that the resemblances between the sculpture and the poetic picture, which we
have been considering, are accidental and not intentional
resemblances; and that the one was so little the model of the
other that they need not even have had the same kind of model
before them. Nevertheless, had he supposed such an imitation
to be evident, he would certainly have had to declare for the
former. For he is satisfied that the Laocoön dates from the
times in which art among the Greeks attained the summit of its
perfection—from the time, that is to say, of Alexander the Great.

"The kind Fate," he says, "which has still kept watch over
the arts, even in their destruction, has preserved for the whole
world's admiration a work from this age of art, as an evidence
of the truth of history regarding the splendour of so many
vanished masterpieces. Laocoön with his two sons, wrought
by Agesander, Apollodorus, and Athenodorus of Rhodes, is in
all probability of this age, although one cannot positively
determine the date, or, as some have done, declare the Olympiad
in which these artists flourished."

In a note he adds: "Pliny says not a word of the time in
which Agesander and his assistants in this work lived; Maffei,
however, in his treatise on *Ancient Sculpture*, makes out that
they flourished in the 88th Olympiad, and to this decision
some others, including Richardson, have subscribed. But
Maffei, in my view, has taken an Athenodorus among the pupils
of Polycletus for one of our artists, and as Polycletus flourished
in the 87th Olympiad, his supposed pupil has been placed an
Olympiad later; other grounds Maffei can have none."

Quite certainly he could have no other; but why does Herr
Winckelmann rest satisfied with merely adducing this supposed
reason of Maffei's? Does it confute itself? Not quite; for
although certainly it is not supported by any other evidence,
still it surely makes a little probability for itself when one
cannot otherwise show that Athenodorus, Polycletus' pupil,
and Athenodorus, the assistant of Agesander and Polydorus,
cannot possibly have been one and the same person. Fortunately this can be shown, even from the place of their nativity.
The first Athenodorus, according to the express testimony of
Pausanias, was from Klitor in Arcadia; the other, on the
contrary, as Pliny testifies, was born in Rhodes.

Herr Winckelmann cannot have had any object in passing by without completely confuting, by adducing this circumstance, the allegation of Maffei. Much rather must the grounds which, with his undoubted knowledge, he deduces from the artistic quality of the work have appeared to him weighty ; for he did not trouble himself whether or not the opinion of Maffei had still any probability. He recognises without hesitation in the Laocoön too many of the *arguticæ* which were peculiar to Lysippus, with which this master first enriched art, to allow of its being considered a work of earlier date.

Yet even if it is proved that the Laocoön cannot be older than Lysippus, is it also proved, then, that it must be of about his time, and cannot possibly be a much later work? If I overlook altogether the ages in which Greek art down to the commencement of the Roman monarchy by turns raised its head high and by turns sank again, why might not Laocoön have been a happy fruit of the rivalry which the wasteful luxury of the first emperors must have excited amongst the artists? Why might not Agesander and his assistants have been the contemporaries of a Strongylion, an Arcesilaus, a Pasiteles, a Posidonius, a Diogenes? Did not the works of these masters share the esteem bestowed on the best which art had then produced? And if undoubted works from their hands were yet extant but the period of their authors unknown, and were no conclusions to be drawn from anything but their art, what divine inspiration is to guard the critic from placing them in the very times which Herr Winckelmann deems alone worthy of the Laocoön?

It is true Pliny does not expressly note the time in which the artists of the Laocoön lived. Yet if I had to argue from the entire context of the passage whether he desires to reckon them with the ancient or with the modern artists, I confess that I seem to discover in it a greater probability for the latter. Let who will, decide it.

After Pliny has spoken in considerable detail of the oldest and greatest masters in sculpture—of Phidias, of Praxiteles, of Scopas—and thereupon has named the rest (especially some whose works were to be seen in Rome) without any chronological order, he continues in the following strain : *Nec multo plurium fama est, quorundam claritati in operibus eximiis obstante numero artificum quoniam nec unus occupat gloriam, nec plures pariter nuncupari possunt, sicut in Laocoonte, qui est in Titi imperatoris domo, opus omnibus et picturae et statuariae artis praeponendum. Ex uno lapide eum et liberos draconumque mirabiles nexus de consilii sententia fecere summi artifices, Agesander et Polydorus et Athenodorus Rhodii. Similiter Palatinas domus Cæsarum replevere probatissimis signis Craterus cum Pythodoro, Polydectes cum Hermolao, Pythodorus alius cum Artemone, et singularis Aphrodisius Trallianus. Agrippae Pantheum decoravit Diogenes Atheniensis, et caryatides in columnis templi ejus probantur inter pauca operum : sicut in fastigio posita signa, sed propter altitudinem loci minus celebrata.*

Of all the artists named in this passage Diogenes of Athens is the one whose date is most indubitably determined. He decorated the Pantheon of Agrippa; he lived, therefore, in the time of Augustus. But if we consider the words of Pliny more carefully, I believe we shall find the time of Craterus and Pythodorus, of Polydectes and Hermolaus, the second Pythodorus and Artemon as well as Aphrodisius Trallianus, just as incontestably settled. He says of them : *Palatinas domus Caesarum replevere probatissimis signis*. I ask, Can this mean no more than that the palaces of the Caesars were full of these excellent works? in the sense, that is, that the Emperors sought them in all quarters and had them set up in their dwellings? Surely not ; they must have wrought these works expressly for these palaces of the Emperors and must have lived in that age. That there were late artists who wrought only in Italy may surely be concluded from the fact that one finds them mentioned nowhere else. Had they wrought in Greece in earlier times Pausanias would have seen one or other of their works and have preserved a record of them for us. A certain Pythodorus he does indeed allude to, but Harduin is quite wrong in taking him for the Pythodorus named by Pliny. For Pausanias mentions the statue of Juno from the studio of the former, which he saw at Coronea in Boeotia, ἄγαλμα ἀρχαῖον, which appellation he bestows only on the works of those masters who lived in the most primitive and rudest periods of art, long before a Phidias and a Praxiteles. And with works of that sort certainly the Emperors would not have decorated their palaces. Still less weight attaches to the further supposition of Harduin, that Artemon is perhaps the painter of the same name whom Pliny mentions in another place. Identity of name offers only a very slight probability, which is far indeed from warranting us in doing violence to the natural interpretation of a genuine passage.

If consequently it is beyond any doubt that Craterus and Pythodorus, that Polydectes and Hermolaus with the rest lived in the age of the Emperors, whose palaces they filled with their splendid works; then in my opinion one can assign no other age to these artists either whose names Pliny passes over along with theirs with a mere *similiter*. And these are the masters of the Laocoön. Let us only consider it : if Agesander, Polydorus, and Athenodorus were masters as ancient as Herr Winckelmann takes them to be, how improper were it not for a writer with whom precision of expression is no trifling matter, if he must spring at one bound from them to the most recent masters and make this spring as if it were but an ordinary step !

Yet some may object that this *similiter* refers not to the relationship in respect of period, but to some other circumstance which these masters may have had in common. Pliny, that is to say, may be speaking of such artists as worked in association, and on account of this association remained less well known than they merited. For as no one can appropriate to himself alone the honour of the joint work, and to name on every occasion all who had a share in it would be too long-winded (*quoniam nec unus occupat gloriam, nec plures pariter nuncupari possunt*); in this way their collective names would be neglected. This may have happened to the artists of the Laocoön, as to so many other masters whom the emperors employed for their palaces.

This I grant. But even then it is highly probable that Pliny is speaking here only of later artists who worked in association. For if he had desired to speak also of more ancient masters, why should he have mentioned the artists of the Laocoön only? Why not others also? An Onatas and a Calliteles; a Timokles and Timarchides, or the sons of this Timarchides, from whose hands a jointly-wrought Jupiter existed in Rome. Herr Winckelmann himself says that one might make a long list of this kind of ancient works which had more than one father. And should Pliny have bethought him only of the single Agesander, Polydorus, and Athenodorus, if he did not wish expressly to confine himself to the most recent times?

If, moreover, a conjecture becomes so much the more probable the more and greater the difficulties that can be explained by it, then certainly this one—that the artists of the Laocoön lived under the first Emperors—is so in a very high degree. For had they wrought in Greece at the period in which Herr Winckelmann places them, had the Laocoön itself in earlier days stood in Greece, then the complete silence which the Greeks observed concerning such a work (*opus omnibus et picturae et statuariae artis praeponendum*) is extremely surprising.

It must be extremely surprising if masters so great had wrought
nothing else or if Pausanias had never come across their other
works in all Greece, no more than the Laocoön itself. In Rome,
on the other hand, the greatest masterpiece could remain hidden
for a long time, and even had the Laocoön been already finished
under Augustus, it need not therefore appear singular that it is
Pliny who first makes mention of it; Pliny first, and last. For
let us only recall what he says of a *Venus* of Scopas that stood
in a temple of Mars at Rome, *quemcunque alium locum nobili-
tatura.   Romae quidem magnitudo operum eam obliterat, ac magni
officiorum negotiorumque acervi omnes a contemplatione talium
abducunt : quoniam otiosorum et in magno loci silentio apta
admiratio talis est.*

Those who would gladly see in the Laocoön group an imitation
of the Virgilian Laocoön will accept with satisfaction what I
have said above. Yet another conjecture has occurred to me
which they might not much disapprove. Perhaps (so they
may think) it was Asinius Pollio who had the Laocoön of Virgil
wrought out by Greek artists. Pollio was a particular friend of
the poet, outlived the poet, and appears even to have written
a book of his own about the *Æneid*. For where else than in a
work of his own concerning that poem can the detached notes
so properly have stood which Servius cites from him? Pollio
was at once a lover and a connoisseur of art, possessed a rich
collection of the most splendid works of the older masters,
employed the artists of his own time to make new ones, and
with the taste which he showed in his choice so bold a composition as the Laocoön was completely in keeping : *ut fuit
acris vehementiae sic quoque spectari monumenta sua voluit.*
Nevertheless, as the collection of Pollio in Pliny's time, when
Laocoön stood in the palace of Titus, appears to have been
undispersed and all collected in one special Gallery, this conjecture of mine might in its turn lose something of its probability. And why could not Titus himself have done what we
wish to ascribe to Pollio?

XXVII

In this view that the artists of the Laocoön flourished under
the first Emperors, and at any rate cannot be so old as Herr
Winckelmann makes out, I am confirmed by a little piece of
news which he himself now for the first time makes public.
It is this :—

At Nettuno, formerly Antium, the Cardinal Alexander Albani in the year 1717 discovered, in a great vault which lay under the sea, a vase made of the dark-grey marble now called " Vigio," in which the group is inserted and upon which stands the following inscription :—

ΑΘΑΝΟΔΩΡΟΣ   ΑΓΗΣΑΝΔΡΟΥ
ΡΟΔΙΟΣ   ΕΠΟΙΗΣΕ

" ' Athanodorus, son of Agesander of Rhodes, made this.' We learn from this inscription that father and son wrought on Laocoön, and presumably Apollodorus (Polydorus) was also Agesander's son ; for this Athanodorus can be no other than he whom Pliny names. Further, this inscription proves that more works of art than merely three, as Pliny asserts, have been found on which the artists have set ' made ' in the perfect tense, that is to say, ἐποίησε, *fecit ;* he informs us that the other artists out of modesty expressed themselves in the imperfect tense, ἐποίει, *faciebat.*"

In all this Herr Winckelmann will find but little to contradict the supposition that the Athanodorus of this inscription can be no other than he of whom Pliny makes mention amongst the artists of the Laocoön. Athanodorus and Athenodorus, moreover, is but one name ; for the Rhodians used the Dorian dialect. But concerning what he further infers from it I have something to say. First, that Athenodorus was a son of Agesander may pass : it is very probable, only not incontestable. For it is well known that there were old artists who, instead of naming themselves from their fathers, preferred to be called after their teachers. What Pliny says of the " brothers " Apollonius and Tauriscus is hardly susceptible of any other interpretation.

But how? This inscription—shall it, then, confute Pliny's allegation that not more than three works of art have been found the makers of which made themselves known in the *perfect* tense (instead of ἐποίει, by ἐποίησε)? This inscription ! Why are we to learn for the first time from it what we might have gathered long before from many others? Have we not already found upon the statue of Germanicus "Κλεομένης ἐποίησε"? on the so-called *Deification* of Homer "'Αρχέλαος ἐποίησε"? on the famous vase at Gaeta "Σαλπίων ἐποίησε," and so on?

Herr Winckelmann may say : " Who knows this better than I? But "—he will add—" so much the worse for Pliny ! His

allegation is then so much the oftener contradicted, so much
the more certainly refuted."

Not quite ! For how, if Herr Winckelmann makes Pliny say
more than he actually wants to say? and if, therefore, the
examples cited confute not Pliny's assertion, but merely the
surplusage which Herr Winckelmann has imported into it?
And so it is in reality. I must cite the whole passage. Pliny
in his dedicatory epistle to Titus wants to speak of his work
with the modesty of a man who is best aware how far it falls
short of perfection. He finds one noteworthy instance of such
modesty among the Greeks whose boastful book-titles, large in
promises (*inscriptiones propter quas vadimonium deseri possit*),
he rather makes game of, and says : *Et ne in totum videar
Graecos insectari, ex illis nos velim intelligi pingendi fingendique
conditoribus, quos in libellis his invenies, absoluta opera, et illa
quoque quae mirando non satiamur, pendenti titulo inscripsisse :
ut* APELLES FACIEBAT, *aut* POLYCLETUS; *tanquam inchoata
semper arte et imperfecta ; ut contra judiciorum varietates super-
esset artifici regressus ad veniam, velut emendaturo quidquid
desideraretur, si non esset interceptus. Quare plenum verecundiae
illud est, quod omnia opera tanquam novissima inscripsere, et
tanquam singulis fato adempti. Tria non amplius, ut opinor,
absolute traduntur inscripta* ILLE FECIT *quae suis locis reddam :
quo apparuit, summam artis securitatem auctori placuisse, et ob
id magna invidia fuere omnia ea.* I would ask particular attention to Pliny's words : *pingendi fingendique conditoribus.*
Pliny does not say that the custom of acknowledging one's work
in the imperfect tense was universal or had been observed by
all artists at all times ; he says expressly that only the first
old masters—those creators of the plastic arts, *pingendi fingendique conditores*, an Apelles, a Polycletus and their contemporaries—had had this wise modesty ; and as he names these
only, he thereby intimates by silence, but plainly enough, that
their successors, especially in the more recent periods, had
manifested more self-confidence.

But taking this for granted, as one must, the inscription here
mentioned of one only of the three artists of the Laocoön may
be perfectly accurate, and it may nevertheless be true that, as
Pliny says, only about three works were extant in the inscriptions of which their authors made use of the perfect tense—
that is to say, among the older works from the time of Apelles,
Polycletus, Nicias, Lysippus. But, then, it cannot be accurate
that Athenodorus and his assistants were contemporaries of

Apelles and Lysippus, as Herr Winckelmann would make them. We must argue rather : if it is true that amongst the works of the older artists, Apelles, Polycletus and the rest of this class, there were only about three in whose inscriptions the perfect tense was employed ; if it is true that Pliny has himself specified these three works, then Athenodorus, who is author of none of these three works, and who nevertheless uses the perfect tense upon his works, cannot belong to those old artists : he cannot be the contemporary of Apelles and Lysippus, but must be assigned to a later period.

In short, I believe it might be taken as a quite trustworthy criterion that all artists who used the ἐποίησε have flourished long after the times of Alexander the Great and shortly before or under the Emperors. Of Cleomenes it is unquestionable; of Archelaus it is in a high degree probable ; and of Salpion at any rate the contrary can in no way be shown. And so of the rest, Athenodorus not excepted.

Herr Winckelmann may himself be judge in the matter. But I protest at once in anticipation against the contrary proposition. If all artists who used the ἐποίησε belong to the later schools, it does not follow that all who used the ἐποίει belong to the earlier. Among the later artists it may be that some actually possessed this modesty, which so well becomes a great man, and that others affected to possess it.

XXVIII

After the Laocoön, on no point was I more curious than on what Herr Winckelmann might have to say of the so-called Borghese Gladiator. I fancy I have made a discovery about this statue on which I pique myself as much as one can about discoveries of the kind. I was already apprehensive that Herr Winckelmann would have anticipated me in it. But I find nothing of the sort in his book, and if anything could make me distrustful of its correctness it would be just this, that my apprehension has not been justified. " Some people," says Herr Winckelmann, " make of this statue a Discobolus—that is, one who is throwing the discus or a metal quoit, which was also the opinion of the celebrated Herr von Stosch in a letter to me, without, I imagine, a sufficient consideration of the posture in which this kind of figure should be placed. For a man who is about to throw something must withdraw his body backwards, and when the throw is being made his weight rests on his right leg, while the other is free; but here the posture is just the opposite. The whole figure is thrown forward, and rests on the left leg, the right being behind and outstretched to the utmost. The right arm of the statue is new, and in the hand a piece of a javelin has been placed; on the left arm one sees the strap of a shield which he has been holding. If one considers that the head and the eyes are directed upwards and that the figure appears to guard itself with the shield against something coming from above, one might with more justification take this statue as a representation of a soldier who has particularly distinguished himself in a perilous situation : on public gladiators the honour of a statue was presumably never bestowed among the Greeks, and this work appears to be older than the introduction of gladiators amongst them."

There could not be a juster conclusion. This statue is just as little of a gladiator as it is of a quoit-player; it is really the representation of a warrior who distinguished himself in such a posture at some moment of danger. But as Herr Winckelmann guessed this so happily, why did he not go further? How is it that the very warrior did not occur to him, who in this very posture averted the complete defeat of an army and to whom his grateful country erected a statue in the identical posture? In one word, the statue is Chabrias.

The proof of this is the following passage of Nepos in the life of this general : *Hic quoque in summis habitus est ducibus; resque multas memoria dignas gessit. Sed ex his elucet maxime inventum ejus in proelio, quod apud Thebas fecit, quum Boeotiis subsidio venisset. Namque in eo victoriae fidente summo duce Agesilao, fugatis jam ab eo conductitiis catervis, reliquam phalangem loco vetuit cedere, obnixoque genu scuto projectaque hasta impetum excipere hostium docuit. Id novum Agesilaus contuens, progredi non est ausus, suosque jam incurrentes tuba revocavit. Hoc usque eo tota Graecia fama celebratum est, ut illo statu Chabrias sibi statuam fieri voluerit, quae publice ei ab Atheniensibus in foro constituta est. Ex quo factum est, ut postea athletae ceterique artifices his statibus in statuis ponendis uterentur, in quibus victoriam essent adepti.*

I know people will still hesitate a moment to give me their assent, but I hope, too, really for only a moment. The posture of Chabrias seems to me to be perfectly identical with that of the Borghese statue. The forward-thrown spear, *projecta hasta*, is common to both, but the *obnixo genu scuto* the commentators explain by *obnixo in scutum, obfirmato genu ad scutum :* Chabrias showed his men how they should firmly prop the shield by the knee and behind it receive the enemy—the statue, on the contrary, holds the shield high. But how if the commentators were mistaken? How if the words *obnixo genu scuto* were not to be associated, and one must rather read *obnixo genu* by itself, and *scuto* by itself or along with the immediately following *projectaque hasta ?* One needs but a single comma and the resemblance is at once as perfect as possible. The statue is a soldier, *qui obnixo genu, scuto projectaque hasta impetum hostis excipit ;* it shows what Chabrias did, and is the statue of Chabrias. That the comma is actually required is shown by the *que* attached to *projecta,* for if *obnixo genu scuto* were to be read together it would be superfluous, as, indeed, for that reason it is omitted in some editions.

With the high antiquity which would thus be attributable to this statue the form of the letters in the artist's inscription found upon it perfectly agrees, and Herr Winckelmann himself has concluded from the same that it is the most ancient of the existing statues in Rome on which the artist has acknowledged the authorship. I leave it to his penetrating glance whether he has noticed any other point of art that would conflict with my view. Should he honour it with his concurrence, then I might flatter myself that I had furnished a rather better example how happily the classic writers are illustrated by the works of ancient art, and these in their turn by them, than is to be found in all Spence's folio.

XXIX

Herr Winckelmann brings to his work a limitless erudition and an exact and all-embracing knowledge of art, and has yet at the same time wrought with the noble confidence of the ancient artists, who devoted all their diligence to their main subject, and, as for subsidiary matters, treated them with an apparently deliberate negligence or handed them over entirely to the first comer. It is no small merit to have fallen only into such errors as anyone might have avoided. They strike one on the first cursory perusal, and if they are to be noticed at all, it must be merely with a view to remind certain people who imagine nobody has eyes but themselves that they do not require to be noticed.

In his treatises on the Imitation of the Greek masterpieces

Herr Winckelmann has already been more than once misled by Junius. Junius is a very insidious writer; his whole work is a Cento, and as he is always trying to speak in the words of the ancients, he not seldom applies passages from them to painting which in their proper place treat of anything rather than painting. When, for example, Herr Winckelmann wishes to teach us that the highest in art just as little as in poetry is to be reached by the mere imitation of Nature, that both poet and painter must choose the impossible that is probable rather than the merely possible, he adds : " The ' possibility and truth ' which Longinus demands from a painter in opposition to the ' incredible ' of the poet can quite well exist alongside of it." But this postscript would be better away, for it shows the two greatest critics in a disagreement that is wholly without grounds. It is not true that Longinus ever said such a thing. He says something similar of eloquence and poetry, but by no means of poetry and painting. Ὡς δ' ἕτερόν τι ἡ ῥητορικὴ φαντασία βούλεται, καὶ ἕτερον ἡ παρὰ ποιηταῖς, οὐκ ἂν λάθοι σε, he writes to his Terentian ; οὐδ' ὅτι τῆς μὲν ἐν ποιήσει τέλος ἐστὶν ἔκπληξις, τῆς δ' ἐν λόγοις ἐνάργεια. And again,—Οὐ μὴν ἀλλὰ τὰ μὲν παρὰ τοῖς ποιηταῖς μυθικωτέραν ἔχει τὴν ὑπερέκπτωσιν καὶ πάντη τὸ πιστὸν ὑπεραίρουσαν· τῆς δὲ ῥητορικῆς φαντασίας κάλλιστον ἀεὶ τὸ ἔμπρακτον καὶ ἐναλῆθες. Only Junius here edges in " painting " instead of " eloquence," and it was in Junius, and not in Longinus, that Herr Winckelmann read : Praesertim cum Poeticae phantasiae finis sit ἔκπληξις, Pictoriae vero ἐνάργεια. Καὶ τὰ μὲν παρὰ τοῖς ποιηταῖς, ut loquitur idem Longinus, and so on. Very good ; Longinus' words indeed, but not Longinus' meaning !

The same thing must have happened to him in the following observation :—

" All actions," he says, " and postures of the Greek figures that are not marked with the character of wisdom, but were overpassionate and wild, fell into a fault which the ancient artists called Parenthyrsus." The ancient artists ? That could only be shown from Junius. The Parenthyrsus was a technical term in rhetoric, and perhaps, as the passage in Longinus appears to indicate, only to be found in Theodorus. Τούτῳ παράκειται τρίτον τι κακίας εἶδος ἐν τοῖς παθητικοῖς, ὅπερ ὁ Θεόδωρος παρένθυρσον ἐκάλει· ἔστι δὲ πάθος ἄκαιρον καὶ κενόν, ἔνθα μὴ δεῖ πάθους· ἢ ἄμετρον, ἔνθα μέτριον δεῖ. Indeed I really doubt whether this word can be applied to painting at all. For in eloquence and poetry there is a kind of pathos that can be carried as high as possible without becoming Parenthyrsus, and only the highest pathos in the wrong place is Parenthyrsus. In painting, however, the highest pathos would be Parenthyrsus always, well as it might be excused by the circumstances of the person who expresses it.

To all appearance, then, various inaccuracies also in his *History of Art* have arisen simply from the fact that Herr Winckelmann has in his haste taken counsel with Junius only, and not with the originals themselves. For example, when he tries to show by instances that with the Greeks everything excellent in all kinds of art and work was particularly esteemed, and the best workman in the most insignificant department of labour could make his name illustrious, he introduces amongst other things the following : " We know the name of a maker of very exact balances or weighing-machines—he was called Parthenius." Herr Winckelmann can only have read the words of Juvenal, to which he here appeals, *lances Parthenio factas*, in the catalogue of Junius. For had he referred to Juvenal himself, he would not have been misled by the ambiguity of the word *lanx*, but would at once have recognised from the context that the poet did not mean scales or balances, but plates and dishes. Juvenal is at the moment praising Catullus because in a dangerous storm at sea he acted like the beaver which bites away its own flesh in order to escape with its life, and caused his costliest things to be thrown into the sea, in order not along with them to sink with the ship. These treasures he describes, and says amongst other things :—

> *Ille nec argentum dubitabat mittere, lances*
> *Parthenio factas, urnae cratera capacem*
> *Et dignum sitiente Pholo vel conjuge Fusci.*
> *Adde et bascaudas et mille escaria, multum*
> *Caelati, biberat quo callidus emtor Olynthi.*

Lances, which stand here amongst goblets and kettles, what else can they be but plates and dishes? And what does Juvenal mean to say but this, that Catullus caused to be thrown overboard all his table silver, amongst which were dishes of chased work by Parthenius? *Parthenius*, says the ancient commentator, *caelatoris nomen*. But when Grangaeus in his notes on this name adds, " *sculptor, de quo Plinius*," he must only have written this as a good guess; for Pliny mentions no artist of this name.

" Yes," continues Herr Winckelmann, " even the name of the saddler, as we should call him, has been preserved who made Ajax's leathern shield." This, too, he cannot have taken from the source to which he refers his reader, the Life of Homer by Herodotus. For here, certainly, the lines from the *Iliad* are cited in which the poet assigns the name of Tychius to this worker in leather; but it is at the same time expressly stated that in reality a leather-worker of Homer's acquaintance bore this name, to which he wished to show friendship and gratitude by inserting it in his poem : Ἀπέδωκε δὲ χάριν καὶ Τυχίῳ τῷ σκυτεῖ, ὃς ἐδέξατο αὐτὸν ἐν τῷ Νέῳ Τείχει προσελθόντα πρὸς τὸ σκυτεῖον, ἐν τοῖς ἔπεσι καταζεύξας ἐν τῇ Ἰλιάδι τοῖσδε.

> Αἴας δ' ἐγγύθεν ἦλθε, φέρων σάκος ἠΰτε πύργον,
> Χάλκεον, ἑπταβόειον, ὅ οἱ Τυχίος κάμε τεύχων,
> Σκυτοτόμων ὄχ' ἄριστος, Ὕλῃ ἔνι οἰκία ναίων.

It is therefore precisely the opposite of what Herr Winckelmann avers; the name of the saddler who had made the shield of Ajax was already in Homer's time so completely forgotten that the poet took the liberty of inserting an altogether different name in place of it.

Various other minor errors are mere slips of memory, or relate to things which he introduces merely by way of incidental illustration. For instance, it was Hercules, and not Bacchus, of whom Parrhasius boasted that he had appeared to him in the form in which he painted him.

Tauriscus was not a man of Rhodes, but of Tralles in Lydia.

The *Antigone* is not the first tragedy of Sophocles. But I refrain from gathering together a heap of such trifles. It could not, of course, appear censoriousness; but whoever knows my high esteem for Herr Winckelmann might take it for fastidiousness.

NATHAN THE WISE

A DRAMATIC POEM IN FIVE ACTS

BY

GOTTHOLD EPHRAIM LESSING

PERSONS

SULTAN SALADIN.
SITTAH, his sister.
NATHAN, a rich Jew in Jerusalem.
RECHA, his adopted daughter.
DAJA, a Christian, but in the house
　· of the Jew as companion to Recha.
A young Knight Templar.
A Dervish.
The Patriarch of Jerusalem.
A Friar.
An Emir, with various Mamelukes of Saladin.

ACT I—Scene I

Scene : *Apartment in Nathan's house*

Nathan returning from a journey.   To him Daja

Daja. 'Tis he ! 'tis Nathan !   Now may God be praised
That you at last, at last return again.
Nathan. Yes, Daja; God be praised !   But why *at last?*
Have I then hoped for earlier home-coming?
And was it in my power?   Think !   Babylon
By such a road as I perforce must follow,
Now left, now right, is from Jerusalem
At least two hundred leagues ; and then my task,
To gather in the debts the merchants owed me,
Was scarce a business to make for speed,
'Tis no such off-hand matter.
Daja.   Nathan, Nathan,
How wretched meanwhile all things might have been
To greet you on return !   Your house. . . .
Nathan.   On fire !
So much I've heard already; now God grant
That this is all the evil I must hear of !
Daja. So near it was to burning to the ground.
Nathan. Then, Daja, we had built another house ;
And one to suit us better.
Daja.   True enough !
Yet Recha by a hair's breadth only 'scaped
Of burning with it.
Nathan.   Burning?   Recha?   She?
That no one told me.   Then indeed no house
I should have wanted more.   My Recha burned,
Within a hair's breadth !—Ha ! she is, in truth !
Has actually perished !   Say the word !
Out with it !   Kill me, torture me no longer—
Yes, yes, she was burned with it.
Daja.   Were it so,
Would it be from my lips that you would hear it?

I   113

Nathan. Why do you fright me, then? O Recha mine!
   My Recha!
Daja.   Yours? Your Recha call you her?
Nathan. How should I ever disaccustom me
   To call this child my own?
Daja.   Do you name all
   That you possess with only so much right
   Your own?
Nathan.   Nothing with greater! Everything
   I else possess Nature and Fortune's grace
   Rained down on me. This property alone
   I owe to virtue.
Daja.   At how dear a rate
   You make me pay for your pure goodness, Nathan!
   If goodness, with such purpose exercised,
   Can be called goodness!
Nathan.   Such a purpose, say you?
   What, then?
Daja.   My conscience . . .
Nathan.   Daja, first of all,
   Listen and hear me tell . . .
Daja.   My conscience, I . . .
Nathan. What a rare stuff I bought in Babylon,
   Tasteful and worthy of you, so rich and fine,
   Even for Recha I scarce have brought a finer.
Daja. What use? For, Nathan, I must tell you freely
   My conscience will no longer be deceived.
Nathan. And how the bracelets, and the golden chain,
   The ear-rings and the brooch will pleasure you,
   Which in Damascus booths I rummaged out;
   Ask me to show them.
Daja.   Ever 'twas your way!
   Only at ease when giving costly gifts!
Nathan. Be you as glad to take as I to give—
   Nor speak of them!
Daja.   Nor speak! Nathan, who doubts
   That you are honour's self, great-heartedness?
   And yet . . .
Nathan.   And yet—am but a Jew—is't not
   What would you say?
Daja.   Nathan, what I would say
   You know far better.
Nathan.   Well, no words!

Daja.   I'm dumb.
  What God may see herein deserving doom
  And which I cannot alter or prevent—
  Cannot, I say—come on you !
Nathan.   Come on me !—
  But now where is she ? Where lies hid ? O Daja,
  Are you deceiving me ? Does she not know
  That I am come ?
Daja.   That ask I you, her father !
  The fright still quivers in her every nerve,
  Whate'er her fancy shapes is only fire,
  Nothing but fire. In sleep her spirit wakes,
  And sleeps in waking ; now an animal,
  And now more than an angel.
Nathan.   Dear my child !
  What are we human creatures !
Daja.   Long she lay
  This morning with closed eyes, and was as dead.
  Sudden she started up and cried, " O hearken !
  My father's camels come : I hear their tread,
  I hear his gentle voice ! "—as suddenly
  Her eye grew dim again, and so her head,
  Her arm's support withdrawn, dropped on the pillow.
  I, out at gate ! and there beheld your face !
  What wonder ! her whole soul was every hour
  With you, with you alone—and him.
Nathan.   With him ?
  What him ?
Daja.   With him who saved her from the fire.
Nathan. Saved her ! Who was he ? Who ? And where is he ?
  Who saved for me my Recha ? Tell me, who ?
Daja. 'Twas a young Templar Knight whom just before,
  Brought here a prisoner, Saladin set free.
Nathan. A Templar ! What ! Whom Saladin let live ?
  And did no meaner miracle suffice
  To save my Recha ? God !
Daja.   No. Without him
  Venturing once more his new-won life, she perished !
Nathan. Where is he, Daja, this heroic man ?
  Where is he ? Come and lead me to his feet.
  But first you gave him, not reserving aught,
  The treasure I had left you ? Gave him all ?
  Promised him more—much more ?

Daja.   Alas ! we could not.
Nathan. Not? Not?
Daja. He came, and no one knows from whence;
   He went, no one knew whither. Without word,
   Led by his ear alone, with fore-spread mantle,
   Boldly through flame and smoke he sought the voice
   That called to us for help. We gave him lost,
   When suddenly from out the smoke and flame he stood,
   In his strong arm holding her high. Unmoved
   And cold before our sobbed-out thanks, he set
   His prize down gently, thrid the crowd, and vanished !
Nathan. Vanished ! But not for ever, I will hope.
Daja. When the first days were past we saw him go,
   Under the palm-trees walking up and down,
   Yonder, that shade the Holy Sepulchre.
   With trembling I approached him, spoke my thanks,
   Besought, entreated, conjured him but once
   To see the gentle girl who could not rest
   Until her thanks were wept out at his feet.
Nathan. Well?
Daja.   Vain, in vain ! To our entreaty deaf,
   He poured even bitter mockery on me . . .
Nathan. Till you were frighted from him . . .
Daja.   No, in truth !
   For I assailed him every day anew;
   And every day endured new mockery.
   What did I not bear from him ! What had not
   Willingly borne ! But many days now past
   He comes no more to seek the palm-trees' shade
   Girdling the quiet grave of the Redeemer;
   And no man knows where now he lives retired—
   You are amazed ! You ponder !
Nathan.   I but think
   What feeling this in such a soul as Recha's
   Surely begets. To find herself disdained
   By one proven worthy of so high regard;
   So driven away, and still to be so drawn;
   A long contention sets of heart and head,
   Whether misanthropy shall win the day
   Or melancholy; often neither wins,
   And fantasy that mixes in the strife
   Makes of us dreamers in whom, ill exchange !
   The head acts heart, and heart acts head by turns;

The latter is, if I have not misread her,
My Recha's case : she dreams.

Daja.   She's dutiful,
And all love-worthy !

Nathan.   Still she dreams, she dreams !

Daja. One special crotchet—may we dare to call it ?—
She cherishes.   'Tis that her Templar Knight
Can be no earthly creature, born of woman ;
One of the angels rather, whose sweet guard
She trusted in from her blest infancy,
Flew from his veil wherein even in the fire
He hovered round her, took the Templar's form
To save her—do not smile !   Who knows ? who knows ?
Even if we smile, we'll leave her this illusion
In which the Jew, the Christian, and the Muslim
Are joined in one—surely a blessed dream !

Nathan. Even to me 'tis blessed ! Go, brave Daja ;
See what she does ; if I can speak with her—
This wondrous angel-guardian then I'll find,
And if it pleases him still here below
To play the pilgrim, still his knightly part
To fill, sure I shall find and bring him hither.

Daja. You undertake things harder than you know.

Nathan. Then the sweet dream to actuality
More sweet will yield its place, for, trust me, Daja,
To men a human creature is more dear
Than any angel, so you will not grieve
To see this angel-mania exorcised.

Daja. You are so good, and yet you are so wicked !
I go—but listen, see !—here Recha comes.

SCENE II

Recha, and the foregoing

Recha. Home safe and sound, my father, home once more ?
I feared 'twas but your voice sent to announce you.
But come ; no hills, or wastes, or rivers part
Us now ; we breathe within the self-same walls.
Why haste you not your Recha to embrace ?
Poor Recha ! who meanwhile was burned with fire,
Almost, but almost only : Shudder not
It is a horrid death, to die in fire !

Nathan. My child, my darling child !

Recha.   And you must over
  Euphrates, Tigris, Jordan; over who knows
  What waters ?   O how often have I trembled
  For you, before the fire came close to me !
  Since then I think to die in water were
  Refreshment, comfort, safety; but in truth
  You did not drown, nor did I die in fire—
  Let us be glad and lift our heart to God.
  He bore you and the vessel on the wings
  Of His *invisible* angel-host across
  The treacherous rivers.   He too gave the sign
  To my good angel that he *visibly*
  On his white wing should bear me through the fire.

Nathan. (White wing ! Ah, yes, the Templar's fore-spread
  cloak.)

Recha. Visibly, visibly, should bear me through
  The scorching flame, safe covered by his wing;
  Thus I have seen an angel face to face,
  And *my own* angel.

Nathan.   Recha were worthy that,
  And would in him see nought more beautiful
  Than he in her.

Recha [*smiling*].   Whom flatter you, my Father ?
  The angel, or yourself ?

Nathan.   Yet, had a man,
  Even such as Nature gives us every day,
  Done you this service, he must then appear
  To you an angel.   Yea, he must and would.

Recha. No, not that kind of angel; no ! a real,
  An actual angel he !   Have not yourself
  Taught me 'tis possible that angels are,
  That God for good to them that love Him can
  Work wonders ?   And I love Him.

Nathan.   He loves you,
  And works for such as you His hourly wonders;
  Ay, has indeed from all eternity
  Wrought them.

Recha.   I love to hear that doctrine.

Nathan.   How ?
  That it would sound so natural, commonplace;
  If a mere Knight had saved you, were it then
  Less miracle ?   Chief miracle it is

That the true miracles become to us
So commonplace, so everyday.   Without
This universal miracle could it be
That thinking men should use the word like children,
Who only gape and stare upon what's strange,
And think what's newest is most wonderful.

Daja. [*To Nathan.*] O will you, Nathan, with such subtleties
Break her now o'er-stretched brain?

Nathan. Hear me!   For Recha
Were it not miracle enough to find
Her saved by one whom first a miracle
Must himself save?   Yea, no small miracle!
For what man ever heard that Saladin
Spared a Knight Templar's blood? or such a Knight
Did ever ask or hope that he should spare him,
Or offered more for freedom than the belt
Carrying his weapon, or at most his sword?

Recha. My father, that proves all, and argues clear
It was no Templar, but the semblance only,
For if no captive Templar ever came
Into Jerusalem but to certain death;
Nor any such was ever granted freedom
To walk Jerusalem streets, then how could one
Spring up at midnight for my rescue?

Nathan.   See!
She argues well.   You, Daja, answer her.
You tell me he came here a prisoner;
Then doubtless you know more.

Daja.   Well, yes; I know
What common rumour says—that Saladin
Showed mercy to him for his dear resemblance
To a child-brother Saladin had loved.
Yet as full twenty years have run their course
Since the boy died—his name I know not what;
He dwelt, I know not where—the story seems
An idle tale strange and incredible!

Nathan. Nay, Daja, why were this incredible?
Is it rejected only to make room
For things less credible, as happens oft?
Why should not Saladin, who loves his race,
As all men know, have had in younger years
A brother whom he specially beloved?
Was 't never known two faces should be like?

Can an old passion not return again?
Like causes, do they not work like effects?
Since when? Tell me, what's here incredible?
Ah, my wise Daja, it were then no more
A miracle; *your* miracles alone,
Demand, or shall I say deserve, belief?

Daja. You mock.

Nathan.   But first you mocked at me. Yet, Recha,
Even so your great deliverance remains
A miracle and possible alone
To Him who by weak threads can turn—His sport
If not His mockery—the stern resolves
And deep-laid plans of monarchs.

Recha.   O my father!
My father, if I err, you know I err
Unwillingly.

Nathan.   Nay, more, you wish to learn:
But see! A brow so moulded or so arched;
Bridge of a nose, this way or that way shaped;
Eyebrows that on a blunt or sharper ridge
Rest full or pencilled delicate, a line,
A bend, a fold, an angle, or a mole,
Or what else, on some Western countenance,
And you escape the fire, in Asia!
Were that no wonder, miracle-hungry folk?
Why trouble, then, an angel?

Daja.   Why, what harm—
Nathan, if I may speak—what, after all,
What harm to wish an angel for a saviour
Rather than man? For so one feels the First
Ineffable Cause of one's salvation drawn
Much closer.

Nathan.   Pride, mere pride! The iron pot
Wants silver tongs to draw her from the furnace,
That she may dream she's made of silver too.
Pah! ask you what's the harm? Then, I would ask,
What profit? " That's to feel God so much nearer "—
Your thought—is folly, if not blasphemy.
The thought is harmful, does the soul a mischief.
Come, hear me for a moment. To this being
Who saved you, be he angel or but man,
Would you not render service in return
With a glad heart, repaying what you might?

How then and what, if angel?   What of service,
Say what great service can you do for him?
Thank him, you'll say, and sigh to him or pray,
Dissolve in rapturous tears before him, fast,
Give alms and celebrate his Festival.
All nothing !   For methinks thereby far more
Yourself and your dear neighbours gain than he.
Your fasting will not fatten him, your expense
Not make him rich, nor will your rapturous worship
Add to his glory, nor your faith in him
Make him a mightier angel.   Is't not so?
But, if a human creature !

Daja.   Certainly,
I know a human creature's needs had given
More opportunity to serve ; God knows
How ready we were for it !   But he wished,
He needed, nothing ; in himself content,
And with himself at peace as only angels
Are or can be.

Recha.   At last, when he quite vanished . . .

Nathan. Vanished !   How mean you, vanished?   Shown him-
   self
Under the palms no more?   Then, did you make
More eager search elsewhere?

Daja.   We did not.   No !

Nathan. No, Daja, no?   But thereof may come sorrow !
Fond dreamers !   Should your angel now be sick?

Recha. Sick !

Daja.   Sick !   O say not so !

Recha.   What shuddering
Strikes my heart dead !   Feel, Daja, this cold brow—
So warm it was, and suddenly 'tis ice !

Nathan. He is a Frank, a stranger to our clime ;
He's young ; unused to hunger and to vigil,
And heavy labours laid upon him now.

Recha. Sick !

Daja. Nathan means only it were possible.

Nathan. Well, there he lies !   Without a friend, or gold
To buy friends for him.

Recha.   Father, O this heart !

Nathan. No tendance, counsel none, nor friendly talk,
The spoil of pain, perhaps of death, he lies !

Recha. Where? where?

Nathan.   He who for one he had not seen
  Nor ever knew—enough, a fellow creature—
  Plunged in the fire . . .
Daja.   O spare her, spare her, Nathan !
Nathan. Who would not nearer come or further know
  What he had saved, to spare himself the thanks.
Daja. O pity her, Nathan !
Nathan.   Further, who desires not
  To see her more, unless again to save—
  Enough—a fellow creature.
Daja.   Cease, and look !
Nathan. He on his bed of death, nor comfort hath
  But memory of this deed !
Daja.   O Nathan, cease !
  You kill her !
Nathan.   Him you killed, or might have killed.
  Recha ! My Recha ! this is medicine,
  Not poison that I bring. Come to yourself !
  He lives, mayhap is not even sick !
Recha.   In truth ?
  Not dead ? Not sick ?
Nathan.   Not dead ; for sure, not dead !
  For God rewards good deeds, even here rewards them.
  But come ! I need not teach you what you know :
  How easier far is dreaming pious dreams
  Than acting bravely ; how a worthless creature
  Will dream fine dreams, in order to escape—
  (Though oft his object's hidden from himself)—
  Some serviceable labour.
Recha.   Ah, my father !
  Never again leave Recha to herself !
  May it not be that he is only gone
  Upon a journey ?
Nathan.   Yes, without a doubt.
  I see, below, a Mussulman who scans
  With searching gaze my camels and their load.
  Who is he ? Know you him ?
Daja.   It is your dervish.
Nathan. Who ?
Daja. Why, your chess-companion—your dervish !
Nathan. Al-Hafi ! my Al-Hafi ?
Daja.   Purse-bearer
  To the Sultan now.

Nathan. Al-Hafi ! Are you dreaming ?
'Tis he ! in truth, 'tis he ! He comes this way—
In with you, quick ! And now what shall I hear ?

Scene III

Nathan and the Dervish

Dervish. Do not be startled, open your eyes wide !
Nathan. Is't you ? Or is it not ? In silk attire,
A dervish !
Dervish. Well, why not ? Can nought be made
Out of a dervish, nothing ? Tell me why ?
Nathan. O much, no doubt ! But I have ever thought
The true, the genuine dervish, would refuse
To be aught else than dervish.
Dervish. By the prophet !
That I'm no genuine dervish may be true.
Yet when one must—
Nathan. What ! *must*—a dervish *must* ?
No man needs must, and shall a dervish, then ?
What must he ?
Dervish. What a true man asks of him
And he sees clear is right ; that must a dervish !
Nathan. By Heaven, thou speak'st the truth. Come hither, man,
Let me embrace thee. Thou art still my friend ?
Dervish. Dost thou not ask first what I am become ?
Nathan. Despite what thou'rt become !
Dervish. But might I not
Be now a fellow of State whose friendship were
To thee inopportune, a burden ?
Nathan. If thy heart
Is Dervish still, I'll trust it. For State office,
That's but a garment !
Dervish. Which still must be regarded ;
What think you ? Now advise me—at your court
What should I be ?
Nathan. A Dervish, nothing more.
Yet later, very probably, a cook.
Dervish. And thus with you unlearn my handicraft ?
Just cook ! Not waiter also ? Now confess
Saladin knows me better—I am made

His Keeper of the Treasure.
Nathan.   Thou ? By him ?
Dervish. The smaller Treasure, be it understood ;
  The chief, that of his House, his father guards.
Nathan. His House is large.
Dervish.   And larger than thou thinkest,
  For every beggar is a member of it.
Nathan. Yet Saladin so hates the beggar tribe—
Dervish. That root and branch he means to blot them out,
  Though in the attempt himself become a beggar.
Nathan. Bravo ! That mean I ; Saladin, well done !
Dervish. And beggar he is now, in spite of one !
  For every sunset sees his treasury
  Emptier than empty. For however full
  The morning's flood, the ebb comes ere midday.
Nathan. By channels drained, alike impossible
  To fill or close.
Dervish.   You hit the bull's eye there.
Nathan. I know it.
Dervish.   Truly, it is little good for princes,
  Vultures to be among the carcases ;
  But ten times less when they are carcases
  Among the vultures.
Nathan.   Not yet that, my dervish.
  Not that !
Dervish.   Your speech is wisdom, sir.   Now come
  What will you give to have my place from me ?
Nathan. What does your place bring in ?
Dervish.   To me ?   Not much.
  To you it would be wondrous profitable.
  For were the Treasure at ebb, as oft it is—
  Then you would raise your sluices ; make advances
  And take in usury whatever pleased you.
Nathan. With interest on interest again ?
Dervish. Ev'n so !
Nathan.   Until my capital were interest
  And nothing more.
Dervish.   Is that no lure for you ?
  Divorce then, nothing else, is what remains
  To us two friends and our past happiness !
  For verily I reckoned much on you.
Nathan. Verily ?   Reckoned !   How ?
Dervish.   That you would help me carry

My office with all honour, and offer me
An ever-open treasury.　You tremble.
Nathan. Well, let us understand each other.　Here
Is room for difference.　Thou, my friend, art thou.
Al-Hafi, dervish, to my uttermost
Is welcome, but Al-Hafi, Saladin's
Attorney—why, to him—
Dervish.　　　　　　　Ah ! I guessed right.
Thou would'st be kind if prudence should allow,
Prudent and sage.　But patience ! Thou would'st make
Of one Al-Hafi two ; but presently
Those two may separate.　See this robe of honour
Saladin gave me, look before it fades
And turns to rags, such as may clothe a dervish,
Hangs on a nail in old Jerusalem,
And I am by the Ganges, where barefoot
I lightly tread the hot sand with my teachers.
Nathan. That would be like you !
Dervish.　　　　　　And play chess with them.
Nathan. Your chiefest joy !
Dervish.　　　　　　Think only, what seduced me !
That I should be no more a beggar, rather
Might play the rich man 'mongst the beggars, might
Perchance, hey presto ! change the richest beggar
Into a poor rich man ?
Nathan.　　　　　　No, no ; not that !
Dervish. No, something more absurd ! For the first time
Flattery trapped me, the good-hearted fancy
Of Saladin it was that overcame me.
Nathan. What fancy ?
Dervish.　　　　" Only a beggar could interpret
The soul of beggars, only a beggar learn
How rightly to give alms.　Your predecessor,"
So said he, " was too cold by half, too rough ;
When he did give, he gave ungraciously ;
Blustered enquiry of the wretch he gave to ;
Not satisfied to know the need, must learn
First how the need arose, and then weighed out
According to the cause, a stingy dole.
But not so will Al-Hafi ! Nor in him
Will Saladin appear unkindly kind.
Al-Hafi is not as choked pipes that yield
In mud and foam what they received so pure,

The limpid waters.   No ; Al-Hafi thinks,
Al-Hafi feels as I do."   Such the tune
The fowler's pleasing pipe played in mine ear
Till the bullfinch was netted.   O a fool !
Fool of a fool am I !

Nathan.   Gently, my Dervish,
Gently !

Dervish.   Eh, what !   Were it not foolery
To tread men underfoot by scores of thousands,
Starve, rob, enslave, lash, stab and crucify them,
Then to a handful play philanthropist ?
Were it not foolery to ape the mercy
Of the All-Highest, Who sends sun and rain
Alike upon the evil and the good,
On wilderness and pasture, to ape this
And not to have the overflowing riches
Of the Almighty?   What ! were it not folly. . . .

Nathan. No more, Al-Hafi, cease !

Dervish.   Nay, of my share
In this wild folly let me question you.
Were it not foolish in these fooleries
To note the good side only, and be partner
For the good's sake in folly?   Answer me !

Nathan. Al-Hafi, ask you counsel ?   Hear it, then ;
Make haste, return into the wilderness !
With men you might, dehumanised, forget,
Unlearn to be a man.

Dervish.   This fear I too.
Farewell !   [*Exit.*

Nathan. What ! what ! so fast away ?   Dost then imagine
The desert will take wings ?   Would he but wait
And hearken to a friend !   Ho ! ho ! Al-Hafi !
He's gone ; and I so wished to question him
About our Templar.   In all likelihood
He knows him.

SCENE IV

Enter Daja hastily.   Nathan

Daja. Nathan !   Nathan !
Nathan.   Well, how now ?
Daja. He has appeared again !   He has returned !

Nathan. Who, Daja? who has come again?
Daja.   He ! He !
Nathan. Well, he ! But who ? Why name him simply " he " ?
  That's not becoming, even if he is an angel.
Daja. He's pacing up and down amongst the palms,
  And plucks as he goes by dates from the boughs.
Nathan. And eating ?—and a Templar ?
Daja.   Why torment me ?
  Her eager looks through the close-column'd palms
  Divined him ere they saw, and fixedly
  Now follow him. She begs, beseeches you
  Without delay to seek him there. O hasten !
  She from her window casement will make sign
  Which way he turns, nearer or further off.
  Hasten !
Nathan.   What, travel-stained, just as I lighted
  From off the camel ? Were that well ? Go thou
  In haste to him ; tell him of my return.
  For think, the worthy man has but declined
  Entering my doors in absence of the host,
  And will come readily when he invites him.
  Go, tell him I invite him heartily.
Daja. Utterly vain ! He will not ; one word says it—
  He darkens not the door of any Jew.
Nathan. Then go, if nothing more, to follow him :
  Keep him in sight ; your eyes accompany him.
  I follow straight.   [*Nathan goes in, and Daja out.*

Scene V

SCENE : *An open space with palm-trees, amongst which the
     Templar walks up and down. A friar follows him at some
     distance on one side, seeming as if he would address him.*

Templar. He follows me as once before ; and look,
  See how he peers behind his hands ! Good brother,
  Should I perhaps say " Father " ? Is it so ?
Friar. " Brother," not more ; lay-brother at your service.
Templar. Well, brother, if one self had anything !
  But, as God lives, I have not—
Friar.   None the less
  Warm thanks, and God give thee a thousandfold
  What thou wouldst joy to give. The will, the will

Makes givers, not the gift.   Neither for alms
Was I sent after thee.
Templar.   Yet, thou wert sent?
Friar. Yes, from the cloister.
Templar.   Where I even now
Had hoped to find a simple pilgrim-meal?
Friar. The table was already laid; come only,
Come back, my lord, with me.
Templar.   Whither?   And why?
I have not eaten flesh for many a day;
What matters it?   I find the dates are ripe.
Friar. Nay, let my lord beware of this cold fruit.
Unwholesome, for it much obstructs the spleen,
Thickens the blood, brings melancholy thoughts.
Templar. I'm prone to melancholy and welcome it.
But for this warning's sake you were not sent,
I know, to seek me.
Friar.   No; it was to learn
Something about you, just to sound and probe you.
Templar. And this thou tell'st me boldly to my face?
Friar. Why not?
Templar. [*Aside.*] Crafty brother!   Has the cloister
More of thy kind?
Friar. I know not, my good lord,
I must obey.
Templar.   And there, is it your custom
To listen and obey and never question?
Friar. Were it obedience else, I ask my lord?
Templar. (How near simplicity will come to truth!)
Confide, to me thou may'st, who is the man
Would know me better; not yourself I'll swear.
Friar. Would it become me or advantage me?
Templar. Then whom becomes it or advantages,
This eager prying?
Friar.   Who's the inquisitor?
The Patriarch, I must believe—he 'twas
That sent me after you.
Templar. Knows he not, then, the red cross on white mantle?
Friar. Even to me 'tis known!
Templar.   Well, Friar, listen;
I am a Templar and a prisoner.
Would you know more?   Ta'en prisoner at Tebnin,
The fort which in the last hour of the truce

We thought to scale and then to rush on Sidon.
Yet more? taken with twenty, me alone
Saladin spared; with this the Patriarch knows
All he need know, and more ev'n than he need.

Friar. But scarcely more than he knew yesterday.
He would learn, too, the reason why my lord
Was pardoned by the Sultan, and he only.

Templar. Do I myself know why? Already I knelt,
My mantle on the ground, and with bared neck
Waited the stroke, when with a searching look
Saladin springs towards me, gives a sign;
They raise me and unfetter; when to thank him
I turn, his cheek is wet with teardrops; dumb
He stands, dumb I; he leaves me there. And now
What this strange story means, there! that's a riddle
The Patriarch may guess at.

Friar.   Thus he reads it—
That God for great things, great things has preserved you.

Templar. Yea, for great things indeed. To save from fire
A Jewish girl; to guide some curious pilgrims
To Sinai's mountain—great things truly!

Friar.   " Great things "
Will come in time; meanwhile such trifles serve:
Perhaps the Patriarch himself has ready
Affairs of weightier import for my lord.

Templar. What, Friar! Mean you that? Has he said aught?
Whispered? Dropped hint?

Friar.   Yea, not uncertainly;
Only my lord must first be probed to learn
Whether he's just the man.

Templar.   Oh, merely probed!
(We'll see first how the probing goes!) Well, sir?

Friar. The short way is the best way—that my lord
Be told in plain terms what the Patriarch wills.

Templar. Speak out then plainly.

Friar.   It would please him much
If by my lord into the proper hands
A letter might be brought.

Templar.   By me? By me?
I am no errand-runner. And was this
The business planned, an employment worthier
Than snatching Jewish maiden from the flames?

Friar. Yea, and with reason. For, the Patriarch says,

K

That with this missive's import is bound up
Christendom's fortune. Says the Patriarch,
" Carry this letter safe, and earn a crown
Which by and by the King of Heaven will give,
A crown none," says the Patriarch, " is worthier
To wear than thou."

Templar.   None worthier than I?

Friar. " For," says the Patriarch, " no man on earth
Can win this crown more certainly."

Templar.   Than I?

Friar. " He hath full freedom here, goes everywhere,
Well understands how cities may be stormed
And how defended "—says the Patriarch—
" He best can judge the weakness or the strength
Of that new-builded inner battlement
Of Saladin and plainliest describe it "—
So says the Patriarch—" to the host of God."

Templar. Good friar, were it right that I should hear
The content and the intent of the letter?

Friar. That know I not in its entirety.
'Tis for King Philipp's hands. The Patriarch—
Often I wonder how a saint who else
Lives wholly in Heaven can stoop and condescend
To be so intimate with things o' the world.
For they must vex his soul.

Templar.   Well, then, the Patriarch?

Friar. Knows with exactest certainty how, where,
And in what strength and from what quarter Saladin,
In case the truce be broken and strife renewed,
Opens afresh his campaign.

Templar.   This he knows?

Friar. Yea, would be glad King Philipp also knew,
That, with this knowledge fortified, the King
Might judge the risk, whether so terrible
That at all costs the truce must be renewed
With Saladin, the truce your Order bravely
Hath broken already.

Templar.   What a Patriarch !
The dear man wants no common messenger
In me ; he wants a spy. Well, good friar,
Tell this your Patriarch : that when you probed me
You found me useless ; that I hold myself
A prisoner still ; and more, that the one calling

Of Templars ever was to drive the foe
With naked spear, never—to play the spy.
Friar. I thought as much ! and will not blame my lord.
The best is yet to come. The Patriarch
Lately has gathered how the hold is named,
And where it lies in Lebanon, wherein
The untold sums are hid that Saladin's
Provident father stores to pay the army
And face the war's expense. Now, Saladin
From time to time to this stronghold resorts
By ways remote, with meagre company ;
Perceiv'st thou ?
Templar. No, not I.
Friar. A simple thing
To ambush then the Sultan, take him captive,
And give him his quietus ; what were easier ?
You shudder ? Two God-fearing Maronites
Offer the deed, if once some gallant man
Were found to guide them.
Templar. And the Patriarch
Has chosen me to act the gallant man ?
Friar. He thinks King Philipp then from Ptolemais
Would surely send his aid.
Templar. Friar ! To me ?
To me ? Hast thou not heard, or hear'st thou now
For the first time what debt of obligation
Binds me to Saladin ?
Friar. I've heard the tale.
Templar. And still ?
Friar. The Patriarch thinks that's well enough,
But God's rights and your Order . . .
Templar. These change nothing !
Suggest me not a knave's trick.
Friar. No, good faith !
Only the Patriarch thinks a knavish trick
In man's sight needeth not be so in God's.
Templar. That I might owe my life to Saladin,
And yet take his ?
Friar. O fie ! The Patriarch thinks
That Saladin were still a foe to Christ,
Therefore can have no claim to be your friend.
Templar. Friend ? Since I will not play the villain to him,
The thankless villain ?

Friar.   Why, of course, of course !
The Patriarch's mind is, we are quit of thanks,
Quit before God and man, when service done
Was not for our sake done, and rumour tells,
Saladin spared you for that he discerned
His brother's likeness in your look and ways.
Templar. Ah, this too knows the Patriarch, and still?
Would it were true ! Ah, Sultan Saladin !
How? Nature framed in me one feature only
After your brother's pattern, should not then
Something within me answer to the same?
And shall this something in my soul be shifted
To please a Patriarch? No, Nature, no !
Thou dost not lie ! God does not contradict
Himself in His own works ! Hence, friar, hence !
Wake not my anger; leave me to my thoughts.
Friar. I go; and I go happier than I came.
My lord will pardon me. We cloister people
Are under rule, we must obey the heads.

SCENE VI

*The Templar and Daja, who has been observing the Templar at a
distance for some time, and now approaches him.*

Daja. The friar, methinks, left him in no good humour.
But I must chance my errand.
Templar.   Excellent !
Who says the proverb lies—that monk and woman.
Woman and monk, are Beelzebub's two claws?
To-day he flings me from the one to the other.
Daja. What do I see? You, my brave knight? Thank God !
I thank Him for His grace ! So long a time
You have been hidden. You have not been, I'll hope,
Retired in sickness?
Templar.   No.
Daja.   In health, then ?
Templar.   Yes.
Daja. We have been deep in trouble for your sake.
Templar. So ?
Daja.   Surely wert on a journey ?
Templar.   You have guessed it !
Daja. And art to-day returned ?

Templar   No ; yesterday.

Daja. To-day, too, Recha's father is returned,
  And surely Recha now dare hope?

Templar.   For what?

Daja. For what she prayed of you so often.   Come ;
  Her father now himself most pressingly
  Invites you.   He has come from Babylon,
  A train of richly-laden camels with him,
  And everything that's costliest in spices,
  Jewels and stuffs that only India,
  Persia and Syria or China can provide.

Templar. I'm not a buyer.

Daja.   He's honoured of his people.
  As princes are, and yet, I wonder often
  Their title of honour is " Nathan the Wise,"
  And not " Nathan the Rich."

Templar.   Ah ! to his people
  Are *rich* and *wise* perhaps identical.

Daja. Rather " the Good " should they have named him.   For
  It's not expressible how good he is.
  That moment when he learned what Recha owed you
  What would he not have done for you, or given !

Templar.   Ay !

Daja. But try, but come and see !

Templar.   What then ?   How fast
  A moment passes !

Daja.   Think, were it not so,
  Were he not this good man, that I so long
  Had dwelt within his gates?   Think you perhaps
  That I forget my worth as Christian?
  O no, it was not sung beside my cradle
  That I should company my lawful spouse
  Only for this to Palestine, to tend
  A Jewish maiden.   A noble squire my spouse
  In Kaiser Friedrick's host.

Templar.   And was by birth
  A Swiss on whom the honour was bestowed
  With his Imperial Majesty to drown
  I' the self-same river-bed ; woman, how often
  Already have you told me this same tale?
  Will you not cease at last, then, to pursue me?

Daja. Pursue?   O gracious God !

Templar.   Yes, yes, pursue.

And once for all I will not see you more,
Nor hear ! nor have recalled thus endlessly
A deed in which my thoughts had never part,
Which when I think of it becomes a riddle
Ev'n to myself.   Regret it I must not—
But see, if such should hap again ; your fault
It were, if I should act less rashly, should
Enquire beforehand—and let burn, what would.

Daja. That, God forbid !

Templar.   I beg you from to-day
Do me at least this favour : know me no longer.
For Jew is Jew.   And keep the father off.
I'm a rough hind.   Long since the maiden's image
Passed from my soul, if it was ever there.

Daja. Ah ! but from her soul yours hath never passed.

Templar. What, then, is one to do ?   Say what.

Daja.   Who knows !
Men are not always what they seem.

Templar.   Yet seldom
Anything better.   [*He turns to go.*

Daja.   But wait a moment.   Why
This haste ?

Templar. Woman, these palms I loved and their green shade,
You make them hateful.   [*Exit.*

Daja.   Go then, German bear !
Go ! Yet I follow, not to lose the trail.

                          [*Follows at a distance*

ACT II—Scene I

Scene : *The Sultan's Palace.   Saladin and Sittah at chess.*

Sittah. Where now, where are you, Saladin ?   You dream.

Saladin. I thought the move a good one.

Sittah.   Good perhaps
For me ; but take it back.

Saladin.   Why, then ?

Sittah.   The knight
Is left uncovered.

Saladin.   True.   Well, then, so !

Sittah. That forks your pieces.

Saladin.   Well, then, I call check !

Sittah. How does that help you? See, I cover it,
  And you are as you were.
Saladin.   From this dilemma,
  I see no way but sacrifice. Let be !
  Take you the knight.
Sittah.   I want him not; I pass.
Saladin. Thank you for nothing : better strategy
  Prompts you to leave the knight in place.
Sittah.   May be.
Saladin. Make not your reckoning without the host.
  See ! Do you overlook what you would gain?
Sittah. By no means. For I could not think you held
  So lightly of your queen.
Saladin.   I, of my queen?
Sittah. I see quite well to-day I shall not win
  My thousand dinars—no, not even a heller.
Saladin. How so?
Sittah.   Canst ask? Because with all your cunning
  And all your skill you mean to lose. But that
  I have no mind to, for besides such sport
  Is not quite entertaining, did I not ever
  Win most with you in games that I have lost?
  For then to comfort me for my lost game
  You gave me twice the stake.
Saladin.   Then, sister dear,
  You should have tried with all your might to lose.
Sittah. It well may be, at least, your liberal hand,
  Dear brother, bears the blame if I play ill.
Saladin. We'll stop the game : 'tis late, we'll make an end.
Sittah. And leave it so? Then check ! and double check !
Saladin. Truly I had no thought of such a check—
  That takes my queen as well. . . .
Sittah.   Could it be helped?
  Let's see.
Saladin.   No, no; I must resign the queen.
  Never with this piece was I fortunate.
Sittah. With this piece only?
Saladin.   Take it off?—No good !
  For so all is protected as before.
Sittah. How courteously one must behave to queens
  You've taught me often . . .   *[Lets it stand.*
Saladin.   Take it or take it not.
  I have no move.

Sittah.   But take, what need of that?
   Check!   Check!
Saladin.   Proceed.
Sittah.   Well, check! and check! and
      check!
Saladin. And mate!
Sittah.   Not quite; for you can move that man
   Between, or make what move you will; no matter.
Saladin. Right! you have won: Al-Hafi straight will pay,
   Let him be called: Sittah, you guessed the truth;
   My mind was not i' the game: I was distracted.
   Besides, who gives us aye these polished pieces
   Perpetually? all smoothed away to nothing.
   What matter?   Losing needs excuse.   But not
   The unform'd pieces, Sittah, made me lose;
   Your art, your swift and quiet glance . . .
Sittah.   Even so
   You try to soothe the smart of the lost game.
   Enough! you were distracted; more than I.
Saladin. Than you?   What had you to distract you?
Sittah.   Truly
   Not your distractions.   O my Saladin,
   When shall we play so eagerly again?
Saladin. All the more eagerly when occasion comes!
   Ah! since the war resumes, you mean.   Well, let it!
   On! on! I have not sought it.   Willingly
   Had I prolonged anew our armistice, and gladly,
   How gladly first had found a manly spouse
   For my dear Sittah, and that were Richard's brother
   Brother of Richard, think!
Sittah.   Your Richard's praise
   Is ever on your lips!
Saladin.   If brother Melek
   Had, after, Richard's sister for his mate:
   Ha! what a house together!   Of the first,
   Best houses in the world the best and first.
   You find I am not slack in my self-praise,
   Deeming me not unworthy of my friends—
   Ah, 'spousals such as these would bring us men!
Sittah. Have I not often laughed at your fair dream?
   You know not Christians, nay, you will not know them.
   Their pride is to be Christians, not to be men;
   For even that which from their Founder's day

Hath seasoned superstition—humanity—
They love, not for its human quality,
But that Christ taught it, that Christ did the like—
Well for them that He was a man so good ;
Well for them they can take in utter faith
His virtues ! But what virtues ? Not His virtues,
No, but His Name, which must be spread world-wide
To cloud with slander and obliterate
The names of all good men. The Name alone
Is everything.
Saladin.   Why else, you mean, should they require
Both you and Melek take the name of Christian
Ere Christians will permit you talk of marriage.
Sittah. Even so ! As if by Christians only love
Were to be looked for, love wherewith the Maker
Endowed woman and man.
Saladin.   Christians believe
So many pitiful things that they can swallow
Even this ! And yet there you mistake. The Templars—
They are the cause ; they, they alone by whom
Our hopes are frustrate : they will not let go
That pleasant town which should be brought to Melek
By Richard's sister as her bridal dower ;
They fix their claws on Acre. And not to lose
The privilege of the knight, they play the monk,
The simple monk. And thinking they may shoot
A fortunate arrow at the bird in flight,
They scarce can wait the passing of the truce.
So be it ! I'm prepared. On, gentlemen !
If all besides were only as it should be.
Sittah. Ah, what, then, troubles you ? What goes not straight ?
What makes you tremble ?
Saladin.   Even that which for so long
Has made me tremble. I was in Lebanon—
Our father, our good father, is succumbing
To his sore burdens.
Sittah.   O, 'tis pitiful !
Saladin. He can no more. 'Tis pressure everywhere ;
Where'er we look is failure.
Sittah.   What, then, fails ?
What presses ?
Saladin.   What I almost scorn to name ;
What when I have it seems superfluous,

And when I want it indispensable.
Where stays Al-Hafi? Have none gone after him?
This pitiful cursed money! Ha, Al-Hafi!
'Tis well that you are come.

SCENE II

The Dervish Al-Hafi. Saladin. Sittah

Al-Hafi.   Th' Egyptian moneys
Have now, methinks, arrived; and Allah grant
That they be in great plenty.
Saladin.   Have you news?
Al-Hafi. I? No; I thought I should receive it here.
Saladin. To Sittah pay the stake—a thousand dinars
                         [*Goes to and fro, in thought.*
Al-Hafi. Pay! Pay! and not receive! O excellent!
Instead of something—less, still less than nothing.
To Sittah? evermore to Sittah? Lost?
And lost again at chess. And there's the board!
Sittah. You do not grudge me luck?
Al-Hafi. [*Examining the board.*] What grudge you?—If——
But you know all.
Sittah. [*Signing to him.*] Hush, Al-Hafi, hush!
Al-Hafi. [*Still examining the board.*] First grudge it not yourself.
Sittah.   Al-Hafi, hush!
Al-Hafi. Were yours the white? Did you give check to him?
Sittah. Good that he did not hear!
Al-Hafi.   Is it his move?
Sittah. Say out aloud that I can have my money.
Al-Hafi. Why, yes; you'll get it, as you always get it.
Sittah. How? Are you mad?
Al-Hafi.   The game's not finished yet.
You have indeed not lost it, Saladin.
Saladin. [*Scarcely attending.*] Still, pay, my good Al-Hafi; we
    must pay.
Al-Hafi. Pay! Pay! Your queen still stands.
Saladin. [*Still moody.*]   It makes no odds,
The piece is taken.
Sittah.   Have done, Al-Hafi, and say
That I can have my money when I please.
Al-Hafi. [*Still absorbed in the game.*] O that's of course, as
    always—Yet even now

Even if the queen is taken, you are not therefore
Check-mated . . .

Saladin. [*Steps up and throws the pieces down.*]   Yes, I am, and
wish it so.

Al-Hafi. I see, to play's to win; and payment follows.

Saladin. [*To Sittah.*] What says he? What?

Sittah. [*From time to time signing to Al-Hafi.*]   You know him:
how he loves

To oppose and be petitioned. Envious too,
Or I mistake him.

Saladin.   Surely not of you—
Not of my sister. What is this, my Hafi?
Envious?

Al-Hafi.   Maybe, maybe; gladly I'd have
Myself a brain like hers, and such a heart.

Sittah. And yet he ever pays in honesty,
And will to-day: leave him alone for that!
But go, Al-Hafi, go! Shortly I'll send
To fetch the money.

Al-Hafi.   No; for further part
In this mad mummery is not for me.
Sooner or later he must learn the truth.

Saladin. Learn? Who? and what?

Sittah.   Is't thus you keep your promise,
Al-Hafi? Break not oaths!

Al-Hafi.   How could I think
That it would go so far?

Saladin.   Well! What's in hand?
Am I not to be told?

Sittah. I conjure you, Al-Hafi, be discreet.

Saladin. This is most strange! This solemn, earnest prayer
Speaks Sittah to a stranger, to a Dervish,
And not to me, her brother. Solve the riddle,
Al-Hafi, I command you. Speak out, Dervish!

Sittah. Let not a trifle, brother, trouble your spirit:
More than its meanness warrants. Once or twice
Of late, you know, I won from you at chess
Just such a stake, and since I have no need
At present for such moneys; since, besides,
Al-Hafi's treasure-chest is not too full,
And posts have not arrived. But trouble not,
For I'll not make it a present to you, brother,
Not yet to Hafi or his treasure-chest.

Al-Hafi. Ah ! were it only that !
Sittah.   And some such trifles.
  That, too, 's untouched which once you set apart
  For me ; for some few months untouched it lies.
Al-Hafi. That is not all.
Saladin.   Not all ? Then will you tell me ?
Al-Hafi. Since we have waited for the gold from Egypt
  Hath she . . .
Sittah.   Why hear him ?
Al-Hafi.   Hath she not only
  Ta'en nothing . . .
Saladin.   The good girl ! she has besides
  Helped from her own. Is't so ?
Al-Hafi.   Yea, all the court
  She hath maintained, herself alone hath borne
  Your whole expenditure.
Saladin.   Ha ! that's my sister !
                                    [*Embracing her.*
Sittah. Who made me rich enough for this but you,
  Brother ?
Al-Hafi.   Who'll make you soon as beggar-poor
  As he himself is.
Saladin.   Poor ? the brother poor ?
  When had I more ? or when have I had less ?
  One coat, one sword, one charger, and—one God.
  What want I more ? And when shall these come short ?
  Yet, Hafi, I could chide you.
Sittah.   Do not chide,
  Brother ; if only I could lighten as much
  Our father's burden—
Saladin.   Ah ! Ah ! there you strike
  My joy again to earth ! Though for myself
  I nothing lack, nor can lack. Ha, 'tis he
  Whose want is sorest, and with him we suffer.
  What shall I do ? From Egypt our supplies
  Delay their coming, we may wait them long,
  And why, God knows : for all is quiet there.
  Cut down, draw in, and spare—that will I gladly ;
  Nothing will please me better, if alone
  Thereby I suffer, and none else. What helps it ?
  I still must have my horse, my coat, my sword.
  And with my God 'tis easy bargaining.
  For He is satisfied with one small gift,

Which is my soul.—Much I had reckoned, Hafi,
Upon the surplus in thy treasure-chest.

Al-Hafi. Surplus? Yourself confess I had been strangled,
    Perhaps impaled had you in vain demanded
    Of bankrupt me this surplus. Fraud, embezzlement,
    Were then my one resource.

Saladin.   Now, what remains?
    But tell me, Hafi, why you turn to Sittah
    And borrow her small store: are there not others?

Sittah. And could I see this privilege torn from me,
    To further you, my brother? No, this joy
    I'll not surrender till I must: my fortunes
    Are not yet foundered quite.

Saladin.   Only not quite!
    It wanted only this! Hafi, at once
    Contrive, take up from whom you can, nor halt
    On nice considering of means and ways:
    Go, borrow, pledge. Yet, Hafi, borrow not
    Of those whom I made rich. To borrow of them
    Might seem reclaiming. Ask the covetous,
    For they will be the readiest; they know well
    How fast with me their moneys multiply.

Al-Hafi. I know none such.

Sittah.   Hafi, did I not hear
    Your friend from his far journey had returned
    To his own dwelling?

Al-Hafi.   Friend? My friend? To whom
    Give you that name?

Sittah.   Your much-belauded Jew.

Al-Hafi. Belauded Jew! Lauded by me?

Sittah.   Whom God—
    Such were the terms that once you used of him—
    Whom God of all the good things of this world,
    With least and greatest in abundancy
    Had crowned.

Al-Hafi.   And said I so? What meant I then
    By that?

Sittah.   The least was, Wealth; the greatest, Wisdom.

Al-Hafi. How? Of a Jew? I said so of a Jew?

Sittah. What would you not have said of your good Nathan?

Al-Hafi. Oh! 'tis of him! of Nathan! Has he truly
    At last returned again? If this be so,
    Surely his journey prospered. And 'tis true

The folk call him the Wise, call him the Rich.

Sittah. Yea, more than ever now he's called the Rich.
And the whole city hums of rarities,
The stuffs and jewels in his caravan.

Al-Hafi. So then it is the Rich has come again;
And with him comes, who knows? the Wise as well.

Sittah. What think you, Hafi? Could not you approach
him?

Al-Hafi. For what, suppose you? Not to borrow, surely?
Ah, there you touch him! Nathan lend? His wisdom
Lies just in this: that he will lend to no man.

Sittah. That's not the picture once you drew of him.

Al-Hafi. To men in utmost need he lendeth goods—
But money? money never! Tho' for the rest
He's such a Jew as there be seldom found.
Has brains, knows how to live, can play good chess;
But marks him out in bad points as in good
From other Jews. I warn you, reckon not
On him. 'Tis to the poor he gives; to them
Even with open hand like Saladin,
If not so largely, with as good a will;
Without respect of persons. Christian and Jew,
And Mussulman and Parsee, all is one
To him.

Sittah.   And such a man . . .

Saladin.   How comes it, then,
I have not known this man, nor heard his name?

Sittah. Would he not lend to Saladin? To him,
To him who only cares for others' wants,
Not for his own?

Al-Hafi.   Herein you see the Jew,
The common, vulgar Jew! And yet, believe me,
He envies you the most on score of giving,
So jealous is he; grasping, for himself,
At all God's-hire that offers in the world;
And 'tis for this alone he lends to none:
That he have more to give. His reason, this!
That Charity is in the law commanded,
The law commands not to oblige a neighbour;
So Charity itself has made him quite
The least obliging friend in all the world.
In truth, of late I am in ill accord
With him. Still, think not therefore I will speak

Unjustly of him, good and true-hearted he,
Everyway good, except for only this.
No, not for this.   I'll go at once and knock
At other doors . . . and I have just bethought me
Of a rich Moor, a covetous man—I go !
Sittah. Hafi, what needs your haste?
Saladin.   O, let him !   Let him !

Scene III

Sittah.   Saladin

Sittah. What haste he makes, as though he were rejoiced
If he could so escape me.   What means that?
Has he in truth deceived himself in Nathan,
Or would perhaps deceive us?
Saladin.   How deceive?
You question me who hardly know of whom
The talk was, me who never heard until to-day
Of this your Jew, your Nathan.
Sittah.   Is it possible
A man remained hid from you who, they say
Has found the graves of David and Solomon,
And with a mighty secret word can break
Their seals? and then bring forth from time to time
To daylight treasures inexhaustible
No meaner source could furnish.
Saladin. His wealth if this man finds in graves, 'tis sure
They're not the graves of Solomon and David.
Fools lie there buried !
Sittah.   Criminals, mayhap !
Besides, his wealth's source is more fertile far,
More inexhaustible than any grave
Of Mammon.
Saladin.   He's a merchant, so you told me.
Sittah. All highways are his mule-tracks, every waste
Has seen his caravans, his vessels lie
In all the havens.   So Al-Hafi to me once
Declared, and added, with a joyful pride
How greatly, nobly this his friend employed
What in his wisdom he did not disdain
To gather by his diligence ; and added, too,
How free from prejudice his soul, how open

His heart to every virtue, how attuned
To all things beautiful.   Ah ! how he praised him.
Saladin. Yet Hafi spoke of him uncertainly,
　And coldly . . .
Sittah.　　　　　　No, not coldly, but perplexed.
　As though he held it dangerous to praise him,
　And could not blame him undeservedly.
　Or might it not be that the noblest Jew
　Cannot deny his kindred, is still Jew ;
　That Hafi for this feature is ashamed
　Of his dear friend ?   Be't with him as it may,
　The Jew be more Jew or be less, what matter
　If only rich ?   This is enough for us !
Saladin. And yet you would not, sister, take from him
　By force what is his own ?
Sittah.　　　　　　What call you force ?
　With fire and sword ?   No, no, what violence
　But their own weakness need we with the weak ?
　But come a moment now into my harem
　And hear a singer-girl whom yesterday
　I bought.   Meantime perhaps a shrewd design
　I have upon this Nathan will grow ripe—
　Come.

SCENE IV

*In front of Nathan's house, where it is close to the palm trees.
Enter Recha and Nathan.   To them Daja*

Recha. O, you've tarried long, my father.   Hardly now
　Can we have hope to meet him . . .
Nathan.　　　　　　　　Never fear ;
　If not among the palms, then otherwhere
　We find him.   Only calm yourself.   And see,
　Is that not Daja this way hastening ?
Recha. But she has lost him, that is all too certain.
Nathan. Why so ?
Recha.　　　　　For then she'd come with speedier foot.
Nathan. She has not seen us yet, perhaps.
Recha.　　　　　　　　　　O now
　She sees us.
Nathan.　　　Look ! with quicken'd pace she comes.
　Only be calm, be calm !

Recha.   But could you wish
  A daughter who were calm in such a case?
  Untroubled for his weal whose great deed saved
  Her life—her life that's only dear to her
  Because to you she owes it.
Nathan.   O my wish
  Is not to have you other than you are :
  Even if I knew that something new and strange
  Stirred in your loving heart.
Recha.   What, then, my father?
Nathan. What ask you?   Are you then so shy with me?
  What's passing now deep in your inmost soul
  Is innocence and nature.   Let it not
  Trouble your spirit ; mine it does not trouble.
  But promise me that when your heart has spoken
  With clearer voice, you will not hide from me
  Your wishes.
Recha.   Nay, the possibility
  Nigh makes me tremble—the thought that I might wish
  To veil my thoughts from you.
Nathan.   No more of this.
  'Tis done with once for all.   And here is Daja—
  Well?
Daja.   Still he walks among the palms, and soon
  Will come by yonder hedge.   Look, there he comes !
Recha. Ah ! and appears unsure which path to take.
  Whither? if right? if left? uphill or down?
Daja. No, no ; he'll take the footway round the cloister
  Yet once or twice, and then he needs must pass
  Hereby.—What matter?
Recha.   Have you spoken with him
  Already?   How is he to-day?
Daja.   As ever.
Nathan. Carefully !   Warily !   Do not be seen.
  Step back a pace or two : Rather, go in.
Recha. Just one more look ! just one, but ah ! the hedge.
  It steals him from me.
Daja.   Come ! the father's right.
  You run the danger that if he but sees you,
  Upon the spot he'll turn.
Recha.   Ah me ! the hedge !
Nathan. If he turn suddenly by it, infallibly
  He'll spy you.   So go in, go in.
  L

Daja.   Come, Recha;
   I know a window where we're safe.
Recha.   So, Daja?

                        [The two go in.

Scene V

Nathan and presently the Templar

Nathan. Almost I shrink from this strange man.   And almost
   His rugged virtues shake me.   That one man
   Should thus be able to perplex another !
   He comes.   By Heaven !   A stripling like a man.
   I love right well this strong, defiant glance !
   And this brave carriage.   Sure the shell alone
   Is bitter here, and not the kernel.   Where,
   Where have I seen one like him?   Pardon me,
   My noble Frank . . .
Templar.   What say'st thou?
Nathan.   Pardon me . . .
Templar. What, Jew?   Why pardon?
Nathan.   That I venture thus
   To greet you.
Templar.   Can I hinder?   But be brief.
Nathan. Forgive me.   Pass not by so hastily
   And with so scornful brows; slight him not thus
   Whom you have bound to you eternally.
Templar. How bound?   Ah, almost I guess !   You are . . .
Nathan. My name is Nathan, am that maiden's father
   Whom your brave heart delivered from the fire;
   And come to . . .
Templar.   If to thank me—spare your pains !
   I have endured for this mere trifle's sake
   Too heavy a load of thanks.   Assuredly
   You owe me nothing, nothing.   Could I know
   This maiden was your daughter?   'Tis our rule,
   The Templars' duty, thus to run to the aid
   Of whomsoever in the hour of stress.
   Moreover, at that moment to my soul
   My life was burdensome.   How gladly, then,
   I rushed to snatch the opportunity
   Thus for another's life to chance my own,
   Another's, were it but a Jewish girl.
Nathan. Yes, that's the hero's way, to do great deeds

And yet not boast of them, but to hide rather
Behind a modest shame t'avoid applause :
But when he thus disdains the offering
Of grateful praise, tell me what offering then
Will he not scorn?   And, Knight ! were you not here
A stranger and a captive, not thus boldly
I'd put you to the question.   Speak, command :
How can I serve you?

Templar.   Serve me?   In no wise.

Nathan. See ! I am rich.

Templar.   But rich Jew never was
With me the better Jew.

Nathan.   Would you for that
Decline what notwithstanding he possesses
Of good, and take no help of his full hands?

Templar. Nay, as for that, I'll speak no austere vows
Even for my mantle's sake.   When it shall be
Not part, as now, but wholly rags threadbare,
When seam nor stitches longer hold, I'll come
And borrow of you something for a new one,
Money or stuff.—Nay, eye me not so close,
You're still secure, 'tis not yet so far gone.
'Tis still in fair condition ; just one spot
Here on the lappet's foul—where it was singed.
And that it got when out of the fierce flame
I bore your daughter.

Nathan. [*Who seizes the lappet and gazes at it.*]   Now 'tis
     wonderful
That such a foul spot, such a touch of fire
Should bear the man a better testimony
Than his own mouth.   Now would I kiss it straight,
This rusty fleck !   Forgive me ; 'twas not wilful.

Templar. What?

Nathan.   'Twas a tear fell on it.

Templar.   That's no matter !
Has had more drops than that.—(This Jew will soon,
I fear, bewilder me).

Nathan.   Were I too bold
To beg such kindness, that you once would send
Your mantle to my child?

Templar.   Why, for what purpose?

Nathan. That she, too, press her lips upon this fleck.
For she now wishes, though the hope is vain,

Herself to embrace your knees.
Templar.   But, Jew—
  Your name is Nathan?—Truly, Nathan, you have spoken
  To me such words—so kind—so delicate
  You have startled me . . . but certainly . . . I would . . .
Nathan. Pose and disguise you, as you will.   Even here
  I find you out.   You were too good, too modest,
  To be more courteous.   For—the girl, all feeling;
  Her woman-ambassador, all zeal to serve;
  The father far removed—your only care
  Was all for her good name; you fled temptation,
  Fled, that you might not conquer: now I thank you—
Templar. I see you know how Templar Knights should think.
Nathan. And only Templars? only they? and only
  Because the Order's rule commands it so?
  I know how good men think, and I know too
  All lands bear good men.
Templar.   Yet, with difference?
Nathan. O true, difference in colour, dress and form.
Templar. But more or fewer in the different climes.
Nathan. I hold that this distinction is but small.
  Everywhere great men need great spheres, and when
  Too thick they're planted, they then break away
  Their branches.   But the medium men like us,
  On the other hand, are everywhere in crowds.
  Only, the one must not abase the other;
  Only, the halt must tolerate the lame;
  Only, the hillock must not vaunt itself,
  Or think it the one summit in the world.
Templar. Most nobly said!   But know you not the people
  That first abased all others?   Know you not
  What nation first of all proclaimed itself
  The Chosen Race?   How, if I could not cease
  This people, not indeed to hate—not hate—
  But for their pride to dis-esteem?   Their pride
  Which they bequeathed to Muslim and to Christian,
  That their God was the true God, and theirs only!
  You start to hear a Christian and a Templar
  Speak thus.   But tell me when and where this madness,
  This pious rage to have the better God,
  And to impose this better God as best
  On the whole world, more in its blackest form
  Been shown than here and now?   From whose dimmed eyes

The scales fall not? But yet be blind, who will !
Forget what I have said, and let me go.   [*Is going.*
Nathan. Ha ! know you not with how far firmer grasp
I now would hold you. Come, we must, we must
Be friends. Despise my people if you will.
Nor I nor you have chosen our people. Are we
Our people? People? What means then the people?
Are Jew and Christian rather Jew and Christian
Than men? Ah, had I found in you one more
Whom it suffices to be called a Man !
Templar. And so, by God, Nathan, you have, you have !
Your hand ! am shamed to have mistaken you
Even for a moment.
Nathan.   And I'm proud of it.
Only the common rarely is misjudged.
Templar. And what is rare one seldom can forget,
Yes, Nathan, yes; we must, we must be friends.
Nathan. Already are. My Recha will rejoice !
And what a happy future opens up
Before my vision ! You must know her first.
Templar. My heart's on fire within.—Who rushes yonder
Forth of your threshold? Is it not your Daja?
Nathan. Yes surely, and in trouble.
Templar.   Can it be
Mishap befallen our Recha ?

SCENE VI

The former, and Daja in haste

Daja.   Nathan ! Nathan !
Nathan.   Well?
Daja. Forgive me, noble Knight, that I break in
Thus on your converse.
Nathan.   Well, what is't ?
Templar.   What is't ?
Daja. A message from the Sultan : he would speak
With you. My God ! the Sultan !
Nathan.   Me? the Sultan?
Curious perhaps to see what novelties
I have brought home. Say only there's but little
Or almost nought unpacked.
Daja.   O Nathan, no ;

He will see nothing, he will speak with you,—
With you in person, now, with no delay.
Nathan. I come at once. Do you return to Recha.
Daja. Take it not ill of us, worshipful Knight,—
God, we are troubled, guessing not what means
The Sultan.
Nathan.   That we'll learn. Go, only go !

Scene VII

Nathan and the Templar

Templar. You do not know him yet ; I mean, in person ?
Nathan. The Sultan ? No, not yet, though I have never
Avoided him, nor have I sought to meet him,
So loud the general voice spoke in his praise,
That I must rather wish to think it just,
Than see. But now, even were it otherwise—
He has, by sparing of your life . . .
Templar.   Ah, true ;
That certainly is truth ; the life I live
It is his gift—
Nathan.   And thereby gave he me
A double, threefold life. This, I confess,
Has altered all between us ; thrown a cord
At once about me, binding me to him,
And to his service. Scarce now can I wait
To know what he commands me ; ready for all
Am I ; and ready, too, to tell him what
I do is for your sake.
Templar.   Nor I myself
Have yet had chance to thank him, and have crossed
Ofttimes his path in vain : for that impress
I made on him came like a lightning flash
And vanished even as quickly ; who can tell
Whether he has me still in memory ?
And yet he must, once more at least, recall me
To fix my fate. 'Tis not enough that I
Still live at his command, and by his will :
I must await the word, after what rule
And what direction I must spend my days.
Nathan. Doubtless, and therefore I delay no longer.
Perhaps a word will fall may give occasion

To speak of you.   Permit me, pardon me—
I hasten thither.   When, when shall we see you
Within my gates?
Templar.   When may I?
Nathan.   When you will.
Templar. To-day, then.
Nathan.   And your name, if I may ask?
Templar. My name was, sometime, Curd von Stauffen—Curd!
Nathan. Von Stauffen?   Stauffen?   Stauffen?
Templar.   You are startled?
Why start you?
Nathan.   Stauffen?   Branches of this house,
I know, are many.
Templar.   Here in this very soil
Do several rest and rot of this same race.
My uncle—nay, my father as I call him—
Is one—Why turn on me a gaze so keen,
So searching?
Nathan.   Nothing! nothing!   How can I
Grow tired of seeing you?   And for this cause
I leave you.
Templar.   Searcher's eyes not seldom find
More than they seek for.   Nathan, this gives me pause.
Let our acquaintance build on gradual time,
Not prying upon glances.   [*Goes off.*
Nathan.   What said he?
" Searchers find often more than they desire."
As if he read my soul!   'Tis even so.
This might befall me also.—Not alone
Wolf's figure and Wolf's walk; but his voice, too;
The carriage of his head—Wolf to the life;
And how he bare his sword upon the arm
And stroked his eyebrows, as did Wolf, to hide
The ardour of his gaze, so full of fire.
How such sharp-printed pictures yet can sleep
At whiles within, till word or tone recalls them.
Von Stauffen! right, 'tis right; Filnek and Stauffen—
I'll search this soon to the depths, but first must I
To Saladin.   But how?   Is not that Daja
Lurking and listening?   Come, my Daja, come.

Scene VIII

Daja. Nathan

Nathan. What now? Something, to-day, pricks both your hearts
    Quite other news to know than what the Sultan
    Will ask of me.
Daja.   And do you blame her for it?
    You had begun to talk in friendlier mood
    That moment when the Sultan's message came
    And drove us from the window.
Nathan.   Tell her now
    That any moment she may look for him;
    He promised this.
Daja.   For sure? for sure?
Nathan.   My Daja,
    I trust you and will trust. Be on your guard,
    Be dutiful, be true, leave no regrets
    For after conscience—See that you destroy not
    One point of all my plan. Only relate
    And question still with maiden modesty
    And due reserve . . .
Daja.   That you at such an hour
    Could yet remember this! I go; and you
    Must also, for, behold! there comes in haste
    From Saladin a second messenger,
    Al-Hafi, your good Dervish.

Scene IX

Nathan. Al-Hafi

Al-Hafi. Ha, ha! the very man whom I was seeking.
Nathan. Is there such haste? What asks he at my hands?
Al-Hafi. Who?
Nathan.   Saladin. Tell him I come! I come!
Al-Hafi. To whom? To Saladin?
Nathan.   Has he not sent you?
Al-Hafi. Me? No; already has his message come?
Nathan. Yea, verily.
Al-Hafi.   Then everything is right.
Nathan. What? What is right?

Al-Hafi.   That no blame lights on me :
  God knows I'm not to blame.   What have I not
  Said, whispered, lied of you to turn it off?
Nathan. To turn what off?   What's this that you call right?
Al-Hafi. That you're his right-hand now, his Chancellor.
  I pity you.   Yet second thoughts forbid.
  For from this hour I go ; go, you have heard
  Already whither, and you know the road.
  Upon the way can I do ought for you?
  Am at your service.   It must be only what
  One naked can drag with him.   Speak : I go.
Nathan. Bethink you now, Al-Hafi, once bethink you ;
  That I as yet know nothing of these things
  Whereof you're voluble.   What means it all?
Al-Hafi. But you will bring the sack along with you.
Nathan. Sack?
Al-Hafi.   Well, the gold you'll lend to Saladin.
Nathan. And is this all?
Al-Hafi.   Perhaps I should look on
  And watch him bleed you to the very toes?
  And see the waste of his sweet charity
  Draw from the once-full barns and draw again
  Until the wretched aborigines,
  Ev'n the poor mice, are starved?   Perhaps you dream
  That he who's thirsty for your gold will take
  Your counsel also?   Ha ! he follow counsel !
  Since when has Saladin suffered advice?
  Think rather, Nathan, what's just chanced to me.
Nathan. What, then?
Al-Hafi.   I came on him as he played chess
  With sister Sittah : she's a clever player ;
  And the game Saladin imagined lost
  Stood yet upon the board.   I gave a glance
  And saw the contest neither lost nor won.
Nathan. For you a find indeed !   You trembled then.
Al-Hafi. A move with king on pawn was all required
  To give her check.   If I could only show you !
Nathan. I well can trust you there.
Al-Hafi.   For so the rook
  Were freed, and she were done.   This I would show him,
  And call him.   Think !
Nathan.   He was not of your mind?
Al-Hafi. He would not listen, and contemptuously

He brushed the game down.
Nathan.   Is it possible?
Al-Hafi. Saying, for once at least he'd take checkmate;
  He wished it.   Is that play?
Nathan.   Hardly, in sooth:
  'Tis playing with the play.
Al-Hafi.   Like that, it's worth
  A rotten filbert.
Nathan.   Money here or there!
  That is the least.   But not to listen to you,
  Upon so weighty a point not once to listen,
  Not to admire your eagle vision!   That,
  That cries out, think you not, for its revenge?
Al-Hafi. You jest!   I told you this that you might know
  The kind of brain he is; brief, in one word,
  His whimsies weary me, and I have done.
  Here am I running among filthy Moors
  To ask the use of filthy purses.   I,
  Who never in my days begged for myself,
  Am now for others borrowing.   Borrowing's as bad
  Almost as begging, and the lending so
  At usury as bad almost as theft.
  Amongst my people by the Ganges shore
  I shall need neither, nor need I be
  Of either, instrument.   For by the Ganges,
  The Ganges only you'll find men, but here
  No man save you were worthy of the boon
  To live by Ganges shore.   Come you with me.
  Leave Saladin the plunder, at his will.
  He'll bring you step by step to beggary,
  And all your baggage with you.   For a guide
  And warrantor I'll stand.   I pray you, come.
Nathan. Methinks, indeed, 't might be our last resort.
  Yet, Hafi, I must ponder it.   Wait you . . .
Al-Hafi. Ponder it?   Such things abide no pondering.
Nathan. Only till I return from Saladin;
  Till leave-takings . . .
Al-Hafi.   To hesitate and ponder
  But asks excuses not to dare.   The man
  Who cannot at a wink decide to live
  His self-poised life, must live another's slave
  For ever.   As you will!   Farewell, as seems
  You best.   My way lies yonder: your way here.

Nathan. Hafi ! You'll settle first your treasurership ?
Al-Hafi. A jest. The total of my treasure-chest
Is not worth reckoning. And for my account
Yourself or Sittah shall be warranty—
Farewell ! [*Exit.*
Nathan. Be warrant for him ! Yes, I know him
Savage and kind and faithful; the true beggar,
When all is said, is the one genuine King !

ACT III—Scene I

In Nathan's house. Recha and Daja

Recha. Daja, what were my father's words to-day ?
" I might expect him any moment now " ?
Surely that sounds as though he might at once
Appear. Has not a world of moments gone ?
Ah, well, who thinks of moments that are fled ?
In each " next minute " I'm resolved to live ;
That one will surely come that brings him here.
Daja. O that accursed message of the Sultan !
But for it Nathan would have brought him straightway.
Recha. And when this longed-for moment has arrived,
With its fulfilment of my tenderest wish——
What then ? what then ?
Daja. What then ? Why, then, I hope
The tenderest of *my* wishes too shall move
To its fulfilling.
Recha. What can take its place
Then, in my heart, that will have quite unlearned
To throb without some one o'ermastering wish ?
If nothing—that were terror !
Daja. My, my wish
Will enter then the place of that fulfilled ;
My wish to know you in safe hands, in Europe,
In hands all worthy to have *you* in keeping.
Recha. Strangely deceived ! For what makes this wish yours,
The same forbids it ever should be mine.
Your country is the magnet which attracts you,
And shall my own, my own not hold me back ?
Shall the image of your loved ones vividly
Rise on your inward vision, and prevail,

More than mine round me, seen and felt and known?
Daja. Struggle you will, but struggle as you will,
  The ways of Heaven are still the ways of Heaven.
  What if it were then he who rescued you,
  Through whom his God for Whom he fights should lead you
  Back to the soil whose daughter you were born?
Recha. Daja, you speak most strangely; your wild brain
  Does breed the queerest fancies.   His?   " His God "
  " For Whom he fights."   Then whom does God belong to?
  What kind of God who to one man belongs,
  Who needs be fought for by His worshippers?—
  Nay; who shall tell for what soil we were born
  If just that spot where we were really born
  Not claims us?   If my father heard you speak !
  What would he do to you, who image ever
  My happiness removed afar from him?
  What do to you, finding you wantonly
  Mixing the seed of reason, that in my soul
  He sowed so pure, with your land's weeds and flowers?
  Daja, dear Daja, no; he will not suffer
  Your motley growths to root upon my ground.
  And I must tell you I myself have felt
  How beautiful so'er these blossoms show,
  My ground enfeebled and consumed thereby;
  Feel in their soul-sweet fragrance heart and brain
  Made giddy and bewildered.   Your own head
  Can bear it, being used.   Nor do I blame
  Therefor your stronger nerves, that can support it :
  Only it suits me not; and even your angel
  Comes little short of quite befooling me.
  I am ashamed here in my father's house
  Of such a folly.
Daja.   Folly !   As if all reason
  Had its home here !   Folly !   Folly !   Folly !
  O if I dared but speak !
Recha.   And dare you not?
  When was I not all ear whene'er you pleased
  To tell me of the heroes of your faith?
  For their great deeds was I not ever ready
  With admiration;   from their martyrdoms
  Have I withheld the tribute of my tears?
  Their faith, indeed, did ne'er appear to me
  What's most heroic in them.   Yet more welcome

Ever to me the doctrine, that devotion
And piety towards God cannot depend
On our beliefs or fancies about God.
Dear Daja, this my father often said :
And you consented with him to its truth :
Why undermine you what with him you builded ?
Daja, this is no talk wherewith to prelude
The meeting with our friend—For me perhaps
'Tis fitting, for to me so much depends—But hark,
A knocking at the gate !   What if 'twere he !

Scene II

*Recha.   Daja and the Templar, to whom someone outside opens the
  door with the words :*

Enter, sir Knight !

Recha. [*Starts back, composes herself, and is about to fall at his feet.*]
                                   It is ! it is my rescuer !

Templar. This to escape I made my coming tardy
  And yet . . .

Recha.   Before this proud man's feet I kneel
  Only to thank my God and not the man.
  The man refuses thanks, wishes for that
  As little as the water-pail that at the fire
  Did show itself so zealous, filled itself
  And poured itself, and filled, nor cared a whit ;
  So, even so, the man ; he, too, was thrown
  With like indifference upon the flame,
  And there, as chanced, I fell into his arm ;
  And then, by chance, remained, as might a spark
  Upon his mantle, lying on his arms ;
  Till something, what I know not, flung us both
  Out of the burning.   What is here for thanks ?
  In Europe wine will urge to other deeds
  Braver than these.   The Templars, too, must ever
  Stand ready for the like, they must, we know,
  Just like to hounds a little better trained,
  Snatch men both from the water and the fire—

Templar. [*Who has looked on surprised and disturbed.*]   O Daja,
  Daja ! if at troubled moments
  My fretted spirit dealt with you unkindly,
  Why every folly that escaped my lips

Brought you to her?   That was too sharp revenge.
Ah, Daja ! from this hour in happier light
Set me before her.
Daja.   But, sir Knight, I think
These little thorns you threw against her heart
Did you small damage there.
Recha.   What? you had trouble?
And were more avaricious of your cares
Than of your life?
Templar.   My sweet and gracious child !—
But all my soul's divided between eye
And ear ! Sure this was not the maid ; no, no,
This was not she I drew from out the fire
For who that knew her had not dared the same?
Who   would   have   waited   for   me?—True—disguised—the
     terror

        [*Pause, in which, gazing at her, he seems to lose himself.*
Recha. You are not changed—I find you still the same
[*Pause ; until she continues in order to interrupt his astonished gaze.*
Now tell us, Knight, where you have been so long?
Might I not almost ask—where you are now?
Templar. I am,—where mayhap I've no right to be.
Recha. Where you have been, perhaps where you've no right?
That is not well.
Templar.   On—on—what is the mountain?
On Sinai.
Recha.   Ah, upon Sinai?   Beautiful !
Now can I learn at last from trusty lips
Whether 'tis true . . .
Templar.   What? whether it is true
That still the self-same spot is to be seen
Where Moses stood with God, when . . .
Recha.   No, not that
Where'er he stood, 'twas before God ; whereof
All that I need I know ; but whether true
That this same height is far less hard to climb
Than to descend?   For, with all hills I've scaled,
As yet, 'twas ever just the opposite.
How, Knight, why turn away?   Would you not see me?
Templar. I turn from seeing you to hear you better.
Recha. More that I may not mark you when you laugh
At my simplicity, and how you smile,
When I no weightier questions ask of you

About this holiest of all holy hills.
Is it not so?

Templar.   Then I must look again
Into your eyes.   What? do you shut them fast?
Now stifle you your laughter?   What need I
To read in looks, in questionable looks,
What ears can tell me plainly—audibly
You speak—But silent now?   Ah, Recha! Recha!
Sure he spoke truly " Know her only first!"

Recha. Who has—by whom—that told you?

Templar.   " Only know
Her first"; it was your father's word to me,
Spoken of you.

Daja.   And not I, too, by chance?
And not I, too?

Templar.   But he, where is he, then?
Where is your father, then?   Is he perhaps
Still with the Sultan?

Recha.   Doubtless.

Templar.   Still, still there?
O me forgetful!   No, it cannot be
That he's there still.   Down by the cloister wall
He would await my coming; so 'twas fixed,
So settled when we parted.   Pardon me,
I hasten to bring him . . .

Daja.   That is my affair;
Rather, remain.   I bring him instantly.

Templar. Not so, not so.   He looks to meet me there,
Not you.   Besides he might—no man can tell—
So easily with Saladin have fallen
On disaccord—you do not know the Sultan—
Sure he's in danger if I go not.

Recha.   How?

Templar. Danger, danger, for me, for you, for him,
If in all speed I go not.

SCENE III

Recha and Daja

Recha.   What means it, Daja?
All in a moment!   Why?   What's come to him?
What drives him?

Daja.   Patience, let him be.   I think
  'Tis no bad sign, perhaps.
Recha.   But sign of what?
Daja. Something takes place within him.   Something boils
  Which yet must not boil over.   Leave him only.
  'Tis your turn now.
Recha.   My turn; Daja?   You grow,
  Like him, past comprehending.
Daja.   Soon you can
  Requite him the disquiet he has caused you.
  Be only not too hard, or too revengeful.
Recha. Of what you speak, perhaps yourself may know.
Daja. Are you already quite at rest again?
Recha. That am I; yes, that am I . . .
Daja.   Or at least
  Confess your unrest gives more joy than pain,
  And that you thank his unrest for the rest
  That you enjoy.
Recha.   Then all unconsciously!
  For what at most I might confess to you,
  Were this that it surprises even myself
  How such a calm within so suddenly
  Can follow in the wake of such a tempest.
  This nearer sight of him, his talk, his tone
  Have—have . . .
Daja.   Left you quite satiate?
Recha.   No, not quite :
  Nay, that I will not say; nay, far from that.
Daja. Only the first fierce hunger stilled.
Recha.   Well, yes.
  If so you'll have it.
Daja.   I?   O, not at all.
Recha. To me he must be dear and ever dearer
  As the days pass, even if my pulse change not
  When I but hear his name; no more my heart
  Beat faster, stronger when I think on him—
  What am I babbling?   Come, dear Daja, come
  Just once more to the window that looks out
  Upon the palms.
Daja.   Ah! the fierce hunger, then,
  Is not quite stilled.
Recha.   At least I'll see the palms
  Yet once again, not only him amongst them.

Daja. This chill begins, I doubt, another fever—
Recha. What chill? I feel no chill. And verily
　　See not less gladly what I see in calm.

SCENE IV

An audience chamber in Saladin's palace.　Saladin and Sittah

Saladin. [*In entering, speaks towards door.*]
　　Soon as the Jew arrives, let him come here.
　　He does not seem to hasten over-much.
Sittah. Perhaps not found at once, or gone abroad.
Saladin. O sister! sister!
Sittah.　　　　　　　　　　　Saladin, you act
　　As if a battle were in prospect.
Saladin.　　　　　　　　　　　　　Yes;
　　And that with weapons I have never practised.
　　I have to pose and keep a careful guard;
　　To lay traps, too, to stand upon smooth ice.
　　When could I so? When studied I such tricks?
　　Must do them now. Ay me, for what? for what?
　　To fish for money! Money! to extort by dread
　　The money of a Jew. To such mean arts
　　Am I at last reduced, to gain myself
　　The meanest of mean things.
Sittah.　　　　　　　　　　　The meanest thing,
　　Too much despised, will take revenge, brother.
Saladin. Alas! 'Tis true! And if this Jew of ours
　　Be wholly that good man, so wise, humane,
　　The dervish painted once?
Sittah.　　　　　　　　　　　If such he be,
　　Why, then we need no snares. The snare awaits
　　Only the fearful, cautious, greedy Jew—
　　The good and wise is ours without a snare.
　　A pleasure you've before you, even to hear
　　How such a man will speak, with what bold strength
　　Either he'll snap the cord, or it may be
　　With what shy prudence he'll slip past the net:
　　This joy's before you.
Saladin.　　　　　　　　　True, and I await it
　　As a new pleasure—
Sittah.　　　　　　　　Why, then nothing further
　　Can disconcert you. See, 'tis merely one

M

Out of the multitude; merely a Jew
Like other Jews : would not you be ashamed
To seem to him what he thinks all men are ?
And thinks the better, the humaner, man
The more a fool.

Saladin.   I must do wickedly,
You mean, so that the wicked may not think
Wickedly of me ?

Sittah.   True, if wickedness
Be treating things according to their kind.

Saladin. Ah ! let a woman frame what scheme she will,
Trust her to fit it with a fair disguise.
If I but touch a ware so delicate,
It breaks in my coarse hand. For things like that
Whoso invented them must carry through,
With artful sleight and cunning craftiness.
Be it as 'twill ! I dance as best I can—
And think I'd rather do it ill than well.

Sittah. Trust not yourself too little. You will win
If you resolve it. Ever men like you
Would fain convince us 'tis the sword alone,
Only the sword that gained them victory—
The lion who went hunting with the fox,
Of his companion doubtless was ashamed,
Not of his cunning . . .

Saladin.   O, women are so happy
When they seduce men to their level. Go !
Go, Sittah ! I have learned my lesson quite.

Sittah. What, must I go ?

Saladin.   Surely you would not stay ?

Sittah. If not stay with you—in the presence here—
Then in the ante-chamber . . .

Saladin.   There to hearken ?
No, sister, no ; if I may once insist.
Away ! the curtain rustles, he is here ;
I'll see to it you have not long to wait.

[*While she leaves by one door, Nathan enters by the other ; and
    Saladin sits down.*

SCENE V

Saladin and Nathan

Saladin. Come nearer, Jew ! Approach ! Come closer yet—
   And fear not.
Nathan.   Fear be to your enemies.
Saladin. You are called Nathan ?
Nathan.   Yes.
Saladin.   Nathan the Wise ?
Nathan. No.
Saladin.   By yourself, O no, but by the people.
Nathan. May be; the people !
Saladin.   Yet you think not, surely,
   I hold in scorn the judgment of the people ?
   Long have I wished that I might know the man
   Whom they call wise.
Nathan.   Ev'n if in mockery
   They named him ? Ev'n if to the people " wise "
   Should mean no more than prudent ? prudent but he
   Who reckons cleverly his own advantage—
Saladin. His true advantage, mean you, his true good ?
Nathan. Then verily were the man of selfish mind
   Most prudent. Then indeed were wise and prudent
   But one.
Saladin.   You seek to prove, what you would contradict.
   Men's true advantages the people know not.
   You know them, or at least have sought to know ;
   Have weighed them, pondered them ; and this itself
   Already makes the wise man.
Nathan.   Which no man
   But thinks he is.
Saladin.   Enough of modesty,
   Too much of that, when one expects dry reason,
   Can make one sick.   [*Springs up.*
                    Let's come to business.
   But—but—uprightly, Jew ! In honesty !
Nathan. I will so serve you, Sultan, to be deemed
   Worthy your constant custom.
Saladin.   Serve me, how ?
Nathan. The best of all I have, be at your service
   And at the lowest price.
Saladin.   Of what speak you ?

  Not, surely, of your wares? Chaffer and higgle
  My sister may. (That's for the listener !)
  I have no use for merchants and their goods.
Nathan. Then without doubt you will desire to know
  Whatever on my way I chanced across
  Or marked of your foes' arms—if openly—
Saladin. Even of that I nothing ask of you.
  Of that I know already all I need ;
  In short—
Nathan.   Command me, Sultan.
Saladin.   I desire
  Instruction of you in another field,
  Quite other ; and to use your wisdom there.
  Since you are wise, tell me as to a friend,
  What faith, what law, have satisfied you best.
Nathan. Sultan, I am a Jew—
Saladin.   A Muslim I.
  The Christian stands between us. Of these three
  Religions only one can be the true one.
  A man like you will not consent to stay
  Where'er the accident of birth has cast him ;
  Or if he stays, 'twill be of 's own election
  As insight, reason, choice of best things, prompt him.
  Come, then, impart to me your insight : let me hear
  The moving reasons : since for this high quest
  Time was not granted me. Tell me the choice,
  Tell me the grounds—of course, in confidence—
  Which fixed the choice, that I may make it mine.
  How now ! You start, you weigh me with your eye.
  It well may be that of all Sultans yet
  I am the first inspired by such a whim,
  Which yet methinks is no unworthy one
  Even for a Sultan. Not so? Then speak out !
  Speak out. Or would you have a minute's space
  To ponder it? Good ; I will give it you—
  (Has she been listening? I will catch her out :
  And hear how I have managed.) Ponder now ;
  Ponder it swiftly. Presently I'm here.
  [*Goes into the ante-chamber, to which Sittah had betaken herself.*

SCENE VI

Nathan, alone

Nathan. Hm ! Hm ! Marvellous ! What's to happen now ?
  What does the Sultan want ? I came prepared
  For money, and he asks for truth—for truth !
  And wants it paid in ready cash, as though
  The truth were coinage. Yea, even as if
  It were old coinage that was told by weight.
  That might pass, truly ! But such new-coined pieces
  That owe the die their value, must be counted.
  As money into sack, does one sweep truth
  Into one's head ? Who, then, is here the Jew,
  I or the Sultan ? Might he not, perhaps,
  Ask for the truth in truth ? 'Twere a mean thing
  Even the suspicion that he used truth
  As a mere trap to catch me. That were mean ?
  Too mean ? What is too mean for great men's use ?
  True, true. See how he drives the door and storms
  The house ! Surely one knocks and listens first
  When one comes as a friend. So, warily
  I'll walk ! But how, but what ? Wholly to be
  The common Jew, that will not serve me here,
  Still less not to be Jew at all. For if
  Not Jew, he well might ask me, Then why not
  A Mussulman ? That's it ! And that can save me !
  Not children only, we can feed men too
  With fables. Ah ! he comes. Well, let him come !

SCENE VII

Saladin and Nathan

Saladin. (The field is clear now.) Not too soon, I hope,
  Do I return to you ? You are at end
  With your deliberation. Come, then, speak !
  Not a soul hears us.
Nathan.   All the world may listen
  And welcome.
Saladin.   Confident, so confident
  Is Nathan of his cause ? Ha ! such I name
  A wise man ! Who dissembles never truth

But stakes all for it—body, life, and soul.

Nathan. Yes, truly, when 'tis needful and availeth.

Saladin. Henceforward I can hope with right to wear
  A title of mine, reformer of the world
  And of the law.

Nathan.   In sooth, a lovely title !
  Yet, Sultan, ere I trust me to your hands,
  Perhaps you will permit me to relate
  An ancient tale ?

Saladin.   Why not ? I was from childhood
  Lover of tales, well told.

Nathan.   Ah ! ah ! *Well told.*
  That's more than I can claim.

Saladin.   Come, why again
  So proudly modest ? Come, the tale ! the tale !

Nathan. There lived a man in a far Eastern clime
  In hoar antiquity, who from the hand
  Of his most dear beloved received a ring
  Of priceless estimate. An opal 'twas
  Which spilt a hundred lovely radiances
  And had a magic power, that whoso wore it,
  Trusting therein, found grace with God and man.
  What wonder therefore that this man o' the East
  Let it not from his finger, and took pains
  To keep it to his household for all time.
  Thus he bequeathed the jewel to the son
  Of all his sons he loved best, and provided
  That he in turn bequeath it to the son
  Who was to him the dearest ; evermore
  The best-beloved, without respect of birth,
  By right o' the ring alone should be the head,
  The house's prince. You understand me, Sultan.

Saladin. I understand : continue !

Nathan.   Well, this ring,
  From son to son descending, came at last
  Unto a father of three sons, who all
  To him, all three, were dutiful alike,
  And whom, all three, in natural consequence,
  He loved alike. Only from time to time
  Now this ; now that one ; now the third, as each
  Might be alone with him, the other twain
  Not sharing his o'erflowing heart, appeared
  Worthiest the ring ; and then, piously weak,

He promised it to each.   And so things went
Long as they could.   But dying hour drawn near
Brought the good father to perplexity.
It pained him, the two sons, trusting his word,
Should thus be wounded.   What was he to do?
Quickly he sends for an artificer,
To make him on the model of his ring
Two others, bidding spare nor cost nor pains
To make them in all points identical;
And this the artist did.   When they are brought
Even the father scarcely can distinguish
His pattern-ring.   So, full of joy, he calls
His sons, and each one to him separately;
And gives to each son separately his blessing,
Gives each his ring; and dies.   Still hear you, Sultan?

Saladin. [*Who has turned away perplexed.*] I hear, I hear—Only
    bring you the tale
To speedy end.   Is 't done?

Nathan.   The tale is finished.
For what still follows, any man may guess.
Scarce was the father dead, but each one comes
And shows his ring, and each one claims to be
True prince o' the house.   Vainly they search, strive, argue,
The true ring was not proved or provable—
    [*After a pause, during which he waits the Sultan's reply.*
Almost as hard to prove as to us now
What the true creed is.

Saladin.   How? is this to be
The answer to my question?

Nathan.   Nay, it merely
Makes my excuse that I don't trust myself
Exactly to distinguish twixt the rings
The Sire with express purpose had bade make
So that no probing might distinguish them—

Saladin. The rings!   You play with me!   It was my thought
That the religions I have named to you
Were plainly, easily distinguishable,
Down even to clothing, down to meat and drink!

Nathan. Only not so in questions of foundation—
For base not all their creeds on history,
Written or handed down?   And history
Must be received in faith implicitly.
Is 't not so?   Then on whom rest we this faith

Implicit, doubting not? Surely on our own?
Them from whose blood we spring? Surely on them
Who from our childhood gave us proofs of love?
Who never have deceived us, saving when
'Twere happier, safer so to be deceived?
How, then, shall I my fathers less believe
Than you your own? or in the other case,
Can I demand that you should give the lie
To your forefathers, that mine be not gainsaid?
And, yet again, the same holds of the Christians.
Is't not so?

Saladin.   (By high God! The man is right;
I must be dumb.)

Nathan.   Then let us come again
Back to our rings. As we have said—the sons
Appealed to law; and swore before the Judge
Out of the father's hand, immediately,
To have received the ring—and this was true—
After for long he had the promise sure
One day to enjoy the privilege of the ring—
And this no less was true. Each cried the father
Could not be false towards him, and ere he might
Let such suspicion stain him, must believe,
Glad as he were to think the best of them,
His brothers played him false, and he should soon
Expose the traitors, justify himself.

Saladin. And now, the Judge? I'm waiting, fain to hear
What you will make him say. What was his verdict?

Nathan. Thus spake the Judge: Bring me the father here
To witness; I will hear him; and if not
Leave then my judgment seat. Think you this chair
Is set for reading of riddles? Do you wait,
Expecting the true ring to open mouth?
Yet halt! I hear, the genuine ring possesses
The magic power to bring its wearer love
And grace with God and man. That must decide;
For never can the false rings have this virtue.
Well, then; say whom do two of you love best?
Come, speak! What! silent? Is the rings' effect
But backward and not outward? Is it so
That each one loves himself most? Then I judge
All three of you are traitors and betrayed!

Your rings all three are false. The genuine ring
Perchance the father lost, and to replace it
And hide the loss, had three rings made for one.

Saladin. O, splendid! splendid!

Nathan. So, went on the Judge,
You may not seek my counsel, but my verdict;
But go! My counsel is, you take the thing
Exactly as it lies. If each of you
Received his ring from his good father's hand,
Then each of you believe his ring the true one—
'Tis possible the father would not suffer
Longer the one ring tyrannise in 's house,
Certain, he loved all three, and equal loved,
And would not injure two to favour one.
Well, then, let each one strive most zealously
To show a love untainted by self-care,
Each with his might vie with the rest to bring
Into the day the virtue of the jewel
His finger wears, and help this virtue forth
By gentleness, by spirit tractable,
By kind deeds and true piety towards God;
And when in days to come the magic powers
Of these fair rings among your children's children
Brighten the world, I call you once again,
After a thousand thousand years are lapsed,
Before this seat of judgment. On that day
A wiser man shall sit on it and speak.
Depart! So spake the modest Judge.

Saladin. God! God!

Nathan. Saladin, if you feel yourself to be
This wiser promised man . . .

Saladin. [*Who rushes towards him, seizes his hand, which to the end he does not release.*] I, dust? I, nothing?
O God!

Nathan. What would you, Saladin?

Saladin. My good Nathan!
The thousand thousand years of the great Judge
Are not yet up. Not mine His judgment throne.
Go! but abide my friend.

Nathan. Had Saladin
Further no word for me?

Saladin. Not anything.

Nathan. Nothing?

Saladin.　　　　　No, not a jot—Why ask you this?

Nathan. I should have begged an opportunity
　To proffer a petition.

Saladin.　　　　　　　Need you then
　An opportunity?　My friend, speak on!

Nathan. I come from a wide round, whereon my task
　Was gathering in of debts.　Almost I have
　Too much of ready coin.　The time begins
　To assume the look of storm.　I hardly know
　Where safely to bestow it, and have thought,
　Seeing how much this coming war will ask,
　That you, perchance, might use a portion.

Saladin. [*Looking him in the eyes steadily.*]　Nathan!
　I will not ask whether before this hour
　Al-Hafi has been with you, nor enquire
　Whether a suspicion prompts you to this offer
　Of your freewill . . .

Nathan.　　　　　What mean you, a suspicion?

Saladin. Yes, I deserve it.　Pardon.　For what helps it?
　I must confess, I had it in my mind—

Nathan. Not surely to request the same of me?

Saladin. Yea, verily.

Nathan.　　　　　Thus both of us were helped!
　But that I cannot send you all my means
　The Templar gives occasion : sure you know him.
　A heavy obligation must I meet
　To him before all else.

Saladin.　　　　　A Templar, what?
　Surely you will not aid with your good gold
　My worst of enemies?

Nathan.　　　　　I speak of one,
　One only, him whose life you spared.

Saladin.　　　　　　　　Ah what
　You mind me of—Most strange!　I had forgot
　The stripling.　Know you him?　Where is he lodged?

Nathan. Where lodged?　Why, know you not how much of
　　blessing
　Fell to my lot, even through your grace done to him?
　'Twas he, at risk of his new-gifted life,
　That saved my daughter from the flaming walls.

Saladin. He?　did he that?　Truly, he looked like that—
　This surely had my brother likewise done,

Whom he so much resembles.   Is he still
In the Holy City? · Bring him here to me.
I've told so many things to my dear sister
Of this her brother, whom she never knew,
That I must needs show her his counterfeit !
Go, fetch him ! See, of one good action, tho'
It was of simple passion born, so many
Other good deeds flow forth !   Go fetch him hither.

Nathan. [*Letting go of Saladin's hand*.] Straightway ! And of
    the rest, the other matter,
  Does it, too, stand?   [*Exit*.
Saladin.   Ah, had my sister stayed
  To hearken ! Quick, to her ! to her ! For how
  Can all be told that now I have to tell?

                              [*Exit from the other side*.

SCENE VIII

*Under the Palms, in neighbourhood of the cloister, where the
Templar waits for Nathan.*

Templar. [*Walks up and down, struggling with himself, till he
  breaks out*.] Here halts the victim, weary and foredone—
'Tis well ! I would not know or see more clear
What in me passes, and would not foresee
What yet will pass.   Enough ! I've fled in vain,
In vain ! And yet I could nought else but fly.
Well, come what will; the stroke fell far too swiftly
To be escaped ; though hard and long I struggled
To come from under.   To see her, whom yet
To see I had but small desire, to see her
And the resolve never to lose her from
Mine eyes, and yet what speak I of resolve?
Resolve is plan, is act, while I but suffer,
Suffer, not act—to see her and to feel
Bound to her by strong cords, bound up with her,
Was one; is one : from her to live apart
Is thought unthinkable and were my death,
And wheresoever after death we are,
'Twould be even there my death—Is this, then, love?
So the Knight Templar loves assuredly,
The Christian loves the Jewish maid, in truth ;

Hm ! what of that ? In this the Holy Land,
And hereby holy to me evermore,
I have sloughed off a world of prejudices,—
What will my Order say ? As Templar Knight
I'm dead, was dead to them from that self hour
Which made me prisoner to Saladin,—
The head which Saladin restored to me,
Was it my old ?—'tis new ! and clear of all
The lies and stuff they babbled to it once,
Wherewith 'twas slaved ; and 'tis a better one,
Agreeing more with my paternal clime,
I feel it so in truth. For it begins
To think even as my father must have thought
Under those skies, unless those tales be false
They tell of him—Tales ? tales, yet credible
Which never seemed to me more credible
Than here they seem where I but run the risk
Of stumbling, where he fell. Ah, where he fell ?
I'll rather fall with men, than stand with children.
Sure, his example makes me confident
Of his approval. Whose approval else crave I ?
For Nathan's ? Furtherance more than approval
Will not be wanting there. The noble Jew !
Who yet desires not to seem more than Jew !
Here comes he hastening, gladness in his eyes.
Whoe'er came otherwise from Saladin ?
Ho ! Nathan !

SCENE IX

Nathan and the Templar

Nathan.   How ? Is 't you ?
Templar.   It has been long,
    Your converse with the Sultan.
Nathan.   Not so long ;
    For on my way to him I was much hindered.
    Ah, truly, Curd, the man matches his fame.
    His fame is his mere shadow. But now first
    I have a thing to say that will not wait.
Templar. What ?
Nathan. He would speak with you and bids you come
    Without delay. Give me your company
    Now to my house, where first I must procure

A something for his hand, and then we go.
Templar. Over your threshold, Nathan, willingly
  I pass no more.
Nathan.   Meanwhile you have been there
  Already and spoken with her. Come then, tell me
  How Recha pleases you?
Templar.   Beyond all speech!
  Only—to see her more—never will I!
  Never, except I have your promise here
  That I may see her ever.
Nathan.   How will you
  I should interpret that?
Templar. [*After a short pause falling on his neck.*] My father!
  father!
Nathan. Young man!
Templar.   Not son? I pray you, Nathan!
Nathan. Beloved youth!
Templar.   Not son? I pray you, Nathan!
  Beseech you by the tenderest ties of nature!
  O let not later bonds come in between!
  Let it suffice to be a man! nor drive
  Me from you!
Nathan.   Dear, dear friend! . . .
Templar.   And son?
  Not son? Even not then, if gratitude
  Has paved love's way to your loved daughter's heart?
  Not even then, if both hearts only waited
  A father's gracious sign to melt in one?—
  You're silent.
Nathan.   You surprise, you startle me,
  Young knight.
Templar.   Surprise you, Nathan, startle you
  With your own inmost thoughts? You'll not disown them
  Because my lips have spoke them? I surprise you?
Nathan. There's something I must know—who was this Stauffen
  You claim as sire?
Templar.   What say you, Nathan? what?
  Is curiosity, then, all you feel
  At such a moment?
Nathan.   Nay, not so, for, look you,
  I myself knew, knew well in earlier years
  A Stauffen, his name Conrad.
Templar.   Well, what think you?

That same name bore my father.

Nathan.   Verily?

Templar. Myself am so called after him; for Curd
　Is Conrad.

Nathan.   Even so, my Conrad could not be
　Your father.   For my Conrad was like you,
　A Templar, and unwedded.

Templar.   O, for that!

Nathan. How?

Templar. O, for that he still might be my father.

Nathan. Now you jest.

Templar.   And you, you take it
　Quite too precisely.   Say, what were it then?
　Something of bastard or side-blow perhaps!
　Granted, the wound is not to be despised—
　Absolve me of my proof of ancestry,
　And in my turn I will absolve you yours.
　Not truly that I touch with taint of doubt
　Your family tree.   That, God forbid! you could
　Uprear it leaf by leaf to Abraham.
　And beyond that I'll build it up myself,
　Attesting it by oath.

Nathan.   Now you grow bitter.
　Have I deserved it?   Think you I detracted
　Aught from your worth?—But yet, I will not take
　For a word dropped, offence.   No more's to speak.

Templar. Really?   No more to speak.   O, then, forgive me!

Nathan. Come with me only, come!

Templar.   But tell me whither?
　Not to your house?   That never; that I cannot!—
　There's fire there.   I will await you here.   Go you!
　If I see her again; then many times
　I still shall see her.   But if not, why then
　I've seen her far too often . . .

Nathan.   I shall hasten.

SCENE X

The Templar, and soon after Daja

Templar. Enough and more.   The brain of human-kind
　In grasp is almost limitless, yet often
　Suddenly fills to bursting with a trifle!

It matters nothing, nothing; let it be
Even full of what it will—Let patience work;
The spirit soon compounds the turgid stuff,
Makes itself room; order and light return.
Do I then love for the first time? Or what
I once called love, was it not love at all?
Or is love only what I suffer now?

Daja. [*Who has slipped in from the side.*] Sir Knight! sir
  Knight!

Templar.   Who calls? Ha, Daja, you?

Daja. I have slipped past him: but where you now stand
  He still might see us. Come, behind this tree.

Templar. What is it? Why so secret? Tell me why.

Daja. What brings me to you, does concern a secret,
  A secret truly; more, a double one—
  The one only know I, the other you
  Alone can know. How if we made exchange?
  Trust me with yours, then I'll trust you with mine.

Templar. With pleasure, readily; if I may know
  First what you think is mine. But out of yours
  That surely will appear. Only begin.

Daja. O, that would never do; no, no, sir Knight;
  You first; I'll follow; be assured that mine,
  My secret cannot help you by a jot,
  Have I not yours before it. Only quick!
  If I but win it by my questioning,
  Then you've confided nothing. Then my secret
  Remains my secret, and your own escapes.
  Still, you poor soldier! That you men should think,
  O credulous men! that you can keep such secrets
  From us poor women.

Templar.   Secrets we ourselves
  Often don't know we have.

Daja.   That well may be
  Then, to be sure, I'll so far act the friend
  To acquaint you with yourself. Say, what then made you
  So all at once vanish in cloud, and leave
  Your friends deserted? that you do not now
  Return with Nathan? Recha, has she so little
  Worked on you? How? or, should I ask, so much?
  So much! so much! Instruct me how to know
  The fluttering of the poor ensnaréd bird
  Limed to the tree! In brief, confess me here

That you do love her, love her even to madness,
And I will tell——
Templar.   To madness? Verily;
Your insight is astounding.
Daja.   Grant me then
Only the love; I'll let you off the madness.
Templar. Since, I suppose, that may be taken for granted?
A Templar-Knight to love a Jewish girl ! . . .
Daja. Truly there seems but little sense in that—
And yet at whiles there's more of sense in things
Than we surmise ; nor were 't incredible
The Christ should lead us to Himself by ways
The wise man of himself might never find.
Templar. Your words are solemn. (Well, if Providence
Were put in place of Christ, were she not right?)
You breed in me a curiosity
I never knew before.
Daja.   O, 'tis the land
Of miracles !
Templar.   (Well,—the miraculous.
How can it otherwise ? Seeing all the nations
Crowd themselves here together.) My dear Daja,
Consider it confessed—what you desire :
That I do love her, hardly understand
How I shall live without her ; that . . .
Daja. Truly, sir Knight? Here pledge your oath to me
To take her for your own, to save my Recha,
Here, while life lasts ; yonder, eternally.
Templar. And how ? How can I ? Can I swear to do
What stands not in my power?
Daja.   But in your power
It stands. For by a single word I bring it
Within your power.
Templar.   So that not even her father
Could hinder or obstruct ?
Daja.   Eh, Father—what Father !
Her father *must* agree.
Templar.   Must, Daja? Must?
Sure, he's not fallen amongst robbers yet !
There is no *must* for him.
Daja.   I tell you truth ;
He must in the end consent, and gladly too.
Templar. Must, must, and gladly. Daja, how if I say

That I myself already tried to touch
This chord within him?
Daja.   And he would not accord?
Templar. No! No; with such a discord he joined in
As sharply wounded me.
Daja.   What say you?   What!
That you had shown him, even in shadow merely,
Your love for her, and he did not leap up
For joy? but frostily withdrew, and muttered
Of difficulties?
Templar.   So it was.
Daja.   Then I
Will not reflect a single moment more—   [*Pause.*
Templar. And yet—you *are* reflecting?
Daja.   All things else
Prove Nathan kind—myself, how much I owe him!
And now he will not listen!   O, God knows
My very heart bleeds in me, so to force him.
Templar. I pray you, Daja, free me once for all
From these uncertainties.   But if you are
Yourself unsure, whether what you intend
Should good or bad, shameful or worthy praise,
Be called—then, silence!   I'll forget
That you have ought to keep unspoken.
Daja.   Rather
That stings me not to speak.   Then know—our Recha
Is not a Jewess; is,—she is a Christian.
Templar. So?   Wish you joy!   Was the delivery hard?
Shrink you not from the travail!   O go on,
Go on with zeal to populate the skies,
If you can't earth!
Daja. How, Knight?   Deserves my news this mockery?
That Recha is a Christian gives no joy
To you, a Christian and a Templar Knight
Who loves her?
Templar.   Most especially, as she's
A Christian of your making.
Daja.   So you think?
Well, let it be!   But no, for I would see
Him who will make her convert!   'Tis her fortune
To have been long, what now she can't become.
Templar. Explain, or—go!
Daja.   She is a Christian child,

N

And born of Christian parents; is baptized . . .
Templar. [*Abruptly.*] And Nathan?
Daja.   Not her father!
Templar.   Nathan not
  Her father? Know you what you speak?
Daja.   The truth,
  Which many a time has cost me tears of blood.
  No, he is not her father . . .
Templar.   And had her
  Only brought up as a daughter? had the child,
  The Christian child, brought up as Jewish maid?
Daja. 'Tis certain.
Templar.   And she knew not of her birth?
  Had never learnt of him that she a Christian
  Was born and not a Jewess?
Daja.   Never, never!
Templar. And he not merely had brought up the child
  In this delusion, but has left the maiden
  In this deception still?
Daja.   Alas!
Templar.   But—Nathan,
  The wise, good Nathan has allowed himself
  To falsify the voice of nature thus,
  Thus misdirect the outpouring of a heart
  Which, left to itself, would take quite other ways?
  Daja, you have indeed confided here
  A weighty matter—which involves great issues—
  Which quite confounds me—which puts me in doubt
  What I must do. So give me time. Then, go!
  He passes here anon. He might surprise us.
  Therefore, go, Daja!
Daja.   It would be my death!
Templar. Speak with him now I cannot. If you meet him,
  Say only that we two shall presently
  Meet in the Sultan's chamber.
Daja.   But betray not
  To him what you have heard.—This does but give
  The last seal to the matter, takes away
  All scruples from you when you think of Recha—
  And if thereon you carry her to Europe,
  Let me not stay behind. I conjure you—
Templar. I lay that on my heart; but, leave me now.

ACT IV—SCENE I

SCENE : *In the cloisters of the convent*

The Friar and soon thereafter the Templar

Friar. Well, well ; of course the Patriarch is right !
　Although as yet no single enterprise
　He laid upon my shoulders has success.
　Why does he choose only such jobs for me ?
　I have no craving for these artful games,
　I am not made for the persuader's part,
　Nor wish to stick my nose in everything
　Or play the meddler. Am I, then, for this,
　Desiring to be separate, for myself
　Alone, only the more by others' will
　To be the more entangled ?
Templar. [*Entering hastily.*] My good friar !
　We meet again. A long time I have sought you.
Friar. Sought me, my lord ?
Templar.　　　　　　　　Have you forgotten me ?
Friar. No, no ! I only thought that never in my life
　Should I so come to meet my lord again :
　Prayed the good God I might not. For God knows
　How loathsome was the errand laid on me,
　He knows whether I wished an open ear
　To find for it ; and knows how I rejoiced
　That you so spurned, without a moment's thought,
　What misbecame your knighthood. I was glad ;
　But things go all awry ; we meet once more !
Templar. You know, then, why I come, though I myself
　Can hardly guess.
Friar.　　　　　　Perhaps, have thought it over,
　Perhaps discovered that the Patriarch
　Was after all i' the right ; that pelf and honour
　His project might ensure you, that a foe
　Remains a foe, even if he seven times
　Had proved our angel. So with flesh and blood
　You have ta'en counsel, and now come again
　To offer service. God !
Templar.　　　　　　No, my good man !
　Be calm ; for this I come not ; not for this
　Would I consult the Patriarch. What I thought

On that point think I still, and would not lose
For anything the world holds that regard
Of which a man so honest, pious, kind
Has deemed me worthy.   No, I have but come
To beg the Patriarch's counsel . . .

Friar.   You—of him
A Knight, consult a—priest.   [*Looking timidly round.*

Templar.   Indeed, the affair
Is rather priestly.

Friar.   Yet you will not find
The priest consult a knight, however knightly
The business be.   ·

Templar.   'Tis a priest's privilege
To go astray, a privilege none of us
Envies him much.   In truth were it myself,
Solely myself in question, and myself
Solely to answer where were need of Patriarchs?
But there be things I would do faultily
By others' counsel rather than do well
By my sole will.   Besides, I now perceive
Religion too is party, and who thinks
Himself therein no partisan, that man
Is in himself a party.   This being so,
'Tis right it should be.

Friar.   That I speak not of,
Not knowing if I understand my lord.

Templar. And yet ! (let's see what is 't I really want.
Decree or counsel?   Simple counsel or refined?)
I thank you, friar ; thanks for your wise word.
Why Patriarch?   Be you my Patriarch?
I'll rather ask the Christian in the Patriarch
Than Patriarch in Christian.   Now the question—
The matter is . . .

Friar.   No further, sir, no further !
To what good end?   Surely my lord mistakes me.
Who knows too much, has the more care ; for me
One care's enough and more.   O good ! see yonder,
There comes, for my relief, the priest himself.
Stay where you stand.   He has already seen you.

SCENE II

The Patriarch, who comes up with priestly pomp by the one cloister ;
and the foregoing

Templar. I would avoid him. He's not at all my man !
  A portly, rosy, and most friendly prelate !
  And what a splendour !
Friar.   You should only see him
  Going to court ; comes from a sick man now.
Templar. How Saladin must be abashed before him !
Patriarch. [*Approaching, makes a sign to the friar.*] Here !
    Surely that is the Templar. What would he ?
Friar. I know not.
Patriarch. [*Approaching him, whilst the friar and retinue retire.*]
                Well, sir Knight ! Am much rejoiced
  To see the brave young man ! Eh, you are still
  A stripling. Now, by help of God, therefrom
  Something might grow.
Templar.   Scarce more, my reverend lord,
  Than what already is, and mayhap less.
Patriarch. I hope at least that such a pious knight,
  For the good and glory of dear Christendom
  And God's own cause, may flourish many years !
  That surely will not fail, if, as is due,
  Young valour hearken to the ripened wisdom
  Of age ? How else can I now serve my friend ?
Templar. With what to youth is wanting, that's with counsel.
Patriarch. O willingly ! if counsel but be taken.
Templar. And yet, not blindly ?
Patriarch.   Who could ask it ? No,
  For verily none should cease to use his reason,
  God-given reason, in its proper sphere.
  Mark you, its proper sphere, not everywhere !
  O no ! As, for example, when God deigns,
  By one of His good angels—that's to say,
  Some servant of His word—suggest to us
  A means, in some uncommon way of action,
  The weal of Christendom and His great Church
  To further and establish, who shall dare
  Question, by reason, the decree of Him
  Who hath created reason, and to test
  The eternal law o' the Glory of the Heavens

By the small rules of what vain men call honour?
Of this enough, enough.   What is it, then,
Whereon my lord now seeks our counsel?
Templar.   This:
Suppose, most reverend Father, that a Jew
An only child possessed, a little maid,
Whom he had reared up with the utmost care
And in all kindness, loved as his own soul,
And who most piously returned his love,
And now 'twere whispered unto one of us
This maiden was no daughter of the Jew;
That he had chosen her in her infancy,—
Bought, stolen—what you will, and that we learned
The maiden was a Christian, and baptized;
The Jew had only reared her as a Jewess,
Let her remain a Jewess and his daughter;—
Say, reverend Father, what were here to do?
Patriarch. I shudder. Yet before all else my lord explain
Whether the case he pictures is a fact
Or a hypothesis.   That is to say,
Whether my lord has but imagined this
Or whether it has happened, and goes on.
Templar. I thought that were all one; I had but wished
To know your Reverence' mind.
Patriarch.   *One!* look you, sir,
How wide the arrogant human intellect
In spiritual things can err—Sir, no, no!
For if the case proposed be but a sport
O' the brain, it is not worth the taking pains
To think it out in earnest. I leave the case
To theatres, where oft such arguments
Of *pro et con* are with the crowd's applause
Handled at large.   But if my lord have now
No such stage-trifles in his mind, and if
The case is fact, and in our diocese,
Even in our city of Jerusalem,
This thing has happened—then indeed—
Templar.   What then?
Patriarch. Then were the Jew without a day's delay
To undergo the penalty which laws
Both Papal and Imperial denounce
For such an outrage, such a heinous crime.
Templar.   And that?

Patriarch. These laws I speak of for the Jew
  Who leads a Christian to apostasy
  Appoint the stake, the fire . . .
Templar.   What, the dread flame?
Patriarch. And how much more to that most wicked Jew
  Who tears by violence a poor Christian child
  Out of the bond of baptism.   Is not all
  We do to children violence?   That's to say,
  Of course, excepting what the Church may do
  With children.
Templar.   But say only if the child
  Save for the Jew's compassion, were but fallen
  A prey to hunger and to wretchedness?
Patriarch. It matters not!   The Jew must burn.   For better
  It were fallen here to utter misery
  Than be saved thus to its eternal loss.
  Besides, how dares the Jew to forestall God?
  Sure, without him God can save whom He will.
Templar. And also, I should think, in spite of him.
Patriarch. No matter!   He must burn.
Templar.   That touches me
  To the very heart!   The rather that they say
  He has not brought the girl up in his faith
  So much as in no faith, and taught her of God
  No more, no less, than satisfies the reason.
Patriarch. No matter!   He must burn, and were indeed
  On this one count worthy to burn three times.
  What!   Let a child grow up without a faith?
  What!   the great duty of Belief to leave
  Untaught to children?   That is wickedness!
  I wonder much, sir Knight, that you yourself . . .
Templar. Most reverend lord, for what remains, I leave it,
  If God will, to the confessional . . . (*is going*).
Patriarch.   What!   not now
  Render account to me?   The criminal,
  The Jew you'll leave unnamed?   Not now and here
  Produce him?   Well, I think I know the way!
  I'll straightway seek the Sultan.   Saladin,
  In virtue of the sworn Capitulation,
  Which bears his seal, he must, he must protect us;
  Protect us in all rights and in all rules
  To our most holy faith and Church belonging.
  Praise be to God!   we have th' Original,

We have his hand and seal.   Yes, it is ours !
Easily, too, I'll make him understand
How perilous 'tis even for the State
To believe nothing !   Since all civil bonds
Are loosed, are torn asunder, when men dare
Have no belief . . . Away with such an outrage !
Templar. Pity, I cannot now with better leisure
　Enjoy the wise discourse.   I'm called to Saladin.
Patriarch. Indeed ? . . . Well, now. . . . Now   verily. . . .
　Then, then. . . .
Templar. I will prepare the Sultan for your coming
　If that be pleasing to your Reverence.
Patriarch. Oh !—ah !—I know my lord enjoys high favour
　With Saladin !   I beg but to be named
　With my devotion to him.   I am driven
　Evermore purely by the zeal of God.
　Where I exceed, it is for Him.   But will
　My lord yet weigh the matter ?   True, is't not,
　Sir Knight, that question of the Jew we spoke of
　Was nothing but a problem ?   That's to say—
Templar. A problem.   [*Exit.*
Patriarch.   Which I notwithstanding mean
　To fathom deeper, even to the ground ;
　Yet that, again, were really a commission
　For Brother Bonafides.   Here, my son !
　　　　　　　　[*He speaks in going off to the friar.*

Scene III

*A room in Saladin's Palace, into which a number of sacks are
　brought by slaves, and placed side by side on the floor*

Saladin, and soon thereafter Sittah

Saladin. [*Coming in.*] Well, truly now, there seems no end of
　that.
　Is there still much to come ?
A Slave.   Still quite the half.
Saladin. Bear what remains to Sittah.   Where's Al-Hafi ?
　Let him take charge of these forthwith.   Or shall I
　Send them to the old man's stronghold in the hills ?
　Here 'twill slip through my fingers.   Though indeed
　One does grow hard at last, and in the end
　'Twill cost some art to extort one coin from me

Until at least the moneys out of Egypt
Come to these lands, the destitute must find
Elsewhere their bread.   Alms at the Sepulchre,
These must go on, or all the Christian pilgrims
Withdraw with empty hands.   If only I . . .

Sittah. What's this?   What does this money here with me?

Saladin. Therewith repay yourself; the overplus
Lay by for after needs.

Sittah.   And is not yet
Old Nathan with the Templar come to you?

Saladin. He seeks him everywhere.

Sittah.   See what I've found
In looking through my trinkets.

                    [*Showing him a small picture.*

Saladin.   Ha! my brother!
That's he, 'tis he!   *Was* he, *was* he, alas!
Ah brave young hero, whom I lost so soon!
My brother dear, wert thou beside me still,
What had I not accomplished!   Give me, Sittah,
The picture; look, I know it instantly;
He gave it to thy elder sister, Lilla,
One morning when she would not let him go,
Holding him close embraced.   'Twas the last day,
The last that he rode out.   I let him ride,
Alone, alas!   And Lilla died of grief,
And never would forgive me, that alone
I let him ride away.   He came no more.

Sittah. Poor brother!

Saladin.   But let be!   God's will be done!
Once we shall all ride out and come no more.
Besides—who knows?   It is not death alone
Frustrates our plans.   He had his enemies,
And many a time the strongest man succumbs
Like the most weak.   Be 't as it may with him;
I must compare the picture with this Templar,
And see perhaps how much my phantasy
Deceived me.

Sittah.   'Twas for that I brought it.   Yet
Give it to me!   'Tis for a woman's eye
To judge such niceties.

Saladin. [*To an usher who enters.*] Speak, who is there?
The Templar?   Let him enter!

Sittah.   I'll sit here,

Out of your way, nor let my questioning looks
Disturb him.

[Sits aside on a sofa and lets her veil fall.

Saladin.   Well, 'tis well! (Now, for his voice!
How will that prove? The tone of Assad's voice
Sleeps in my memory still, and can awake!)

SCENE IV

The Templar and Saladin

Templar. Dare I, thy prisoner, Sultan . . .
Saladin.   Prisoner?
To whom I make the gift of life, shall I
Not also give him freedom?
Templar.   What fits thee
To do, befits me best to hear, and not
Presume beforehand. But yet, Sultan, thanks,
Especial thanks to thee, for granted life
Accords not with my nature or condition.
'Tis at thy service always.
Saladin.   Only use it
Never against me. One more pair of hands
Truly I need not grudge my enemy.
But one heart more like thine I cannot spare.
For in no point am I deceived in thee,
Young hero! Body and soul thou art my Assad.
See! I might ask thee, where this world of time
Thou hast been hiding? In what cave hast slept?
In what a Guinistan by what kind nurturer
This flower has all this age been kept so fresh?
See! I might call to your remembrance all
We did long since in company, the woods we roamed,
The gallops o'er the free uncumber'd ground,
I might upbraid thee for that thou hast kept
A secret from me, stolen an adventure from me:
Yes, so I might, if only thee I saw
And not myself as well. Now, let it be!
Of this sweet dream remains so much of truth
That in my autumn there blooms up again
An Assad here. Knight, shall we have it so?
Templar. Ay! Whatsoever comes to me from thee,
Be't what it will, is welcome to my soul.

Saladin. Let us try that forthwith ; wilt thou abide
 With me, about me ? As Mussulman, as Christian,
 All one ! in the white cloak, or gaberdine,
 In turban or in helmet, as thou pleasest,
 All one to me ! I never have desired
 That one bark grow on all trees of the wood.
Templar. Else hardly should'st thou be what now thou art,
 The conqueror who would rather by God's grace
 Till his own field.
Saladin.   Well, if thou think'st no worse
 Of me, then surely we are half agreed.
Templar.   Nay, quite !
Saladin. [*Offering him his hand.*] A word ?
Templar.   A man ! receive herewith
 More than thou could'st take from me. Wholly thine !
Saladin. Too much gain for one day. Too much, sir Knight.
 Came he not with thee ?
Templar.   Who ?
Saladin.   Thy Nathan.
Templar.   No ;
 I came alone.
Saladin.   Ah, what a deed was that of thine !
 And what a happy fortune that the deed
 Fell out to his advantage, that great man,
Templar. [*Coolly.*]   O, yes !
Saladin.   So cold ? Not so, young man ! When God
 Does a good deed through us, we must not be
 So cold, nor even for modesty appear
 To be.
Templar. Yet everything in this strange world
 Has many sides ! Of which 'tis often hard to tell
 How they are reconciled !
Saladin.   Hold to the best,
 Only the best, and praise the Lord who knows
 Best how to reconcile them. But, young man,
 If you are so fastidious, then must I
 Be on my guard with you. Unhappily
 I am myself a thing of many sides
 Hard for me often to bring to harmony.
Templar. That grieves me ; for suspicion's not my failing,
 Nor ever was . . .
Saladin.   Well, tell me, then, of whom
 Thou hast it now ? It almost seemed, of Nathan.

 Mistrust of Nathan? Thou? Explain thyself!
 Speak, give me earnest of thy confidence.
Templar. I've nothing against Nathan; 'tis myself
 Alone I'm vext with.
Saladin.   And for what?
Templar.   That I
 Have dreamt a Jew might once perchance unlearn
 To be a Jew, and dreamt it, too, awake.
Saladin. Away with waking dreams—a vain vexation.
Templar. Thou know'st of Nathan's daughter, Sultan. What
 I did for her. I did . . . because I did.
 Too proud to reap thanks where I had not sowed,
 Day after day, disdainful, I refused
 To see the girl again. Her sire was absent;
 He came; he heard; he sought me out; he thanked me;
 Expressed his hope I might approve his daughter;
 Of prospects spoke, of future happy days.
 Well, so I was talked over, came, saw, found
 A maiden such . . . ah, Sultan, I'm ashamed!
Saladin. Ashamed? Ashamed! Why, that a Jewish girl
 Should touch your heart; but that's all past, perhaps?
Templar. That 'gainst this passion my impetuous heart
 Stirred by the father's kind inviting words,
 Should stand so feebly. Miserable drop,
 I fell a second time into the fire.
 For now I wooed, and now was I disdained.
Saladin. Disdained?
Templar.   Well, the wise father did not straightway
 Bid me begone. But the wise father first
 Must make enquiry, must consider first. Of course!
 Did I not do the like? Enquired, considered
 I too not first, when she shrieked in the fire?
 Why, certainly! God! 'tis a pretty thing
 To be so wise and thoughtful!
Saladin.   Now, now, come!
 Have patience with an old man; thou'rt but young.
 How long are these refusals, then, to last?
 Will he perhaps demand of thee that thou
 Shalt first become a Jew?
Templar.   A Jew? Who knows?
Saladin. *Who knows?* Why, he who knows what Nathan is.
Templar. The superstition in which we grew up,
 Doth not, because we see it as it is,

Lose, therefore, all its power upon our souls.
They are not all free men who mock their chains.
Saladin. Most wisely spoken ! But Nathan verily . . .
Templar. The worst of superstitions is to hold
One's own the most endurable.
Saladin.   May be,
Still Nathan . . .
Templar.   . . . which alone poor purblind men
Must trust, till they can stand the daylight, which
Alone . . .
Saladin.   Yes, good ! But, Nathan ! Nathan's lot
Is no such weakness.
Templar.   So I also thought !
If all the same this paragon of men
Were such a common Jew that he would seek
To seize on Christian babes to bring them up
As Jews—how then?
Saladin. And who thus slanders him?
Templar.   The very girl
With whom he would decoy me, hope of whom
He would hold out as payment for the deed
I am not to have done for her in vain ;
This very girl is not his daughter—no
She is a Christian child, some castaway.
Saladin. Whom notwithstanding he'd withhold from you?
Templar. [*Hotly.*] Will he or will he not? He is found out.
This babbler of equality and tolerance
Found out ! And on the heels of this Jew wolf
In philosophic sheep's wool I shall put
Dogs that will undisguise him.
Saladin. [*Earnestly.*]   Calmly, Christian !
Templar. What, calmly, Christian ! Jew and Mussulman
Will have but Jew and Mussulman ; shall Christian
Alone not dare make Christians?
Saladin.   Calmly, Christian !
Templar. [*Composedly.*] The weight of this reproach which Saladin
Crams in one word, I feel it, ah, could I
But know how Assad in my place had taken it.
Saladin. Not so much better ! Perhaps with as much rage !
But who so soon has taught thee even like him
To pierce me with a word ? And verily
If these things be exactly as thou sayest,
I cannot find in them my thought of Nathan.

Meanwhile he is my friend, and friends of mine
Must not one with the other come to strife.
Then, be advised, walk warily.   Give him not
A prey to the fanatics of your rabble !
Stir not the pool ; vengeance on him your priests
Would bind on me for duty.   To no Jew,
No Mussulman, be thou in vain a Christian !
Templar. 'Twere soon too late for that ; but I am warned
Even by the bloodthirst of the Patriarch
Who had in fancy chosen me for his tool.
Saladin. How ? cam'st thou first to him and not to me ?
Templar. Yes, in the storm of passion, in the whirl
Of indecision.   Pardon me.   Now no more,
I fear, wilt thou the features of thine Assad
Trace in my countenance.
Saladin.   Was it not
This very fear that hurt !   Methinks, I know
Error and virtue often dwell together.
Go, seek for Nathan as he sought for thee,
And bring him hither.   'Tis my part to bring you
To reconcilement.   For the maiden's sake
Be serious, and be calm, for she is thine.
Perhaps already Nathan understands
That, even swine's flesh withheld, he has brought up
A Christian child !   Go, find him.

> [*The Templar goes out, and Sittah stands up.*

Scene V

Saladin and Sittah

Sittah.   Strange, how strange !
Saladin. Is it not, Sittah ?   Must not brother Assad
Have been a bright and beauteous boy ?   See here.

> [*Showing the picture.*

Sittah. If he was like this, and the Templar sat not
For this dear picture.   But, my Saladin,
How could'st thou now forget to question him
About his parents ?
Saladin.   And most specially
His mother ? if his mother never came
Into this region ?   What ?
Sittah.   Be sure to ask him !

Saladin. O, nothing were more likely ! Assad was
　　With Christian fair ones such a favourite
　　And to fair Christians so devoted too,
　　That once the story ran—but no, but no ;
　　I will not speak of that.　Enough, I have him
　　Once more !　And will with all his faults
　　And all the fancies of his tender heart,
　　Receive him.　Oh, this maiden that he loves
　　Nathan must give him.　Think'st thou not ?

Sittah.　　　　　　　　　　　　Not *give* him,
　　Leave him.

Saladin.　　　　Certainly !　What right has Nathan,
　　If he is not her father, over her ?
　　He who preserved her in her mortal peril
　　Alone can take the unknown father's rights.

Sittah. Then, Saladin, how if thou did'st straightway
　　Take the girl to thee and withdrew her straight**way**
　　From the illegal holder.

Saladin.　　　　　　　Were that needful ?

Sittah. Not needful, truly.　'Tis my curious heart
　　Alone that drives me to th' advice, because
　　Of certain men I'm fain to know at once
　　What kind of girl they love.

Saladin.　　　　　　　Well, Sittah, send
　　And have her brought to us.

Sittah.　　　　　　　O, may I, brother ?

Saladin. Only, spare Nathan !　Nathan must by no means
　　Believe that one would part the girl by force
　　From him.

Sittah. Be not afraid of that.

Saladin.　　　　　　　And I
　　I must myself see where Al-Hafi hides.

Scene VI

SCENE : *The open court in Nathan's house, opposite the palm-tree*
　　grove, as in Scene I of Act I.　Part of the wares and jewels
　　lies unpacked, of which they are speaking

Nathan and Daja

Daja. O, all are splendid ; choicest of the choice !
　　O, everything as fits your generous hand.
　　Where do they make this lovely silver stuff

Threaded with the gold tendrils? What's its cost?
A wedding dress indeed! No queen could ask
A better.

Nathan. Wedding dress? Why call it so?

Daja. Why, yes; of course you did not think of that
In buying it. But, Nathan, verily
That and nought else it is, a wedding dress
As if bespoken. The white ground, an emblem
Of innocence, the heavy golden threads,
That wind about this ground in every part,
Emblem of riches. See you? It is lovely.

Nathan. Why all this wit? A wedding dress for whom
Do you thus emblemize so learnedly?
Are you, then, bride?

Daja.   I?

Nathan.   Who, then?

Daja.   I? Good God!

Nathan. Who, then? Whose wedding dress is this you prate
of?
All this is yours, and for no other.

Daja.   Mine?
Is meant for me? And is it not for Recha?

Nathan. What I have brought for Recha, they have packed
Apart. Come, take your goods and chattels!

Daja.   Templar!
Not I, were they the treasures of the world,
I will not touch them till you swear to me
To use the happy chance that Heaven has given you
And will not give, perhaps, a second time.

Nathan. Make use? Whereof? A happy chance, of what?

Daja. O, this pretence of blindness! In two words,
The Templar Knight loves Recha. Give her to him;
Therewith at once your sin, your sin whereof
I can no more keep silence, has an end.
So will the girl come once again 'mongst Christians,
Become once more that which she was and is.
And you, for all the goodness you have shown us,
For which our gratitude can never cease,
Shall not have merely heaped up coals of fire
On your own head.

Nathan.   Ah! the old harp again
But only fitted with another string
That neither can be stilled nor kept in tune.

Daja. How so?

Nathan.   I like this Templar, and would rather
  Recha had him than any in the world.
  But yet . . . have patience with me yet a while.

Daja. Patience! O Patience!—is not this your own
  Old harp again?

Nathan.   Only a few days' patience!
  But look! Who comes along? Is't not a friar?
  Go, ask him what he wants.

Daja.   What can he want?

                              [*Goes up to him and asks.*

Nathan. Give it—before he asks—(*aside:* Could I but come
  Closer the Templar, not exposing him
  The reason of my questions! Which if told
  And the suspicion groundless, then for nothing
  I had staked my fatherhood.) What does he seek?

Daja. He asks to speak with you.

Nathan.   Well, let him come.
  Go you meanwhile.

Scene VII

Nathan and the Friar

Nathan. [*Aside.*] (How glad had I remained
  My Recha's father. And, indeed, can I
  Not yet remain so, tho' I lose the name?
  To her herself I should be so forever
  Did she but know the joy that were to me.)
  [*To Daja.*] Go! What service can I do you, holy friar?

Friar. Really, not much. It gives me joy at least
  To find great Nathan well.

Nathan.   You know me then?

Friar. Why, yes; who does not? For so many men
  You have left your imprint in their hands;
  'T has stood in mine these many, many years.

Nathan. [*Reaching for his purse.*] Come, friar, come; I will
    renew the print.

Friar. Have thanks! I should but steal it from a poorer;
  Nothing for me! Permit me only to refresh
  My own name in your memory. I can boast
  To have laid something also in your hand
  Not quite to be despised.

Nathan.   Forgive me, then—

  o

I am ashamed—say what was that? and take
As my atonement seven times its worth.
Friar. But first of all hear now the reason why
Only to-day is brought to my remembrance
The pledge I trusted to you.
Nathan.   Pledge entrusted?
Friar. Not long ago I lay an eremite
On Quarantana, near to Jericho.
There came a robber-band of Arabs, broke
My little chapel down and my poor cell,
And dragged me off, their prisoner. By good chance
Escaped, hither I hied me to the Patriarch,
To beg another little resting-place
Where I could worship God in solitude
Until my quiet end.
Nathan.   Be brief, good friar !
I stand on coals. The pledge ! The pledge entrusted me !
Friar. Forthwith, Sir Nathan. Well, the Patriarch
Promised to find me settlement on Tabor
So soon as place were vacant, bade meantime
That I should dwell in cloister as lay-brother,
Where now I am, sir Nathan, where I long
A hundred times a day for Tabor. For
The Patriarch employs me upon things
That fill me with great loathing. For example :
Nathan. Quick, I beseech you !
Friar.   Well, it comes, it comes !
Some one to-day has whispered in his ear,
That somewhere hereabout there bides a Jew
Who has brought up they say a Christian child
As his own daughter.
Nathan. [*Taken aback.*] How?
Friar.   But hear me out !
As he commissioned me, if possible,
Forthwith to track this Jew ; beside himself
With rage before this horrid sacrilege,
He deemed the sin against the Holy Ghost
Which cannot be forgiven—that is, the sin
That's held the greatest of all sins, altho',
Thanks be to God ! we're not exactly sure
In what the sin consists—there all at once
My conscience woke, and then there came the thought
I might myself sometime have had the chance

To do th' unpardonable sin.   Come, say;
Did once a groom just eighteen years gone by
Bring you a little daughter three weeks old?
Nathan. How? what?   Well, frankly—it is true.
Friar. Ay, look upon me here.   That groom am I.
Nathan. You are?
Friar.   The lord from whom I bro't you her
Was, 'less I err, one lord Von Filnek.   Wolf Von Filnek!
Nathan. Right!   Yes; it was so.
Friar.   For the mother died
In bringing her to birth, and the sad father
Was called all suddenly to march 'gainst Gaza,
Where the poor worm could not accompany,
So sent her unto you.   And met I not
With you in Darun?
Nathan.   Right, quite right!
Friar.   It were
No wonder if my memory should deceive me.
I've had so many masters, and with him
I served so short a term; soon after this
He dwelt at Ascalon; he was to me
Ever a gracious master.
Nathan.   A man indeed!
Whom I have much to thank for; from my head
Not once but many times he warded off
The spear's thrust.
Friar.   Beautiful!   More gladly, then,
To your good care you took his little one.
Nathan. That you may well believe.
Friar.   Where is it, then?
You will not, surely, say the babe is dead?
O let it not be dead!   If only none
Knows of the matter.   There are other ways.
Nathan. What are these ways you mean?
Friar.   Come, Nathan, trust me!
For see, this is my notion; if the good
That I intend to do should touch too close
On what is evil, rather I refrain
From the good deed; for what is ill we can
Without much dubitation recognise,
But not so well what's good.   'Twas natural,
Quite natural, that if the Christian babe
You meant to bring up well and happily

It should be as your own; no unjust claim.
Have you then done so, with a faithful love,
With father-care, to be rewarded thus?
That rings not true to me.   Surely more wise,
More prudent had it been, by other's hand
To have reared up the Christian little one
In Christian faith; but then you had not loved
Your friend's dear babe.   And tender babes need love,
Were 't even a wild beast's love, in their first years,
More than they need our Christianity.
For Christianity there's always time
If the girl only sound in body and soul
Grows up before your eyes, then in God's sight
What she was first, remains she.   And has not
The Christian doctrine, after all, been built
Upon the Jewish?   It has often vexed me,
Has often verily cost me tears to think
That Christians could so utterly forget
The Lord of their Redemption was a Jew.

Nathan. Good brother, you must be my advocate
If hatred and hypocrisy should rise
Against me for one act—ah, for one act!
You only, you alone must know of it.
But take the secret with you to your grave!
For never yet did vanity persuade me
To tell it to another.   To you alone
I tell it.   Pious simpleness alone
Shall hear it.   For simplicity alone
Can understand the wondrous recompense
The godly man may earn for loving deeds.

Friar. I see you moved, a tear stands in your eye.

Nathan. You met with me at Darun with the babe,
Perchance you know not that three days before
In Gath the Christians murdered every Jew,
Man, woman, child of them; perchance know not,
That among these my wife, and with her, too,
Seven hopeful sons were numbered, seven sons,
Who in my brother's house had taken refuge,
Were all together burned.

Friar.   My God, my God!

Nathan. And when you came I'd lain three days and nights
In dust and ashes before God and wept.
Wept?   More; had pleaded, argued it with God,

Raged, stormed, and cursed me and the world;
Sworn to all Christians and their faith a hate
Unquenchable—
Friar.   Ah, I can well believe it !
Nathan. Yet reason by degree came back to me.
She spoke with gentle voice, " And yet God is !
This, too, is the decree of God !   Well, then,
Come, practise what thou long hast understood ;
Which of a surety is not harder than
It is to understand, if thou but wilt.
Rise up."   I rose and cried to God, " I will !
If thou wilt that I will ! "   And at that moment
Did you dismount and handed me the babe
Wrapt in your mantle.   What you told me then
And what I answered, I've forgotten—quite,
Only this much I know : I took the child,
Laid it upon my couch, kissed its soft cheek,
Kneeled on the ground, and sighed " O God, for seven
Already one Thou givest ! "
Friar.   Nathan !   Nathan !
You are a Christian !   By God, you are a Christian !
No truer ever was !
Nathan.   Happy for us,
That what to you makes me a Christian, so
Makes you to me a Jew.   But let us not
Thus make each other weak.   Here we must act !
And though a sevenfold love hath bound me fast
To this lone stranger maiden, though the thought
Already kills me that once more in her
I am to lose my sons—if Providence
Again require her of me—I obey !
Friar. 'Tis finished !   Even the course I have longed
To prompt you to, your own good heart has chosen.
Nathan. Yet it must be no rash first-comer think
To tear her from me !
Friar.   No, truly, God forbid !
Nathan. Whoso hath not a greater right than I,
Must have at least an earlier. . . .
Friar.   Verily !
Nathan. Which blood and Nature warrant.
Friar.   Even so,
That's my thought, too.
Nathan.   Come, then, name me the man

Who stands to her related, brother or uncle,
Cousin, or by what other tie of blood;
From him I'll not withhold her—her so fit,
Created, reared, to be the ornament
Of any house or any faith on earth.
I hope, of this your master and his kin
That you know more than I.

Friar.   No, hardly that,
Good Nathan, you've already heard how short
My time of service with him.

Nathan.   Yet at least
You surely know of what house or what race
Her mother was? Was she, too, not a Stauffen?

Friar. Quite possible. Indeed, I think 'twas so.

Nathan. Was not her brother, that's Conrad von Stauffen,
A Templar?

Friar.   Yes, unless my memory cheats me.
But hold! It comes to me I have a book,
A tiny book belonging to my master,
Still in my hands; I drew it from his bosom
When he was laid in earth at Ascalon.

Nathan. Well?

Friar. 'Tis a book of prayers; a breviary, we call it.
This, tho't I, may a Christian man still use
Unshamed—though really I—I cannot read——

Nathan. No matter! Tell me more.

Friar.   In this small book
First leaf and last, written in his own hand,
There are inscribed the names of all his kin.

Nathan. O blessed news! Go! run! fetch me the volume.
I'll buy it from you with its weight in gold,
And add a thousand thanks. O hasten! run!

Friar. Right willingly—But it's in Arabic
All that my master wrote in't.   [*Exit.*

Nathan.   That's all one.
But bring it only. God! if yet I might
Keep the dear child, and such a son-in-law
Win in addition! if I might! But now
Let be what will be. Who can it have been
Played the informer with the Patriarch?
I must not fail to ask. Could it be Daja?

SCENE VIII

Daja and Nathan

Daja. [*Entering in haste, agitated.*] Nathan, only think !
Nathan.   Well, what has happened ?
Daja.   The poor child
  Was fearfully alarmed when she was called—
  She has been sent for . . .
Nathan.   Who ?   The Patriarch ?
Daja. The Princess Sittah, sister of the Sultan.
Nathan. And not the Patriarch ?
Daja.   No, Sittah !   Hear you not ?
  The Princess Sittah sends and bids her come.
Nathan. Whom ?   Recha ?   Well, if Sittah sends for her,
  And not the Patriarch . . .
Daja.   Why think of him ?
Nathan. Have you of late not heard from him ?   In truth ?
  Nor whispered to him something ?
Daja.   I ? to him ?
Nathan. Where are the messengers ?
Daja.   They stand without.
Nathan. Then for precaution I myself will see them.
  Come you !   If only nothing lurks behind,
  From him.   [*Exit.*
Daja.   And I—I fear quite other things.
  Forsooth, an only daughter of a Jew
  So rich as Nathan is, were no ill match
  Even for a Mussulman.   It is over,
  All over with the Templar, unless I
  Can dare the second step and to herself
  Discover who she is.   Courage, my heart !
  Let me but use the moment well, when next
  I have her by myself, and that may be
  At once, when I accompany her.   A first hint
  At random dropped can do at least no harm.
  Yes, yes ! 'tis now or never !   Boldly on ! [*Follows Nathan.*

ACT V—Scene I

Room in Saladin's Palace, to which the sacks of money were borne,
where they still lie

Saladin, and soon thereafter several Mamelukes

Saladin. [*In entering.*] There stands the gold then still.   And
  none knows where
  To find Al-Hafi, who most probably
  Is somewhere set a fixture at the chess
  Ev'n of himself oblivious, and if so
  Why not of me?   But, patience !   Ho, what now?
A Mameluke. The wished-for tidings, Sultan !   Sultan, joy !
  The caravan is come from Kahira ;
  Safely arrived, with seven years' tribute drawn
  From plenteous Nile.
Saladin.   Bravo, my Ibrahim !
  Thou art indeed a welcome messenger !
  Ha !   Ha !   at last !   at last !   Your Sultan's thanks
  For the good news.
Mameluke. [*Waiting.*] (Well then, come on with it.)
Saladin. Why waitest?   Thou mayst go.
Mameluke.   And nothing more
  By way of welcome?
Saladin.   What?
Mameluke.   To messenger
  No message-fee?   Then I should be the first
  Saladin learned i' th' end to pay with words.
  This is itself a name :   To be the first
  With whom he played the niggard !
Saladin.   Take thou then
  One of the sacks there.
Mameluke.   No, not now !   Thou might'st
  Wish to bestow them all on me.
Saladin.   What pride !
  Come here !   There hast thou two.—In earnest?   Going?
  Out-do me in your magnanimity?
  For sure it costs thee much more to decline
  Than me to give.   O Ibrahim !   What evil chance
  Should thus befall me, thus, so short a time
  Before my going hence, to change my nature?
  Will Saladin not die as Saladin?
  Then neither must he live as Saladin.

2nd Mameluke. Ho ! Sultan !
Saladin.   If thou comest to announce . . .
2nd Mameluke. The caravan from Egypt is arrived !
Saladin.   I know it.
2nd Mameluke. Came I then too late ?
Saladin.   Wherefore
  Too late ?   Take for good-will one or two sacks.
2nd Mameluke. Say three.
Saladin.   I see that you can reckon !   Take them—
2nd Mameluke. There still will come a third, if come he can !
Saladin. How so ?
2nd Mameluke.   How so ?   Most like he broke his neck !
  We three were watching at the water-gate.
  No sooner sighted we the caravan
  Than each man sprang and hasted, sinews strained,
  Up the long road.   The foremost fell, and I
  Won to the front and kept it till we reached
  The City, but there Ibrahim, the scamp,
  Knows street and alley better.
Saladin.   O, he fell !
  Was hurt, perhaps !   Go, friend, ride out to meet him.
2nd Mameluke. That certainly I will, and if he live
  Half of these sacks I'll gladly render him.   [*Exit.*
Saladin. See, what a gallant, noble carle even he !
  And who but me can boast such Mamelukes ?
  And were it not permitted me to think
  That my example helps them ?   Perish the thought
  That at the last they must accustom them
  To quite another sort.
3rd Mameluke.   Hail to thee, Sultan !
Saladin. Art thou the man who fell ?
3rd Mameluke.   No, lord, I come
  To tell thee Emir Mansor, leader of
  The caravan, has dismounted.
Saladin.   Bring him in !
  Ah, he is here !

SCENE II

Emir Mansor and Saladin

Saladin.   Welcome, my Emir !   Well,
  How has all gone ?—Oh, Mansor, Mansor, long
  We've waited thee . . .

Mansor.   This letter will inform you,
   What unrest in Thebais first your captain,
   Your Abdul Kassem, had to quell by battle,
   Ere we could venture to begin the journey,
   The march thereafter I did expedite
   As much as possible—
Saladin.   Trust you for that !
   And now, good Mansor, take without delay . . .
   This, too, thou wilt do gladly . . . wilt collect
   Fresh escort, for at once thou must away
   On further travel, carry the best part
   Of this rich treasure to my father's hold
   On Lebanon.
Mansor.   Most gladly will I do it !
Saladin. And take thou not an escort over weak.
   On Lebanon things are not quite so safe.
   You've heard ?   The Templars are once more afoot.
   Be well upon your guard !   But come—where halts
   The train ? for I must see it, and myself
   Set all in motion.   Then I go to Sittah.

SCENE III

*The Palms near Nathan's house, where the Templar is walking up
and down*

Templar. His house I will not enter ; I'm resolved—
   He'll show himself at last.   How quickly, gladly,
   They used to notice me at this same spot.
   But I may still survive it, if he cease
   To hunt me as he used when I came near.
   Hm !   I am vexed at heart.   What is the cause
   Of my embitterment ?   Sure, he said " yes " ;
   Nor ever yet has he denied me.   Saladin
   Hath promised, too, to bring him to accord.
   Maybe the Christian roots in me more deep
   Than does the Jew in him.   Who knows himself ?
   How otherwise should I so grudge to him
   The little prey he took occasion once
   To stalk down in the Christians' hunting-ground ?
   No little prey, indeed !   That noble creature !
   Creature, but whose ?   O surely not the slave's
   Who set afloat upon life's weary shore

The block, and then made off.   Surely the artist's
Rather, who in the abandoned block perceived
The god-like form within and bro't it forth
By his so potent art?   Recha's true father
Remains, spite of the Christian who begot her,
For evermore this Jew.   So when I think
Of her as merely Christian girl, without
All graces which she only could derive
From such a Jew's upbringing, what, my heart,
Could then in her be found to please thee so?
Nothing, or little!   Even her smile, were that
More than the soft, sweet quivering of a muscle;
Perchance what makes her smile not worth the charm
In which it clothes itself upon her lips;—
No; not her smile even!   For I've seen it spent
In greater charm on idle jest and folly,
On mockery, on flatterer and admirer.
Has it then taken me captive, and inspired
The wish to flutter life away in its
Sweet sunny beams?   In faith, I cannot tell.
And yet I am at odds with him who gave,
Yes, gave alone this higher worth to her,—
How so, and why?   Have I then earned that laugh
Of Saladin at parting?   Bad enough
To think that Saladin conceived me so!
How small he must have thought me, despicable!
And all about a girl.   It must not be,
Curd, Curd, it shall not be.   Then turn and take
Another road.   May it not be that all
That Daja spoke was only idle talk,
And difficult to prove?—See, there at last
He comes, in eager converse, from his house!
Converse, with whom?   With him? with my old friar?
Ha! then he knows it all, and is betrayed
Already to the Patriarch.   What have I wrought
In my perversity!   O that one spark,
One little flash of passion, should avail
To burn away our brain's best elements!
Resolve and quickly what must now be done,
And here aside I'll wait them, if perhaps
By happy chance the friar quit his presence.

Scene IV

Nathan and the Friar

Nathan. [*As he approaches.*]   Once more, good friar, take my
   utmost thanks !
Friar. And you the like, sir !
Nathan.   I ? from you ? for what ?
   For my self-will, that I thus push upon you
   What you've no use for ?   Yes, if but your will
   Had yielded to me, but with all your heart
   You strove against being rich, more rich than I.
Friar. The book, besides, does not belong to me,
   But to the daughter :—it is surely hers,
   The daughter's sole paternal heritage.—
   Of course, she has yourself.   And God forbid
   That you should ever rue t' have done so much
   For her.
Nathan.   That I shall never, never !   Fear not that.
Friar. Ah but ! the Templars and the Patriarchs . . .
Nathan. Whatever harm they do me cannot make
   Me rue what I have done : say nought of that !
   And are you then so perfectly assured
   It was a Templar set the Patriarch on ?
Friar. Can hardly be another.   For a Templar
   Shortly before was with him, what I heard
   Seemed to confirm it.
Nathan.   There is only one
   In all Jerusalem, and him I know—
   He is my friend, a frank and noble youth.
Friar. Quite so ; 'tis he !   But what one is, and what
   The world makes of one, are not quite the same.
Nathan. Alas ! 'tis true !—Let whomsoever do
   His worst or best !   For, friar, with your book
   I can defy them all and go straightway
   Therewith to Saladin.
Friar.   Much luck to you,
   And now I'll say farewell.
Nathan.   And even yet
   You have not seen her—Come again and soon.
   If only nought come to the Patriarch's ear—
   Yet what of that ?   To-day tell what you please.
Friar. Not I !   Farewell.   [*Exit.*

Nathan.   Forget us not, my brother !
God ! I could sink down, under open heavens,
Upon my knees ! to see the threatening knot
That often has appalled me of itself
Unloosen ! God ! How light I feel me now
Since there is nothing further in the world
I have to hide ! and even as in Thy sight
Can walk in men's sight too, who judge a man,
Must judge, by deeds alone.

SCENE V

Nathan and the Templar, who comes forward to meet him

Templar. Ho ! wait me, Nathan ; take me with you.
Nathan.   What !
Sir Knight, I thought to meet you at the Sultan's,
Where have you hid yourself ?
Templar.   O, we have missed
Each other ; do not take it ill.
Nathan.   Not I,
But Saladin . . .
Templar.   You had just left his presence . . .
Nathan. You saw him, then ? 'Tis well.
Templar.   It is his wish
To speak with us together.
Nathan.   All the better,
Come, I was now upon my way to him.
Templar. May I ask, Nathan, who it was that now
Parted with you ?
Nathan.   You do not know the man, then ?
Templar. Was't not that honest father, the lay-brother,
The good retriever that the Patriarch
Likes to make use of ?
Nathan.   Maybe ; he is lodged
Certainly with the Patriarch.
Templar.   No bad trick,
To send simplicity to clear the way
For rascaldom.
Nathan.   Ah, yes, the silly, not the pious.
Templar. No Patriarch believes in piety.
Nathan.   For him
I would go surety. He will give no aid

To 's Patriarch in any villainy.

Templar. At least he so professes.   But did he
Say nothing to you about me?

Nathan.   Of you?
Well, not indeed of you by name; in fact
He hardly knows your name.

Templar.   Hardly, says he?

Nathan. Of a certain Templar, to be sure, he did
Say something . . .

Templar.   What was it?

Nathan.   Something by which
He once for all cannot mean you, my friend.

Templar. Who knows?   But let us hear it.

Nathan.   'Twas that one
Accused me to the Patriarch.

Templar.   Accused you?
Accused?   That is, with his good leave, a lie!
Now hear me, Nathan!   I am not the man
To shuffle and equivocate.   No, what
I have done, I have done.   Nor am I either
One to defend as well done all he does.
Why should I die for shame of one sole fault,
Having the firm resolve to make it good?
And know I not, forsooth, how far repentance
May yet advance a man?   Hear me, Nathan!
I am in truth the Templar named by him,
The friar, am he who did accuse you, doubtless,—
And you yourself know what it was that vexed me,
What made the blood boil in my every vein,
Fool that I am!   I came, my heart aflame
To throw me in your arms.   How you received me!
How coldly, how lukewarmly, which is worse,
Much worse than coldly; and how sedulous
You were to show me out with formal phrase;
And how for answer you did stave me off
With questions all irrelevant, that now,
Even now I cannot think of and be calm—
Still hear me, Nathan!   In my yeasty mood
Came Daja, whispering to my willing ear,
And threw your cherished secret at my head,
Which seemed to me to hold the explanation
Of your mysterious bearing.

Nathan.   How so?   Why?

Templar. Still bear with me !   Yes, I imagined then
 That what one day you captured from the Christians,
 You would not willingly lose to a Christian—
 And the thought came to me to put the knife
 To your throat straightway. . . .
Nathan.   Templar, was it good ?
Templar. Yet hear me, Nathan !   O without a doubt
 I then did wrong ; there was no guilt in you.
 That foolish Daja knows not what she speaks,
 She hates you, and only seeks to entangle you
 In dangerous business—O maybe, maybe !
 But I'm a fool, raving now here, now there,
 Now doing far too much, now far too little—
 And so it maybe now.   Forgive me, Nathan.
Nathan. If this is what you think me.
Templar.   In a word,
 I sought the Patriarch—but have not named you.
 That is a lie, I say again.   I put the case
 Just as a general problem, so to have
 His mind upon it.   Even that, I know,
 I might have left unspoken ; better so !
 For knew I not the Patriarch already,
 The knave he is ? and could I not myself
 Have bro't it home to you ?   How need I, then,
 Bring the defenceless maiden to the danger
 Of losing such a father ?—Well, what next ?
 The Patriarch's knavery, ever the same,
 Has bro't me to myself the shortest way—
 For, hear me, Nathan ; listen, and hear me out !
 Granted, he knew your name—even what of that ?
 He's only able to take the girl from you
 If she be yours alone and not another's ;
 From *your* house only can he drag her off
 Into his cloisters.   So give her to me,
 Give her to me only ; and let him come.
 Ha ! let him try that game, to take my wife
 From me.—Give her to me and quickly.   Whether
 She be your daughter now, or she be not !
 A Jewess, or a Christian or what else !
 All's one !   All's one !   I will not, either now
 Or in my life henceforward, question you
 Upon the matter.   Be it as it will.
Nathan. Perhaps you fancy it were very needful

For me to hide the truth?
Templar.   Be it as 't will!
Nathan. I have not yet to you or any man
  Who had the right to know denied the fact
  That she's a Christian born, and is no more
  Than foster-daughter to me. Wherefore, then,
  You say, remains it undisclosed to her?
  For that—to her alone need I excuse—
Templar. And such excuse you need not even with her—
  Grant to her yet that she may never look
  With other eyes upon you. Spare her yet,
  O spare her the disclosure. You alone,
  You only, have to deal with her as yet.
  Give her to me, I pray you, Nathan, I
  Alone can save you her a second time,
  And will save.
Nathan.   Ah! You could! You could! but now
  No longer can. It is too late for that.
Templar. How so, too late?
Nathan.   Thanks to the Patriarch . . .
Templar. The Patriarch? Thanks? thank him? For what?
  Does he wish to earn our thanks? For what?
Nathan. That we now know to whom she is related,
  Now know to whose hands she can be delivered.
Templar. He who would thank him for yet further good,
  Thank him for this!
Nathan.   'Tis from those hands that now
  You must receive her, not from mine.
Templar.   Poor Recha!
  How all things thrust at you, poor Recha! What
  Were luck for other orphans still becomes
  Ill-luck for you—and, Nathan, where are they,
  These kinsfolk?
Nathan.   Where they are?
Templar.   And who they are?
Nathan. A brother in especial has been found
  It is to him that you must sue for her.
Templar. A brother! What is he, this brother? Soldier
  Or churchman? Let me hear what 'tis I may
  Promise myself.
Nathan.   Of these two I fancy
  He's both or neither. As yet I cannot say
  I know him well.

Templar.   And otherwise?
Nathan.   Most worthy!
  One with whom Recha will agree right well.
Templar. But yet, a Christian!   Now, really at times
  I hardly know what I should think of you :—
  Take it not ill, friend Nathan—Will she not
  Be forced to play the Christian, among Christians?
  And what for long enough she will have played,
  She will at last become.   Will not the tares
  Spring up to choke the pure wheat you have sown?
  And that scarce troubles you.   For, spite of that,
  You still can say that they'll agree right well,
  Sister and brother?
Nathan. So I think and hope!
  If she miss aught with him, does she not know
  She still has you and me, her friends for ever?
Templar. What can she miss with him?   Will not this brother
  With food and clothing, finery and sweetmeats
  Richly enough provide her?   What then more
  Can little sister want?   Oh, certainly,
  A husband!   Well, him too, him too will brother
  Find in good time!   One's always to be found.
  The better the more Christian!   Nathan!   Nathan!
  O what a perfect angle you had formed,
  Whom others now will have the chance to spoil!
Nathan. No fear of that : the man will prove himself
  Worthy of all our love.
Templar.   O say not that,
  Of *my* love say not that, which fills my soul
  As nothing small or great can share with it :
  But stop!   Doth she suspect already aught
  Of what is coming?
Nathan.   Maybe, although I know not
  Whence she might learn it.
Templar.   That's all one!   She shall,
  She must, in either case, know first from me
  What 'tis her fate portends—And so my thought
  Never to see her, or speak with her at all
  Till I could call her mine—that thought is dead.
  I hasten . . .
Nathan.   Stop, whither so fast?
Templar.   To her!
  To see whether this maiden soul is not

P

Yet Man enough, to take the one resolve
    Worthy of her.
Nathan.   Which is?
Templar.   This, now no more
    To ask of you or of her brother aught—
Nathan. And?
Templar.   Then to follow me, even if she had
    Thereby to be wife to a Mussulman.
Nathan. Remain : you will not meet her, she is now
    With Sittah, sister of the Sultan.
Templar.   Why?
    Since when?
Nathan.   And if you'ld find at the same place
    The brother that we spoke of,—come with me.
Templar. The brother? which? Sittah's or Recha's, say?
Nathan. Why, both mayhap. Come only : I pray you, come!

SCENE VI

In Sittah's harem. Sittah and Recha engaged in conversation

Sittah. How glad I am to know you, my sweet girl!
    But look not so oppressed, so shy and timid!
    Be merry. Come, speak freely; I'm your friend.
Recha. O Princess . . .
Sittah.   No! don't call me Princess, call me
    Sittah, your friend, your sister, call me rather
    Your little mother—That's what I should like
    To be to you—so young, so good, so clever!
    What you must know, how much you must have read!
Recha. Read? Sittah, now you mock your silly sister;
    Why, I can hardly read.
Sittah.   "Hardly." Romancer!
Recha. My father's hand a little. But I thought
    You spoke of books.
Sittah.   Why, certainly; of books.
Recha. Now, I find books so really hard to read.
Sittah. In earnest?
Recha.   Quite. My father loves not much
    That cold book-learning, which dead letters cram
    Into the brain.
Sittah.   What! is it so? Indeed,
    He's not far wrong. And yet the thousand things

You know!
Recha.   I only know them from his mouth,
My father, and of most of them I still could tell
How, where and why he taught me.
Sittah.   Everything
Cleaves better so, the whole soul learns at once.
Recha. I'm sure that Sittah, too, has read but little.
Sittah. How so? If so, I am not proud of it.
Why think you so? What reason—now speak out!
Recha. You are so genuine, so unaffected, so . . .
Well, always like yourself. . . .
Sittah.   Well?
Recha.   Books, you know,
Too seldom leave us so, my father says—
Sittah. Ah, what a man your father is!
Recha.   Ah, yes!
Sittah. How sure his hand and eye, they never fail.
Recha. 'Tis true, 'tis true, and this my father . . .
Sittah. What ails you, dear one?
Recha.   O my father!
Sittah.   God!
You weep!
Recha.   My father—father—it must out!
My heart is bursting—give me air—I faint!
        [*Throws herself, weeping unrestrainedly, at Sittah's feet.*
Sittah. Child, what has happened? Recha!
Recha.   I must lose him!
Sittah. You? lose him? What means this? Dear child, be
    calm!
O never, never! Rise, and tell me all.
Recha. In vain your vow is made to be my friend,
My sister.
Sittah.   So I am, I am. Only rise up.
Else must I call for help.
Recha. [*Controlling herself and rising.*] Forgive! forgive!
My pain made me forgetful who you are.
In Sittah's presence no moaning is of use,
And no despair. Reason calm and cold
Alone has power upon her spirit. He
Whose cause has that to aid him will prevail.
Sittah. I understand not.
Recha.   O do not suffer it,
My friend, my sister, never suffer it—

Another father to be forced upon me !
Sittah. Another father ! forced upon you ? Who can
    Do that or even think of doing it, my dear one ?
Recha. Who ? 'Tis my good, my wicked Daja, thinks
    And more than thinks the deed, can do it. Ah !
    You do not know her, this my good, my wicked Daja.
    Well, God forgive it her—and recompense her !
    She has shown me so much good, and so much evil.
Sittah. Evil to you. Then verily little good
    Can live in her.
Recha.   Oh, yes, much good, much good—
Sittah. Who is she ?
Recha.   'Tis a Christian lady who
    Has tended me from childhood, cherished me
    With care so tender that I never missed
    A mother's love. God make it good to her !
    And yet distressed me too, and tortured me !
Sittah. And why, and in what matter ? Tell me, how ?
Recha. Ah ! the poor lady—let me tell you all—
    She is a Christian—tortures me from love ;
    Is one of those enthusiasts who dream
    They know, they only, the true way to God—
Sittah. I understand . . .
Recha.   And feel themselves compelled
    To lead all others who have missed this way
    Back to the same—and scarcely can do other—
    For be it true this way alone can be
    The way of safety, can they be content
    To see their friends upon another road,
    Which leads to loss, to everlasting loss ?
    Thus is it possible, for the self-same people,
    And at the self-same time, to love and hate.
    Yet even this is not what forces from me
    Bitter complaint against her. For her sighs,
    Her warnings and her prayers, her menaces—
    I could have gladly borne—yes, willingly,
    For they have brought ever to my mind such thoughts
    As do one good. And whom does it not flatter
    At heart to find oneself so prized and dear
    To whomsoever that they can't bear the thought
    Of everlasting severance.
Sittah.   That is true !
Recha. But there is something else that goes too far,

For which I have no mental remedy,
Which patience cures not, nor reflection soothes,
Nothing!

Sittah.   What's that?
Recha.   What she just now disclosed.
Sittah. Disclosed, and now?
Recha.   This very moment did.
On our way here we passed a Christian temple,
A ruin. Suddenly she stood still and seemed
To struggle with herself, with tear-dimmed eyes
She looked up first to Heaven, and then on me.
" Come, dear," she said at last, " the shorter way
Which passes through this temple will we take."
She goes; I follow her; my awe-struck gaze
Fixed on the tottering ruin. Now again
She stands; I look and find myself with her
On sunken steps of an altar all-decayed. . . .
How think you 'twas with me, when with hot tears
And claspèd hands she fell before me there,
Lying at my feet. . . .

Sittah.   O Recha, my poor child!
Recha. And by the Almighty, who so many a prayer
Had heard there, and so many a wonder wrought
Besought me to have pity on myself—
At least to pardon, if she must disclose
The claim her church had on me—she went on—
Sittah. O you unhappy one—'twas my foreboding!
Recha. I was of Christian blood; had been baptized;
And was not Nathan's daughter—he not my father!
God! God! he not my father! Sittah! Sittah!
See me again all prostrate at your feet. . . .
Sittah. Recha! Not now; rise up.—My brother comes!

SCENE VII

Saladin and the foregoing

Saladin. What's wrong, here, Sittah?
Sittah.   She is not herself.
Saladin. Who is it?
Sittah.   Ah, you know . . .
Saladin.   Our Nathan's daughter?

What's wrong?

Sittah.   Come to yourself, my child ! The Sultan . . .

Recha. [*Dragging herself on her knees to the Sultan's feet, her head
   bent to the ground.*] I rise not, cannot rise, and cannot see
   The Sultan's countenance, cannot behold
   The bright reflection of eternal justice
   And goodness in his eyes, and on his brow,
   Until . . .

Saladin.   Stand up !

Recha.   Until he promise me . . .

Saladin. Come, then, I promise, be it what it will.

Recha. Not more nor less, to leave to me my father
   And me to him ! Nor know I not who else
   Desires to be my father or can desire it.
   I do not want to know. But is 't alone
   The blood that makes the father, only blood?

Saladin. [*Raising her up.*] I see it all ! Who was so cruel, then,
   To put such fancies in your head. Is this,
   Then, quite already settled, and proved true ?

Recha. O, surely ; Daja has it from my nurse.

Saladin. Your nurse ?

Recha.   Who dying told to her the secret.

Saladin. Oh, dying. Perhaps drivelling too ? And were it
   Even true—You know, the blood, the blood alone
   Can never make the father, hardly makes
   The father of a beast, but gives at best
   The foremost right to earn the name indeed.
   Then be not yet affrighted—cast off fears !
   Hearken, what think you ? When the fathers twain
   Contend for you, leave both, and take a third !
   Take me, then, for your father.

Sittah.   Oh, yes, yes !

Saladin. A right good father I will be to you !
   But stop ! I've thought of something better still.
   What need have you of fathers, after all ?
   Suppose they die ? Let's look about in time
   For one who can keep step with us in living !
   Know you of none ?

Sittah.   Now, do not make her blush !

Saladin. That is exactly what I want to do :
   For blushing makes the ugliest beautiful,
   And will it not make fairer yet the fair ?
   I have your father Nathan here by me

And one besides—bethink you, can you guess?
Hither? If you'll permit me only, Sittah?
Sittah. My brother!
Saladin.   Will you blush before him now?
Recha. Before whom? Blushing?
Saladin.   . . . Little Hypocrite!
Well, then, go pale instead! Even as you will
And can, too.
              [*A female slave steps in and approaches Sittah.*
              What, already are they here?
Sittah. Good; let them enter.—Brother, it is they.

SCENE VIII AND LAST

Nathan and the Templar to the foregoing

Saladin. Welcome, my dear good friends! Nathan, to you,
To you before all else 'tis duty and joy
To tell you that as soon as pleases you,
Your gold can be restored. . . .
Nathan.   Nay, Sultan, nay!
Saladin. Yea, more, am now prepared to further you—
Nathan. Sultan!
Saladin. My caravan is here, and I am rich
Beyond my hopes, richer than e'er I was.
Come, tell me, is there no fine enterprise
Where I can help you, something great? I know
Of ready cash you cannot have too much,
You merchant people!
Nathan.   And why speak you first
Of such a trifle? I see there an eye
In tears; to dry them touches me more closely,
                              [*Goes to Recha.*
You've wept? And why—You still are mine?
Recha.   My father!
Nathan. We understand each other: so, enough!
Be cheerful; be composed. If still your heart
Remains your own! And if no other loss
Does threaten it; for sure your father is
Still yours, unlost!
Recha.   O no, no other loss!
Templar. No loss besides? Then I myself have cheated—
What one fears not to lose, one never thought

That one has held or ever wished to hold—
Let be !—let be ! Nathan, this alters all !
O Saladin, we came at your command,
But now I see I have misled you quite,
Trouble yourself no more !

Saladin.   Young man, again
You puzzle me : and are we bound to read
The riddle that you set ?

Templar.   Sultan, you see,
You hear, is 't not enough ?

Saladin.   Ay, verily ;
'Tis bad enough that you were not more sure
Of what concerns you most.

Templar.   I am sure *now !*

Saladin. He who presumes upon a good deed done,
Takes it all back.   What you have saved is not
Therefore your own possession.   Otherwise
The thief whose greed bade plunge into the fire,
He were your rival here !

             [*Going to Recha, to lead her to the Templar.*
                    Come, dear maid,
Come, judge him not so strictly.   He would be
Another, if he were less warm and proud :
He would have let it be, the saving you.
Set one thing 'gainst another.   Make him shamed !
Do that which would become him best to do,
Confess your love to him ! offer yourself !
And if he should disdain you, or forget
How far, far more in this you do for him
Than what he did for you. . . . What has he then
Done for you !   Let himself be scorched a trifle !
Is that so much ? . . . then say I he has nothing
Of my dear brother's nature, of my Assad,
He bears about his mask but not his heart.
Come, dear one . . .

Sittah.   Go, my dear one, go !   It is
But little this—to tell your gratitude ;
I call it nought.

Nathan.   Stop, Saladin !   Stop, Sittah !

Saladin. You, too ?

Nathan.   Here's one more still to speak a word. . . .

Saladin. Who questions that ?   To such a foster-father
A voice belongs of right ; yea, the first voice—

Hear me; I know the matter through and through.
Nathan. Nay, not yet all.   I speak not of myself.
   There is another, whom, O Saladin,
   I beg you first to hear.
Saladin.   And who is he?
Nathan. Her brother.
Saladin.   Brother of Recha?
Nathan.   Yes.
Recha. My brother?   Have I indeed a brother?
Templar.   Where?
   Where is this brother?   Is he here?   'Tis here
   That I should meet him.
Nathan.   Patience only!
Templar. [*Bitterly.*]   He
   Has found a father to her—will he not
   Contrive to find a brother?
Saladin.   Only that
   Was wanting!   Christian, such a low
   Suspicion had not crossed my Assad's lips.
   Good!   But continue, Nathan!   Pardon him!
Nathan. I do forgive him freely——who can say
   What we in his place, at his age had thought?
                         [*Going to him in friendly manner.*
   Suspicion, Knight, must follow on distrust;
   If you had only granted me to know
   Your true name from the first . . .
Templar.   How?
Nathan.   You're no Stauffen!
Templar. Who am I, then?
Nathan.   Your name's not Curd von Stauffen.
Templar. And what, then, is my name?
Nathan.   'Tis Len von Filnek.
Templar. What?
Nathan.   See, you start!
Templar.   With reason!   Who says so?
Nathan. I; I, who more, much more, can tell you, but
   Accuse you of no lie.
Templar.   No?
Nathan.   'Twell may be
   The other name is also yours of right.
Templar. That I should think!
                     (*Aside :* God gave that word to him.)
Nathan. For, you must hear—your mother was a Stauffen.

Her brother, he who brought you up from childhood,
To whom your parents trusted you in Germany
When, driven from it by the troubled skies,
They landed here for refuge—he was named
Conrad von Stauffen, may have made you child
Of his adoption.   Is it long ago
Since you came hither with him?   Lives he still?

Templar. What shall I say?   It is so, truly, Nathan,
Himself is dead.   I came here with the last
Reinforcement of our Order.   But all this—
What of it—when we speak of Recha's brother?

Nathan. Your father . . .

Templar.   How?   Have you, then, known my father?
Him also?

Nathan.   Yes, my much-loved friend he was—

Templar. He was your friend?   Nathan, is 't possible?

Nathan. Called himself Wolf von Filnek; but was not
A German.

Templar.   Know you that, too?

Nathan.   Yes, he had
A German wife, and only for short time
Accompanied her to Germany. . . .

Templar.   No more,
I beg—but Recha's brother?   Recha's brother?

Nathan. Are you !

Templar.   I?   I her brother?

Recha.   He my brother?

Sittah. Both of one house.

Saladin.   One house !

Recha. [*Going towards him*.] Ah, brother mine !

Templar. [*Drawing back*.] Her brother !

Recha. It can't be, can't be, his heart
Knows nought of it.—We are impostors—God !

Saladin. [*To the Templar*.] Impostors?   How? what think you?
can you think it?
Yourself are an impostor—all things false
In you—face, voice, and bearing !   Nothing yours !
Not to know such a sister.   Templar, go !

Templar. [*Approaching him humbly*.]
Misread not, Sultan, my astonishment !
Mistake not in a moment one in whom
You think that nought of Assad can be seen,
Both him and me !   , [*Hastening to Nathan*.

You give to me and take ;
Both, Nathan, with full hands.   No, no ; you give
More than you take ! yes, infinitely more !
                    [*Falling on Recha's neck.*
Dear sister, sister mine !
Nathan.   Blanda von Filnek !
Templar. Blanda?   Blanda? and not Recha ! no more
Your Recha?   God !   You disinherit her !
You give her back her Christian name and place,
You cast her off for me—O Nathan, Nathan !
Why should she thus atone—why, Nathan, why?
Nathan. Atone? for what?   My children, O my children !
Shall not my daughter's brother be my child,
He also, when he will ?
    [*While he surrenders himself to their embrace, Saladin in
        restless amazement steps up to his sister.*
Saladin.   What say you, sister ?
Sittah. I am so moved to see them—
Saladin.   And I before
Greater emotion still almost recoil—
Brace you against it firmly as you can.
Sittah. How ?
Saladin.   Nathan, but one word with you, one word !
    [*While Nathan approaches him, Sittah goes to the brother and
        sister to express her sympathy, and Nathan and Saladin
        whisper.*
Hear me now, Nathan ! have you told them yet ?
Nathan. What?   That her father was no German born ?
Saladin. What was he, then ?   What other land can claim
him ?
Nathan. That's what himself would never trust me with :
Out of his lips I know no whit of that.
Saladin. And was he then no Frank, no Westerner ?
Nathan. O that he was not that, he freely granted.
He oftenest spoke Persian.
Saladin.   Persian !   Persian !
What need I more assurance ?   It was he !
Nathan. Who, then ?
Saladin.   My brother—O quite certainly
My Assad, 'twas my Assad, without doubt.
Nathan. Well, since yourself have lighted on the fact,
Take confirmation of it from this book !
                    [*Handing him the breviary.*

Saladin. [*Examining it eagerly.*] Ah, his own hand !   That, too,
   I know again !
Nathan. They yet know nothing, rests with you alone
   To tell them what this book contains for them.
Saladin. [*Turning the leaves.*] Shall I acknowledge not my
   brother's children ?
   My nephews not acknowledge—not, my children ?
   Not recognise them ?   Leave them all to you ?   [*Aloud again.*
   'Tis they ! my Sittah, it is they in truth.
   Both of them children of our brother Assad !
                                        [*He runs into their embraces.*
Sittah. [*Following him.*] What do I hear ?   'Twere right no other
   way !
Saladin. [*To the Templar.*] And, proud one, you must love me
   after all !   [*To Recha.*
   Now I'm in fact what I proposed myself,
   Whether you will, or not !
Sittah.   I too !   I too !
Saladin. [*Turning to Templar again.*] My son ! my Assad's son !
   my son, my son !
Templar. I of your blood !   So were those dreams of old
   With which they rocked my infancy to sleep
   Much more than dreams !   [*Falling at his feet.*
Saladin. [*Raising him up.*]   Look at the rascal now !
   Somewhat he knew and yet would have allowed
   Even me to be his murderer—Ah, but wait !

          [*Amidst silent renewal of embraces the*
                    CURTAIN
                 falls.]

MINNA VON BARNHELM

OR

SOLDIERS' FORTUNE

A COMEDY IN FIVE ACTS

BY

GOTTHOLD EPHRAIM LESSING

PERSONS

MAJOR VON TELLHEIM, retired.
MINNA VON BARNHELM.
COUNT BRUCHSALL, her uncle.
FRANCISCA, her lady's maid and companion.
JUST, the Major's servant.
PAUL WERNER, former Sergeant-Major in Tellheim's Regiment.
THE LANDLORD.
A LADY IN MOURNING.
AN ORDERLY.
RICCAUT DE LA MARLINIÈRE.

The Scene is alternately in the Salon of an Inn and a room adjoining.

ACT I—SCENE I

Just. [*Sits in a corner asleep and speaks in his dream.*] Beast!
Beast of a landlord! To us, would you? Look alive, mate!
lay on, mate! [*Draws and wakes up in moving.*] Hullo, there
again! I can't close an eye, but I'm scrapping with him. If
he only had a half of the whacks! . . . But there, it's daylight! Almost time to call my poor master. If I'd my way,
he'd never set foot more in this accursed house. Where can
he have passed the night, I wonder?

SCENE II.

The Landlord.   Just

Landlord. Good morning, Mr. Just, good morning! What, up
so early? Or am I to say, still up, so late?

Just. Say whatever you like.

Landlord. I say nothing but good morning, and that surely
deserves a thank you from Mr. Just.

Just. A thank you!

Landlord. A man is always peevish when he hasn't his proper
sleep. How comes it, the Major hasn't come in? You've
been waiting for him here?

Just. You're first-rate at riddles!

Landlord. I can guess; I can guess.

Just. [*Turning his back and going.*] I'm off!

Landlord. [*Detaining him.*] Not yet, Mr. Just! Eh, surely
you're not still angry, I hope, from yesterday? Who would
keep his anger over the night?

Just. I would; and over all nights to follow.

Landlord. Is that Christian?

Just. As Christian every bit as to turn out of the house, into the
street, an honourable man, because he can't pay on the nail.

Landlord. Shame! Who could be so godless?

Just. A Christian landlord. . . . My master! a man like that!
an officer like that!

223

Landlord. Him have I pushed out of the house? thrown him on
the street? For that, I have far too much respect for an
officer, and far too much pity for a man discharged. I was
obliged to prepare another apartment for him. . . . Think no
more about it, Mr. Just. [*Shouts from the door.*] Hullo ! . . .
I'll make it good another way. [*A boy comes.*] Fetch a glass ;
Mr. Just will take a glass, bring something good !

Just. Don't trouble, Mr. Landlord. The drop would turn to
poison, and—— But I won't take an oath on it ; I've had no
breakfast yet.

Landlord. [*To the boy who brings a bottle of liqueur and glass.*] Give
it here ; go ! Now, Mr. Just : something first-rate ; strong,
sound and tasty. [*Fills the glass and hands it out to him.*]
That will put your innards right in a jiffy !

Just. I almost wouldn't ! . . . But, but—why is *my* stomach to
suffer for *his* insolence? . . . [*He takes it and drinks it off.*]

Landlord. Good health, Mr. Just !

Just. [*Giving the glass back.*] Not bad !—But, Mr. Landlord, you
are still a ruffian !

Landlord. Wait a bit, wait a bit ! One more, quick ! Standing
on one leg is no good.

Just. [*After drinking.*] I must say that's good, first-class !—
Your own brew, Mr. Landlord?

Landlord. Preserve me ! No ! real Danziger double-distilled !

Just. Look here, landlord ; if I could play the hypocrite, it
would be for stuff like that ; but I can't ; it must out. You
are still a ruffian, Mr. Landlord !

Landlord. Never in my life has anyone called me that.—One
more, Mr. Just : all good things are three !

Just. As you like ! [*Drinks*]. Good stuff ! jolly good stuff !—
But the truth, too, is good stuff. Mr. Landlord, you are still a
ruffian !

Landlord. If I were, would I listen to that as I do?

Just. O yes ; there's seldom pluck in a ruffian.

Landlord. Not just one more, Sergeant? A fourfold cord holds
fast.

Just. No, too much is too much ! And what does it help you,
Mr. Landlord? To the very last drop in the flask I would
stick to my word. Shame, Mr. Landlord, to have such good
Danziger and such bad manners ! A man like my master,
who has lived at your house a year and a day, from whom
you've had many a fine dollar, who all his life has never owed
anybody anything ; now, because a couple of months his

payments have been less prompt and he has not spent so freely, you clear out his apartment in his absence.

Landlord. But what if I was compelled to make use of the room? What if I knew quite well that the Major would willingly himself have seen it cleared out, had we only been able to wait for his return? Was I then to turn away an illustrious visitor from my door? Was I wilfully to throw such good business into the jaws of another landlord? And I don't believe for a moment that she could have found an apartment anywhere else in the place. The hotels are chock-full. Was a lady, so young, beautiful, amiable, to be denied admittance? Your master is a good deal too gallant for that! And, after all, what has he lost? Have I not arranged another room in place of it?

Just. Yes, in the top floor back, with a view of the neighbours' chimney-pots . . .

Landlord. The outlook was really quite pretty before my awful neighbour built it up. Otherwise the room is quite elegant, and papered too . . .

Just. Has been !

Landlord. No, no, one wall is so still. And the little room adjoining, Mr. Just; what's the matter with it? It has a fireplace, smokes a bit, no doubt, in winter . . .

Just. But still in summer is quite capital—Sir, I really believe you grudge us even that.

Landlord. Now, now, Mr. Just, Mr. Just . . .

Just. Don't make Mr. Just's head warm, or . . .

Landlord. I make you warm? That's not me! it's the Danziger!

Just. An officer like my master! Or do you think that a retired officer is no longer an officer, who can break your neck? Why were you then in wartime so ready, so obliging, you landlord gentlemen? Why was every officer then a worthy man, and every soldier an honourable gallant fellow? Does the little bit of peace make you so insolent all at once?

Landlord. Why excite yourself so now, Mr. Just?

Just. I *will* excite myself.

Scene III

Tellheim.　The Landlord.　Just.

Tellheim. [*In entering.*] Just!

Just. [*Thinking the landlord has called him.*] Just?—so familiar are we?

Q

Tellheim. Just !

Just. I fancied I was *Mr.* Just for you !

Landlord. [*Who has seen the Major.*] St ! st ! look about you, Mr. Just ; your master . . .

Tellheim. Just, I believe you're squabbling ? Do you remember my orders ?

Landlord. O, your Honour ! squabble ? Heaven forbid ! Your Honour's most obedient servant venture to squabble with one who has the happiness to belong to you ?

Just. O to give him one over his humpback !

Landlord. It's true, Mr. Just speaks for his master, and a bit hotly. But in that he's quite right. I esteem him for it ; I love him for it.

Just. O to give him a punch in the jaw !

Landlord. Pity only that he excites himself for nothing. For I am quite sure your Honour will not take offence, because necessity—er—er—obliged me to . . .

Tellheim. Say no more, my good sir ! I am in your debt : you clear out, in my absence, my apartment ; you must be paid ; I must find another lodging. Quite natural !

Landlord. Another lodging ! You will leave me, your Honour ! I'm lost ! I'm ruined ! No, never ! The lady rather must quit. The Major will not, cannot give up his apartment : it is his ; she must out ; I can't help her—I go, you Honour . . .

Tellheim. No, friend, not two stupid tricks for one ! The lady must remain in possession.

Landlord. And your Honour is to imagine that I, out of distrust, out of anxiety for my money . . . ? As if I did not know that your Grace can pay me whenever you will. Er—er—the sealed packet—" 500 louis-d'or " written on it—er—er—which your Grace had put in the desk—er—is in good keeping.

Tellheim. That I will hope ; like the rest of my things. Just shall take charge of it when he pays your bill.

Landlord. Certainly I got a fright when I came across the packet.—I have always taken your Grace for an orderly, provident man, who never spent all he'd got.—But still—er— er—if I had thought there was ready cash in the desk . . .

Tellheim. You would have treated me more politely. I understand you—Only go now, my good sir ; leave me ; I have to speak with my servant.

Landlord. But, your honour . . .

Tellheim. Come, Just, this gentleman will not permit me to say to you in this house what you are to do. . . .

Landlord. I go at once, your Honour ! My whole house is at your service. [*Exit.*]

SCENE IV

Tellheim. Just.

Just. [*Stamping his foot and spitting after the landlord.*] Faugh !

Tellheim. What's the matter?

Just. I'm choking with rage.

Tellheim. That's as bad as with apoplexy.

Just. And you, sir—I don't know you, my brave master. May I die at your feet if you aren't the guardian angel of this malicious merciless rascal ! Spite of gallows or rack, I could throttle him with these hands, tear him with these teeth.

Tellheim. Don't be a brute !

Just. Better a brute than a fellow like that !

Tellheim. What is it you want, then?

Just. I want you to feel how much you are insulted.

Tellheim. And then?

Just. To avenge yourself—No, the fellow is too small for you ...

Tellheim. But, perhaps, that I should lay it on *you* to avenge me? That was my idea, too. He should not see my face again, and should get his money from your hands. I know you could throw him the handful of coin with a pretty contemptuous look.

Just. So? A fine revenge, that !

Tellheim. But one we must still postpone. I haven't a heller of ready money left ! and don't know how to raise any.

Just. No ready money? What kind of packet is that, then, of 500 louis-d'or which the landlord found in your desk?

Tellheim. That is money entrusted to me for safe keeping.

Just. Surely not the 100 pistoles which your old Sergeant-Major brought you four or five weeks ago?

Tellheim. The same; from Paul Werner. Why not?

Just. Those you haven't used yet? With those, sir, you can do as you like. On my responsibility . . .

Tellheim. Really?

Just. Werner heard from me how wretchedly they teased you about your claims on the Army Treasury. He heard . . .

Tellheim. That I certainly would be made a beggar, if I weren't one already. I am much obliged to you, Just.—And this report of yours induced Werner to share his little bit of poverty with me.—I'm rather glad I've guessed it.—Mr. Just,

make out your own bill at the same time; we are parted
men.

Just. How? What?

Tellheim. Not another word; there's someone coming . . .

Scene V

A Lady in Mourning. Tellheim. Just.

Lady. I beg your pardon, sir !

Tellheim. Whom are you seeking, Madam?

Lady. The very gentleman with whom I have the honour to
speak. You do not remember me? I am the widow of
your former Captain of horse. . . .

Tellheim. Good heavens, my dear Madam ! What a change !

Lady. I've just risen from the sickbed on which the pain of my
husband's loss laid me ! I fear that I am boring you, Major.
I'm going into the country, where a good-hearted but not at
all wealthy friend has offered me a refuge to begin with.

Tellheim. [*To Just.*] Go; leave us for the present.

Scene VI

The Lady. Tellheim.

Tellheim. Speak freely, my good lady. Before me you need
not be ashamed of your ill fortune. Can I help you in
anything?

Lady. I—I—Major ! . . .

Tellheim. I pity you very much, my dear Madame ! In what
can I serve you? You know your husband was a friend of
mine; my *friend*, I say, and I was never lavish with that title.

Lady. Who knows better than I how worthy you were of his
friendship, how worthy he was of yours? You would have
been his last thought, your name the last sound on his dying
lips, had not Nature herself reserved this sad privilege for his
unhappy son, his unhappy wife . . .

Tellheim. Cease, my good Madame ! I would willingly weep
with you; but to-day I have no tears. Spare me ! You find
me in an hour when I might easily be betrayed into murmuring
against Providence. . . . Oh, my honest Marloff ! Quickly
tell me, Madame, what are your commands? If I am in a
position to serve you, if I am . . .

Lady. I must not set out till I have fulfilled his last request. He called to mind just before his end that he was dying your debtor, and implored me to settle this debt with the first ready money.   I have sold his equipment and am come to take up his note.

Tellheim. How, my good lady?   Have you come here for that?

Lady. Exactly.   Permit me to count out the money.

Tellheim. Just a moment, Madame!   Marloff my debtor? That can hardly be.   But let me see. [*Takes out his pocketbook and makes a search.*] I find nothing.

Lady. You have probably mislaid the note, and the note does not matter in the least.   Permit me . . .

Tellheim. No, Madame!   such things I don't usually mislay.   If I haven't got it, that's proof I never had it, or that it was settled, and already given up.

Lady. But . . . but . . . Major!

Tellheim. My dear Madame, it's quite certain.   Marloff owed me nothing.   I cannot even recall that he was ever my debtor. Quite surely, Madame.   On the contrary, he has left me his debtor.   I have never been able to do enough to be quits with a man who for six years shared with me good fortune and ill, honour and danger.   I shall not forget that he has left a son.   He shall be my son, so soon as I can act the father to him.   The difficulties in which I find myself at this moment. . . .

Lady. You noble-minded man!   But do not think too meanly of me.   Take the money, Major; I shall then be at ease about it.

Tellheim. What more do you require for that than the assurance that this money does not belong to me?   Or is it your wish that I should rob the orphan of my friend?   *Rob,* Madame: that it would be and nothing else.   To him it belongs; lay it by for him. . . .

Lady. I understand you; forgive me only if I don't quite know how one should accept benefits.   How comes it that you have found out that a mother will do more for her son than she would for her own life?   I go . . .

Tellheim. Yes, Madame, go, and a happy journey to you!   I do not ask you to send me news of you.   It might arrive at a moment when I could not make use of it.   But there is still another thing, my good lady; I had almost forgotten the most important of all.   Marloff has still claims against the treasury of our former regiment.   His claims are as good as mine are.

If mine be met, his must be met too. I'll be security for that . . . .

Lady. O! my dear sir, but I had rather be silent. So to prepare future benefits is in the eye of God to have already bestowed them. Receive His reward and forgive my tears! [*Exit.*]

SCENE VII

Tellheim. Poor, brave woman! I must not forget to destroy the note. [*Takes from pocket-book papers, which he tears up.*] Who can guarantee that my own need might not some day betray me into making use of it.

SCENE VIII

Just. Tellheim

Tellheim. Are you there?

Just. Yes, sir. [*Wiping his eyes.*]

Tellheim. You've been crying?

Just. I've been making out my bill in the kitchen, and the kitchen is full of smoke. This is it, sir!

Tellheim. Hand it here.

Just. Have pity on me, sir. I know very well people have none for you; but . . .

Tellheim. What do you want?

Just. I'd have sooner expected my death than my dismissal.

Tellheim. I can no longer employ you; I must learn to get along without servants. [*Takes up the bill and reads.*] "*What the Major owes me*: Three and a half months' wages at 6 Thalers a month, makes 21 Thalers. Expended sundries since 1st. instant 1 Thaler, 7 Gr., 9 Pf. Total 22 Thalers, 7 Gr., 9 Pf."—Very good, and it is reasonable that I should pay you the whole of the current month.

Just. Turn over—the other side, Major . . .

Tellheim. O, more? [*Reads.*] "*What I owe the Major*: Paid the army-surgeon on my behalf, 25 Thalers. For nursing and attendance during my sickness, paid for me, 39 Thalers. To my father, raided and burnt out of house and home, remitted at my petition, without reckoning the two captured horses which he sent him, 50 Thalers. Total 114 Thalers. Deducted therefrom the aforesaid 22 Thalers, 7 Gr., 9 Pf., Remains due to Major Tellheim, 91 Thalers, 16 Gr., 3 Pf." You're cracked, man !

Just. I quite believe I've cost you much more. But it would be waste of ink to add it. I can't pay it you; and if you take the livery from me altogether, which, too, I haven't yet earned; you should have let me die in hospital.

Tellheim. What do you take me for? You owe me nothing, and I will recommend you to one of my acquaintances, with whom you will fare better than with me.

Just. I owe you nothing, and still you will drive me away?

Tellheim. Because I don't wish to owe *you* anything.

Just. Is that why? Only that? As surely as I owe much to you, and you nothing to me, so surely you shall not drive me away.—Do what you will, Major : I stop with you; I must stop with you.

Tellheim. And your obstinacy, your defiance, your violent, savage bearing to everybody, your mischievous joy in other people's misfortunes, your revengeful temper . . .

Just. Make me out as bad as you like, I won't for all that think worse of myself than of my dog. Last winter I was walking by the canal in the twilight and heard something whimper. I got down and grabbed at the voice, thinking to rescue a child, and drew a poodle out of the water. Still, "Worth it," thought I. The poodle followed me; but I am no lover of poodles. I chased him away. No use ! I whipped him away. No use! I would not let him be in my room o' nights : he remained on the doorstep. When he came too close to me, I gave him a kick : he howled, looked at me, and wagged his tail. Till this hour he has got not a bit of bread from my hand; and yet I'm the only one he listens to, the only one who dare touch him. He runs in front of me, and shows off his tricks unasked for. He's an ugly poodle, but as good a dog as can be. If he keeps it up I shall have to leave off hating poodles.

Tellheim. [*Aside.*] So will I with him. No, there is nobody altogether inhuman !—Just, we'll stick together.

Just. Rather ! You, sir, manage without a servant? You forget your wounds and that you are lame of an arm. You can't even dress yourself without help. I am indispensable; and am—without cracking myself up, Major—I'm a servant who, if the worst comes to the worst, can both beg and steal for his master.

Tellheim. Just, I'm afraid we *must* part.
Just. That's all right, sir !

Scene IX

A Man-servant. Tellheim. Just.

Servant. Hist ! mate !

Just. What's up?

Servant. Can you, perhaps, bring me to the officer who yesterday occupied this room here? [*Pointing to the one adjoining, from which he has just entered.*]

Just. That's easy. What do you bring him?

Servant. What we always bring when we bring nothing : a compliment. My lady hears that he has been crowded out on her account. My lady knows her manners, and I am to express her regrets to him.

Just. Express them, then ; there he stands.

Servant. What is he? What does one call him?

Tellheim. My friend, I have heard your message. It is a superfluous politeness on the part of her ladyship, which I recognise as I ought. Give her my compliments. What is her ladyship's name?

Servant. What is her name? She calls herself simply Mademoiselle.

Tellheim. And her family name?

Servant. That I've not heard yet, and it's not my business to enquire. I manage generally to have a new master or mistress every six weeks or so. Deuce take all their names !

Just. Bravo, mate !

Servant. To this lady I came first in Dresden a few days ago. She is seeking here, I believe, her fiancé.

Tellheim. Enough, my friend. I wanted to know her ladyship's name; but not her secrets. You may go !

Servant. [*To Just.*] No master that for me, mate !

Scene X

Tellheim. Just.

Tellheim. Arrange, Just, for our getting out of this house. The politeness of the lady visitor affects me more than the brutality of the landlord. Here, take this ring—the only valuable I have left; I had never imagined making such a use of it. Pledge it; ask 80 Friedrichs-d'or for it. The landlord's bill can hardly be more than 30. Pay him, and take away my things—but whereto? . . . Yes . . . Wherever you like. The cheaper the inn, the better. You will find me at the coffee-house close by. I'm off. Manage the business well.

Just. Don't be afraid, Major ! That will be all right.

Tellheim. [*Returning.*] Whatever you do, see that my pistoles are not forgotten : the sack is hanging behind the bed.

Just. I won't forget anything.

Tellheim. [*Coming back again.*] One thing more : be sure to take your poodle along with you; don't forget.

Scene XI

Just. The poodle *will* not be left behind. I can trust him for that. Hem ! the master had the costly ring still, then? and carried it in his pocket instead of on his finger? Good landlord, we are not so bare as we look. I will pledge you with *him* and with nobody else, you lovely little ring. I know he is wild, because you are not to be all spent in his house ! . . .

Scene XII

Paul Werner. Just.

Just. Hullo, Werner ! Come in, Werner ! Welcome to the town !

Werner. The confounded village ! Do what I may, I can't get used to it again. Cheerio, boys, cheerio ! I bring fresh coin. Where is the Major?

Just. He must have passed you; went down the stair this moment.

Werner. I came up the back way. Well, how is he? I should have been with you a week ago; but . . .

Just. Why? what kept you?

Werner. . . . Just, have you ever heard of Prince Heraclius?

Just. Heraclius? I can't think.

Werner. Don't you know the great hero of the East?

Just. The wise men from the East I know well enough who run about after the Star at Christmas.

Werner. Man, I don't believe you read the papers any more
than the Bible.   Don't know Prince Heraclius? the brave man
who has seized Persia and next week will burst the Ottoman
Porte open?   God be thanked there's still war in the world
somewhere !   I have long enough been hoping to see it break
out again in this quarter.   But there they sit, taking care
of their skins.   No ! soldier I was, and soldier I want to be.
One word [*Looking round shyly whether anyone is listening*]
in confidence, Just; I'm off to Persia, to make a couple of
campaigns against the Turks, under His Royal Highness the
Prince Heraclius.

Just. You?

Werner. Yes, I, as you see me here !   Our forefathers constantly
marched against the Turks, and so should we, if we were
honest chaps and good Christians.   Of course, I understand all
right that a campaign against the Turks can't be half so jolly
as one against the French ; but just for that reason it must be
more profitable both in this life and that which is to come.
Your Turks have, every man of them, their sabres set with
diamonds.

Just. In order to have my head split by a sabre like that I
wouldn't go a mile.   You're not going to be mad and leave
your beautiful farm?

Werner. O ! that I'm taking with me !   What do *you* think ?—
The estate is sold . . .

Just. Sold?

Werner. Hist !—I've 100 ducats here, which I got at the sale ;
I'm taking them to the Major . . .

Just. And what is he to do with them?

Werner. What's he to do with them?   Spend them shall he ;
gamble or drink with them—as he pleases.   The man must
have money, and it is bad enough that they make his own so
sour for him !   But I know fine what I should do in his
place !   I should say, " The devil fetch all you people here.
I'm off with Paul Werner to Persia ! "   Damn it all ! The
Prince must surely have heard of Major Tellheim ; even if he
doesn't know his former sergeant-major, Paul Werner.   Our
affair at the Cats-Houses . . .

Just. Shall I tell you that story?

Werner. *You* tell *me*?   I perceive your heart is better than your
head.   I won't cast my pearls before swine.   Here, take the
100 ducats ; give them to the Major.   Tell him to lay them
by for me.   I am going down now to the market ; I have sent

a couple of uniforms there; what I get for them, he can have as well. . . .

Just. Werner, you're a good-hearted fellow; but we can't take your money. Keep your ducats, and your hundred pistoles you can have, too, untouched, as soon as you like.

Werner. So? Has the Major still got some money, then?

Just. No.

Werner. Has he borrowed any?

Just. No.

Werner. Then what does he live on?

Just. We have it on credit, and when they will give us no more credit and show us the door, we pawn what we still have, and proceed. Hearken, Paul, we must play this landlord a trick.

Werner. Has he been annoying the Major? I'm in!

Just. How would it be if we fell upon him in the dusk when he's coming out of the smoking-room and gave him a good thrashing?

Werner. In the dark? Fell upon him? Two on one? That's no good.

Just. Or, if we burned his house over his head?

Werner. Raid and fire? Man, one can tell you've been a baggage rascal, and not a soldier. Faugh!

Just. Or if we played Don Juan with his girl? Though of course she's deuced ugly . . .

Werner. O, that will have happened long ago. Anyway, you need no assistance for that. But what's the matter? What's up?

Just. Come only. There's a surprise in store for you!

Werner. What, is the devil at large hereabouts?

Just. Rather! Come only!

Werner. So much the better! And then—to Persia!

ACT II—Scene I

Minna von Barnhelm. Francisca.

The scene is in Mademoiselle's room

Mademoiselle. [*In négligé, looking at her watch.*] Francisca, we must have got up very early. Time will hang on our hands.

Francisca. Who can sleep in these confounded big towns? The coaches, the watchmen, the drums, the cats, the corporals—there's no end to their rattling, screaming, drumming, mewing, cursing ; exactly as if the night were meant for anything rather than rest.—A cup of tea, Mademoiselle ?

Mad. I hate tea.

Franc. I'll have some of our chocolate made . . .

Mad. Very well.   For yourself ?

Franc. For myself ?   I'd as lief talk for myself alone as drink for myself alone.   Certainly time will hang on our hands. Presently we must dress, and have to settle in what gown we shall deliver the first assault.

Mad. Why talk of assaults when I've only come to demand the terms of capitulation ?

Franc. And Mr. Officer, whom we drove out, and to whom we sent apologies ; he can't be a gentleman of the best breeding, or he would before now have begged permission to call on us.

Mad. All officers are not Tellheims.   To tell you the truth, I only sent him that apology in order to have the opportunity of enquiring of him about our friend.   Francisca, my heart tells me that our journey will be lucky, that I shall find him.

Franc. Your heart, mademoiselle ?   One shouldn't trust one's heart too much.   The heart flatters our wishes a bit.   If mouths were as ready to flatter as our hearts, it would have been fashion long ago to put them under lock and key.

Mad. Ha ! ha ! with your mouth under lock and key ! The fashion wouldn't be amiss !

Franc. Better keep the prettiest teeth hidden than let one's heart jump over them every second.

Mad. What ?   Are you so reserved as that ?

Franc. No, Mademoiselle ; but I should like to be.   We seldom speak of the virtues we have ; but so much the oftener of those we want.

Mad. Do you know, Francisca, you have made a very capital remark.

Franc. Made ?   Does one *make* what just comes in one's head ?

Mad. And do you know why really I find your remark so good ? It is because it has much bearing on my Tellheim.

Franc. But with you what would not have a bearing on him ?

Mad. Both friends and enemies say he is the bravest man in the world.   But who has ever at any time heard him talk of bravery ?   He has a heart made of integrity, but integrity and magnanimity are words never upon his lips.

Franc. What kind of virtues, then, does he speak of ?

Mad. He speaks of none, for he has them all.

Franc. That's what I wanted you to say.

Mad. Wait, Francisca; I remember now. He does speak, often, of economy. Between ourselves, Francisca, I believe the man is a spendthrift.

Franc. Another thing, Mademoiselle. I have very often heard him speak to you of fidelity and constancy. How if he were fickle?

Mad. You miserable creature!—But do you mean that in earnest, Francisca?

Franc. How long is it now since he wrote to you?

Mad. Ah! Since the Peace he has only written me once.

Franc. A sigh even against Peace! Wonderful! Peace ought only to make good again the ill which war has caused, and instead it destroys even the good which its opposite may have brought about. Peace should not be so capricious! And for how long have we had peace now? Time will be beastly long if it bring so little news. What good the post being all right, again! Nobody writes, for nobody has anything to write about.

Mad. "It is peace," he wrote me, "and I approach the fulfilment of my wishes." But, that he has written only once, only one single letter . . .

Franc. That he compels us ourselves to hasten to meet this "fulfilment of wishes." Let us find him only; he will have to pay for that! What if meantime the man had fulfilled all wishes, and we learned here . . .

Mad. [*Anxiously and passionately.*] That he was dead?

Franc. For you, Mademoiselle; in the arms of another.

Mad. Tormentor! Wait, Francisca, he will pay you out for this! But keep on talking, or we shall fall asleep again. His regiment was broken up at the Peace. Who knows into what confusion of accounts and claims that brought him? Who knows to what other regiment or to what outlying province he may have been assigned? Who knows what circumstances—— Someone knocks.

Franc. Come in!

Scene II

The Landlord.   The Same

Landlord. [*Sticking his head in.*] May I come in, your Ladyship?

Franc. Our good landlord?—Just come right in.

Landlord. [*A pen behind his ear, a sheet of paper and ink-stand in his hand.*] I come, your Ladyship, to wish you a humble good morning, and you, too, my pretty child . . .

Franc. A polite man !

Mad. We thank you.

Franc. And wish you, too, a good morning.

Landlord. May I venture to enquire how your Ladyship has rested the first night under my poor roof ?

Franc. The roof is not so bad, landlord ; but the beds might have been better.

Landlord. What do I hear ? Not rested well ? Perhaps the excessive fatigue of the journey . . .

Mad. It may be.

Landlord. Certain, certain ! For otherwise—— Meanwhile, should anything have been not quite to your Ladyship's satisfaction you need only to give your commands.

Franc. Very good, landlord ! We are not at all shy ; and least of all must one be shy in an inn. We shall tell you right out how we want things.

Landlord. And now, at the same time I . . . [*Taking the pen from behind his ear.*]

Franc. Well ?

Landlord. Doubtless your Ladyship is aware of the wise precautions of our police.

Mad. Not in the least, Mr. Landlord . . .

Landlord. We landlords are directed to house no stranger of whatever rank or station for four-and-twenty hours without reporting in the proper quarter in writing his name, home, character, business here, probable duration of stay, and so on.

Mad. Quite right.

Landlord. Your Ladyship, therefore, will perhaps be good enough. [*Stepping to a table and preparing to write.*]

Mad. O, certainly—My name . . .

Landlord. One little moment, if you please . . . [*He writes.*] " Date, the 22nd August, arrived here at the King of Spain."—Now your names, your Ladyship.

Mad. Mademoiselle von Barnhelm.

Landlord. [*Writing.*] " von Barnhelm." Coming ? From where, your Ladyship ?

Mad. From my estates in Saxony.

Landlord. [*Writing.*] " Estates in Saxony." From Saxony ! Ay, ay ! from Saxony, your Ladyship ? From Saxony ?

Franc. Well, why not ? Is it perhaps a sin in these parts to be from Saxony ?

Landlord. A sin ? Preserve us ! that would be a new sort of sin !—From Saxony, then ? Ay, ay ? from Saxony—dear

old Saxony ! But, if I'm right, Saxony is a big place, and has
several—what shall I say ? districts, provinces.—Our police
are very particular, your Ladyship. . . .

Mad. I see ; from my estates in Thüringen, then.

Landlord. From Thüringen ! That's better, your Ladyship ;
more exact. [*Writes and reads.*] " Mademoiselle von Barnhelm, coming from her estates in Thüringen, with a waiting-
woman and two servants."

Franc. Waiting-woman ? I'm to be that, am I ?

Landlord. Yes, my pretty child.

Franc. Now, Mr. Landlord, put down lady's maid instead :
I hear your police are very particular ; there might be a misunderstanding, and some trouble when my banns were published. For I am really only a maid yet, and my name
Francisca ; surname, Willing ; Francisca Willing. I come
from Thüringen, too. My father—on one of her Ladyship's
estates : it is called Klein-Rammsdorf. My brother has the
mill now. I came very young to the big house, and was
brought up along with her Ladyship. We are the same age ;
next Candlemas one-and-twenty. I have learnt all her
Ladyship has. I shall be delighted for the police to know all
about me.

Landlord. Good, my pretty child ; I'll make a note of it in case
of further enquiries.—But, excuse me, your Ladyship, your
present business in our town ?

Mad. My business.

Landlord. Does it concern His Majesty ?

Mad. O no !

Landlord. Or the High Court of Justice ?

Mad. Not at all.

Landlord. Or . . .

Mad. No, no. I am here purely on my own private affairs.

Landlord. Quite right, your Ladyship. But what shall we call
these private affairs ?

Mad. They are called—— Francisca, we're under cross-
examination.

Franc. Surely, Mr. Landlord, the police won't wish to learn the
secrets of a lady.

Landlord. Most certainly, my child : the police want to learn
everything, everything ; and especially secrets.

Franc. Well, now, your Ladyship, what's to be done ? Let me
tell you, then, Mr. Landlord ; but it must be between us and
the police !

Mad. What is the little fool going to tell him?

Franc. We've come to capture one of His Majesty's Officers.

Landlord. How? What? My child!

Franc. Or to let ourselves be captured by him. All the same thing.

Mad. Francisca, are you mad? Mr. Landlord, the saucy creature is pulling your leg.

Landlord. I hope not. She can joke as she pleases with your humble servant; but with the high police . . .

Mad. Do you know what, Mr. Landlord? I don't quite know how to manage this. I fancy you might leave all this registration business until my uncle arrives. I told you yesterday why he had not come with me. He had an accident with his carriage a couple of leagues from here, and was unwilling it should cost me a night's delay. I had to go on. If he is twenty-four hours behind me, that will be the outside of it.

Landlord. Very well, your Ladyship, we'll wait for his arrival.

Mad. He can answer your questions better. He will know to whom and how far he has to declare himself; what he must reveal of his affairs, and what he can keep to himself.

Landlord. So much the better! Certainly, certainly, one can't ask a young girl [*eyeing Francisca with a significant look*] to treat seriously a serious matter with serious people.

Mad. And his rooms are now all ready, landlord?

Landlord. Perfectly, your Ladyship, perfectly; all but the one . . .

Franc. From which perhaps you still have to turn out some honest gentleman?

Landlord. The lady's maids from Saxony, your Ladyship, are wonderfully sympathetic.

Mad. Still, Mr. Landlord, that wasn't right of you. Rather you should have declined to take us in.

Landlord. How so, your Ladyship, how so?

Mad. I hear that the officer whom we crowded out . . .

Landlord. Only an officer on half-pay, your Ladyship . . .

Mad. Even then!

Landlord. He's done with.

Mad. So much the worse! He may be a very worthy gentleman.

Landlord. I tell you, he is discharged.

Mad. The King can't know all deserving men.

Landlord. O certainly, he does; he knows them all.

Mad. Well, at any rate he can't reward them all.

Landlord. They would all be rewarded if they had lived so as to deserve a reward.   But during the war the gentleman lived as if war would last for ever; as if *meum* and *tuum* were for ever abolished.   Now all the inns and hotels are crammed with them; and a landlord has to mind what he's about with them.   I have come off pretty fairly with this one.   If he hadn't any money left exactly, he had at least money's worth; and I fancy I could have let him rest for two or three months yet.   All the same, better is better.   *À propos,* your Ladyship; you probably know something of jewels?

Mad. Not specially.

Landlord. What should not your Ladyship!   I must show you a ring, a costly ring.   Your Ladyship indeed has a very fine one on her finger, and the more I look at it, the more I am astonished how like it is to mine.   Just look at it, look at it! [*Taking it out of its case, and passing it to Mademoiselle.*] What fire!   the centre brilliant alone weighs over five carats.

Mad. [*Examining it.*] Where am I?   What do I see?   This ring . . .

Landlord. Would be cheap at 1500 Thalers.

Mad. Francisca!   See here!

Landlord. I didn't hesitate a moment to lend eighty pistoles on it.

Mad. Don't you recognise it, Francisca?

Franc. The identical one!   Mr. Landlord, where got you this ring?

Landlord. Well, my child?   Surely you have no property in it?

Franc. We no property in this ring?   The inside of the case must bear her Ladyship's initials.   Open it, Mademoiselle.

Mad. It is!   it is!   How did you come by this ring, landlord?

Landlord. I?   In the most honest way possible.   My Lady, my Lady, you don't want to bring me to harm?   How can I tell where the ring properly comes from?   During the war many a thing has changed its owner, with and without knowing it. War is war.   More rings than one will have crossed the border from Saxony.   Give it me again, your Ladyship, give it me again!

Franc. Tell us first from whom you got it?

Landlord. From a man whom I could not believe capable of that sort of thing; from a man in other respects good.

Mad. From the best man under the sun, if you had it from its owner.   Quick, bring the man to me!   It is he himself, or at least he must know him.

R

Landlord. Who, then—whom do you mean, your Ladyship?

Franc. Don't you hear? Why, our Major.

Landlord. Major? Right, he is a Major, who occupied this room before you, and from whom I had it.

Mad. Major von Tellheim?

Landlord. von Tellheim; yes! Do you know him?

Mad. If I know him? Is he here? Tellheim is here? He! He has lodged in this room? He! he has pledged this ring with you? How comes the man to be in difficulties? Where is he? Is he in debt to you? . . . Francisca, the strong-box! unlock it! [*Meanwhile Francisca sets it on the table and opens it.*] What does he owe you? To whom else is he in debt? Bring me all his creditors. Here is cash. Here are notes. All is his!

Landlord. What do I hear?

Mad. Where is he? where is he?

Landlord. An hour ago he was in this house.

Mad. Hateful man! How could you treat him so, and be so hard and inhuman?

Landlord. If your Ladyship will pardon me . . .

Mad. Quick! let him come here immediately.

Landlord. His servant is perhaps still in the house. Would your Ladyship wish that he should fetch him?

Mad. *If* I wish? Hurry, man, run; for this service alone I will forget how badly you have treated him. . . .

Franc. Look alive, Mr. Landlord; quick, be off with you! [*Pushes him out.*]

SCENE III

Mademoiselle. Francisca

Mad. Now I have him once more, Francisca! Look you, I have him once more! I don't know where I am for joy! Do rejoice with me, Francisca. But, after all, why should you? Yet you should, you *must* rejoice with me. Come, my dear, do, and I'll give you a present so that you shall. Say, Francisca, what shall it be? Which of my things suits you best? Take what you like; only rejoice with me. I see, though, you won't take anything. Wait! [*She searches in her satchel.*] There, my dear [*giving her money*]; but what would please you. Ask me for more, if it doesn't run to it. Only rejoice with me. It is poor business, being glad by oneself. Well, take this now. . . .

Franc. I am stealing it from you, Mademoiselle; you are drunk
with happiness. . . .

Mad. Girl, beware, I am quarrelsome drunk; take it, or [*forcing
the money into her hand*]. And if you dare to thank me !—
Wait; well that I thought of it. [*Searches once more in the
satchel for money.*] This, my dear, put on one side, for the first
poor wounded soldier who appeals to us.

SCENE IV

Landlord. Mademoiselle. Francisca

Mad. Well ?   Is he coming ?

Landlord. The obstinate boor !

Mad. Who ?

Landlord. His man.   He declines to take the message.

Franc. Just bring the rascal here.   I know all the Major's
servants quite well.   Which of them can it be ?

Mad. Bring him to us at once.   When he sees us he'll go fast
enough.   [*Exit landlord.*

SCENE V

Mademoiselle. Francisca

Mad. I can't wait a moment.   But, Francisca, you are so
wretchedly cool.   Don't you want to rejoice with me ?

Franc. I want to very much; if only . . .

Mad. If only ?

Franc. We have found the man again.   But how have we
found him ?   By all we hear it must be going very badly with
him.   He must be in trouble.   *That* makes me sad.

Mad. Makes you sad ?   Let me hug you for that, my dear old
playfellow !   I will never forget that.   I am only in love,
but you are good . . .

SCENE VI

Landlord. Just. The Same

Landlord. I've had trouble enough to fetch him.

Franc. A new face !   I don't know him.

Mad. My friend, are you with Major von Tellheim ?

Just. Ay.

Mad. Where is your master ?

Just. Not here.

Mad. But you know where to find him.

Just. Ay.

Mad. Will you be kind enough to fetch him at once?

Just. No.

Mad. You would do me a great favour.

Just. Ay.

Mad. And your master a service.

Just. Perhaps not.

Mad. Why do you suppose that?

Just. Aren't you the strange lady who sent him compliments this morning?

Mad. Yes.

Just. Then it is as I thought.

Mad. Does your master know my name?

Just. No, but he can't stand over-civil ladies any more than over-uncivil landlords.

Landlord. That refers to me, I suppose?

Just. Yes.

Landlord. All the same, don't let her Ladyship pay for that; fetch him as fast as you can.

Mad. [*To Francisca.*] Francisca, give him something. . . .

Franc. [*Pressing money in his hand.*] We don't want your services for nothing.

Just. And I don't want your money for no service.

Franc. One thing for the other.

Just. I can't. My master has ordered me to clear out here. That's what I'm doing, and I beg you not to keep me from the job any longer. When I've done, I will tell him sure enough that he can come here. He is just at hand at the coffee-house; and if he finds nothing better to do, he will come all right. [*Is going out.*]

Franc. Wait a moment. Her Ladyship is the Major's sister.

Mad. Yes, yes, his sister.

Just. I know better. The Major hasn't a sister. He has sent me twice in the last six months to his family in Courland. Of course, there are several sorts of sisters . . .

Franc. Impudence!

Just. One needs a bit of impudence, to run on some people's errands.   [*Exit.*

Franc. What a rascal!

Landlord. I told you so. But let him be. I know now where his master is. I will fetch him myself at once. Only, your Ladyship, I ask you most humbly to apologise for me to the

honourable Major that I was so unfortunate, against my will,
a gentleman of his distinction . . .

Mad. Go now at once, my good landlord. I will make it all
right. [*Landlord goes, and thereupon*] Francisca, run after
him : *he is not to mention my name.*

[*Exit Francisca, after the landlord.*

SCENE VII

Mademoiselle, and, later, Francisca

Mad. I have him again. . . . Am I alone? I will not be alone
to no purpose. [*Folds her hands.*] Nor am I alone ! [*Glancing
upwards.*] One thankful thought to Heaven is the best of
prayers ! I have him, I have him ! [*With outstretched arms.*]
I am happy, I am joyful ! What can the Creator more
delight to see than a joyful creature? [*Enter Francisca.*] Are
you there again, Francisca? You are sorry for him? I'm
not. Misfortune is sometimes gain. Perhaps Heaven took
everything from him, in order to return it all again *in me !*

Franc. He may be here any moment. You are still in your
négligée, your Ladyship. How if you dressed quickly?

Mad. Tut, tut ! In future he will oftener see me so, than drest.

Franc. Ah ! you know yourself, my Lady.

Mad. [*After a moment's thought.*] Really, my dear, you have
hit it again.

Franc. Beauty unadorned is adorned the most.

Mad. Must we be beautiful? I wonder. Probably it is
desirable that we should think ourselves so? No, if only I
am beautiful for him ! Francisca, if all girls are as I now
feel myself, then we are—funny things. Tender and proud,
virtuous and vain, wanton and pious—you will not understand me. I hardly understand myself—joy intoxicates,
turns one's head.

Franc. Compose yourself, my Lady ; I hear someone coming.

Mad. Compose myself? Should I receive him in composure?

SCENE VIII

Tellheim.   Landlord.   The Same

Tellheim. [*Enters, and seeing her, flies to her.*] Ah ! my Minna !—

Mad. [*Running to him.*] Ah ! my Tellheim !

Tellheim. [*Suddenly stops short and draws back.*] Forgive me, your Ladyship—to find Mademoiselle von Barnhelm here. . . .

Mad. Can't be so wholly unexpected by you? [*Drawing nearer to him while he further withdraws.*] Am I still your own Minna? Heaven forgive you rather, that I am still Mademoiselle von Barnhelm!

Tellheim. My dear Lady . . . [*Looks fixedly at the landlord and shrugs his shoulders.*]

Mad. [*Notices the landlord and motions to Francisca.*] My dear Sir . . .

Tellheim. If we are not both mistaken. . . .

Franc. Eh, Mr. Landlord, whom have you brought us? Come along, let us find the right one.

Landlord. Is it not the right one? Surely yes!

Franc. Surely no! Come on; I haven't said good morning to your little daughter yet.

Landlord. O! highly honoured. [*But not moving away.*]

Franc. [*Taking him by the arm.*] Come along, we'll make out the menu-card. Let us see what we're going to have . . .

Landlord. You are to have; first of all . . .

Franc. Hush, hush! If Mademoiselle hears now what she is to eat at noon, it's all up with her appetite. Come on, we must talk of that by ourselves. [*Drags him off.*]

Scene IX

Tellheim. Mademoiselle

Mad. Well? are we mistaken?

Tellheim. Would Heaven it were so! But there is only one, and you are she. . . .

Mad. How formal we are! What we have to say everyone may hear.

Tellheim. You *here?* What are you seeking here, your Ladyship?

Mad. I am seeking nothing now. [*Approaching him with open arms.*] All that I sought, I've found.

Tellheim. [*Withdrawing a little.*] You sought a happy man, a man worthy of your love; and find—a broken wretch.

Mad. Do you love me no longer then? and love another?

Tellheim. Ah! he never loved you, my lady, who could love another after you.

Mad. You pull only one thorn out of my soul. If I have lost

your heart, what matters it whether indifference or mightier
charms have brought me low? You love me no longer, and
yet love no other? Unhappy man, if you love nothing at
all !

Tellheim. You are right, your Ladyship : an unfortunate man
must not love. He deserves his ill-fortune if he cannot maintain this conquest over himself; if he can permit those he
loves to share in his ruin.—It's a hard conquest ! Since
reason and necessity commanded me to forget Minna von
Barnhelm, what agonies I have endured ! I was just beginning to hope these agonies would not forever be in vain; and
you appear again, my lady ! . . .

Mad. Do I understand you aright? One moment, my dear
friend; let us see where we are before we go further astray !
Will you answer me just one question?

Tellheim. Any number, Mademoiselle.

Mad. Will you answer me without any evasion or reserve?
With nothing but a bare Yes or No?

Tellheim. I will—if I can. . . .

Mad. You can. Good ! In spite of the pains you have taken
to forget me—do you still love me, Tellheim?

Tellheim. Mademoiselle, this question. . . .

Mad. You have promised to answer me with nothing but Yes
or No.

Tellheim. And added, " If I can."

Mad. You can : you must know what passes in your own heart.
Do you still love me, Tellheim? Yes or No?

Tellheim. If my heart . . .

Mad. Yes or No !

Tellheim. Well, yes !

Mad. Yes?

Tellheim. Yes, yes ! But . . .

Mad. Patience ! You still love me : that's enough for me.—
Into what a strange tone I have fallen with you ! An unpleasant, melancholy, wretched tone. I take my own again.—
Now, my dear unfortunate ! you still love me, and still have
your Minna, and are unfortunate? Listen now ! What a
silly conceited thing your Minna was—is. She actually
dreamed your whole fortune was herself. Quick, bring out,
let's see this ill-fortune of yours. She wants to try how much
she would outweigh it. Now?

Tellheim. My dear Mademoiselle, I am not given to complaining.

Mad. Very good. I too hardly know what in a soldier, save

boasting, would please me less than complaining. But there is a certain cold, casual way of speaking of his bravery and his ill-luck. . . .

Tellheim. Which yet at bottom is just bragging and complaining.

Mad. O, my dear arguer, then you should never have called yourself unhappy at all. Perfect silence, or out with everything plainly. Good sense, necessity, command you to forget me? I am a great lover of good sense. I have very great reverence for necessity. But just explain to me how sensible this good sense is, how necessary this necessity.

Tellheim. Well, then. listen, Mademoiselle. You call me Tellheim. The name is all right—but you think I am the Tellheim whom you knew in your country : the flourishing man, full of claims, full of ambitions, who was captain of his body and of his soul; before whom the gates of honour and good fortune were opening; who if he were not yet worthy of your heart and hand, might hope to grow daily worthier.—This Tellheim I am just as little as I am my own father. Both are with the past. I am Tellheim, the cashiered, the wounded in honour, the cripple, the beggar. To the one, Mademoiselle, you gave your promise; will you keep it to the other?

Mad. That sounds very tragic ! Yet, my dear friend, until I find that other again—I am so infatuated with the Tellheims—this one will do to help me in my distress.—Your hand, dear beggar ! [*Taking him by the hand.*]

Tellheim. [*Covering his face with his hat and turning away from her.*] This is too much ! Where am I ? Let me go, Mademoiselle ! Your goodness tortures me ! Let me go.

Mad. Why, why? Where would you?

Tellheim. From you !—

Mad. From me? [*Drawing his hand to her breast.*] Dreamer !

Tellheim. Despair will lay me dead at your feet.

Mad. From me?

Tellheim. Yes, from you—never, never again to see you.—Or so resolved, so firmly resolved, to do nothing base, or permit you to do anything rash. Let me go, Minna ! [*Tears himself free, and exit.*]

Mad. [*Calling after him.*] You leave Minna? Tellheim ! Tellheim !

ACT III—SCENE I

SCENE : *the Salon*

Just. [*A letter in his hand.*] Obliged to come into this damned house again ! A bit of a letter from my master to her Ladyship, who wants to be his sister. Hope nothing comes of it, or there will be no end of this letter-carrying. Should like to be rid of this thing, but don't want to enter the room again. These women-folk like asking questions as much as I hate answering them. Ha ! the door opens. Good luck ! the chamber-kitten !

SCENE II

Francisca. Just

Franc. [*Into the door from which she enters.*] Don't be afraid; I'll keep a look-out. There ! [*Seeing Just.*] I've knocked up against something already. But there's nothing to be done with that animal.

Just. Your servant . . .

Franc. I have no use for such a servant. . . .

Just. Now, now; forgive me the figure of speech ! Here's a letter from my master to her Ladyship, the Mademoiselle— *sister !* It was that, wasn't it ? *Sister.*

Franc. Give it me ! [*Snatches the letter out of his hand.*]

Just. My master begs you will be so good as to hand it to the Lady. Then will you be so good, he asks—don't you imagine anything, I won't say what . . .

Franc. Eh, well ?

Just. My master knows what's what. He knows the way to the ladies lies through the maids—so I imagine !—The maid will then be so good, my master begs—as to tell me whether he could have the pleasure of a ten minutes' chat with the maid ?

Franc. Me ?

Just. Pardon me, if I've given you the wrong title. Yes, you ! Ten minutes—no more. But alone, quite alone, *tête-à-tête.* He has something very important to tell you.

Franc. Good ! I have a good deal to say to him, too. Let him come ; I shall be at his disposal.

Just. But when may he come ? When will suit you best, young lady ? After dark, perhaps ?

Franc. What do you mean by that? Your master can come when he chooses. And now you can be off!

Just. Very glad! [*Makes as if to go.*]

Franc. Wait a second; one word more. Where are the Major's other servants?

Just. The others? Here, there and everywhere.

Franc. Where is William?

Just. His valet? The Major has dispensed with him.

Franc. So! And Philip, where is he?

Just. The game-keeper? The Major does not require him any more.

Franc. Because he doesn't shoot any more, no doubt. But Martin?

Just. The coachman? He has ridden away.

Franc. And Fritz?

Just. The footman? He is advanced.

Franc. Where were you, then, when the Major had winter quarters near us in Thüringen? You weren't with him at that time?

Just. Yes, I was; I was groom, but just then in hospital.

Franc. Groom? And what are you now?

Just. Factotum: valet and gamekeeper, footman and groom.

Franc. Well, I never! To dismiss so many smart fellows and to retain the very worst! I should like to know what he saw in you!

Just. Perhaps he found I was an honest man.

Franc. One is deuced little if one's no more than honest. William was a different sort! Did his master let him ride off?

Just. Yes, he did—as he could not prevent it.

Franc. How?

Just. O, William will gather honour on his travels. He has the master's whole stock of clothes with him.

Franc. What? He did not run off with them, did he?

Just. We can't exactly say that; but when we left Nürnberg, he did not follow us up with them.

Franc. O the villain!

Just. He was an all-round chap! Could shave, and curl, and part—and flirt. Couldn't he?

Franc. Well, at all events, if I'd been the Major I wouldn't have parted with the gamekeeper. If he didn't want him for that, he was at any rate a smart fellow. To whom did he recommend him?

Just. To the Commandant of Spandau.

Franc. The fortress? Hunting can scarcely amount to much on the walls there.

Just. O, Philip doesn't do that there either.

Franc. What, then?

Just. Drives a cart.

Franc. Drives a cart?

Just. But only for three years. He arranged a little plot in his master's regiment, and tried to get six men through the outposts. . . .

Franc. I'm amazed! The traitor!

Just. O, he's the smart chap! A gamekeeper who knows all the footpaths, all the byways through woods and marshes for fifteen miles round. And can't he shoot!

Franc. Good that the Major still has the honest coachman.

Just. But has he him?

Franc. I thought you said Martin had ridden away. Then he'll come back again?

Just. What do *you* think?

Franc. Where on earth has he ridden to?

Just. It's well on the tenth week since he rode off with the master's last horse—to the horse-pond.

Franc. And not come back yet? O the gallows-bird!

Just. The horse-pond may have swept the honest coachman away! He was a splendid coachman! He had driven ten years in Vienna. The master won't get such another in a hurry. When the horses were at full gallop he had only to say " Burr ! " and they stood still like walls, in a second. More than that, he was a qualified vet. !

Franc. And now I'm in fear over the footman's promotion.

Just. No, no, that was regular enough. He was made drummer in the garrison.

Franc. I thought so.

Just. Fritz took on with a loose fish, did not come home o' nights, made debts on all hands in his master's name and a thousand beastly tricks. In a word, the Major saw that he violently desired to be elevated [*pantomime of hanging*], so he helped him on the good way.

Franc. O the wretch!

Just. But a perfect footman he was, that's certain. If the master gave him fifty paces start, he could not catch him up with his fastest galloper. Fritz, though, may take a thousand paces start of the gallows, it will catch him up.—These were,

every man of them, your good friends, Miss? William, and
Philip, and Martin, and Fritz? Now, Just applies for the
situation !   [*Exit.*

Scene III

Francisca and later, the Landlord

Franc. [*Looking after him gravely.*] I deserve the cut ! No,
thank you, Just. I set honesty too low. I won't forget
the lesson.—Ah ! the unfortunate man ! [*Turns about and
is going towards her Ladyship's apartment, when the landlord
returns.*]

Landlord. Wait a bit, my pretty child.

Franc. I haven't time now, Mr. Landlord. . . .

Landlord. Only a little moment ! Still no further news from
the honourable Major? That could not possibly be his
farewell !

Franc. What, then?

Landlord. Has her Ladyship not told you? When I left you,
my pretty one, down in the kitchen I happened to come again
into the salon here. . . .

Franc. Happened to come, with the idea of listening a bit.

Landlord. O, my child, how can you think that of me? Nothing
fits a landlord worse than prying.—I was here only a moment
when the door jerked open of her Ladyship's room. The
Major rushed out, the lady after him ; both in an excitement,
with looks, in a situation—something indescribable. She
clasped him ; he tore himself away ; she clasped him again.
" Tellheim ! "—" My Lady ! let me go ! " Whereto? To
the very staircase he dragged her. I was in fear he'd tear her
down with him. But at last he got free. The lady remained
on the top step, looking after him, calling after him, wringing
her hands. All at once she turned about, ran to the window,
from the window again to the stair, from the stair into the
salon, up and down. Here stood I ; here she passed me three
times without seeing me. At last it seemed as if she noticed
me ; but, God bless me, I believe the lady took me for you,
my child. " Francisca," she cried, turning her eyes upon
me, " am I, then, the happy one? " Then stared at the
carpet, and, once more, " Am I indeed happy? " Wiping
tears from her eyes, she smiled, and asked me again, " Francisca, am I, then, so happy? "—Really, I hardly knew where
I was ; till she ran to her door. There she turned to me once

more with " Come along, Francisca ; whom do you pity now ?"
And with that, in !

Franc. O, Mr. Landlord, you've dreamed that.

Landlord. Dreamed ? No, my dear child : one does not dream
all those particulars.—Yes, I'd give a good deal—I don't
want to pry—but I'd give a good deal to have the key to this
business.

Franc. The key? To our door, Mr. Landlord? The key is
on the inside : we took it in last night ; we are timid.

Landlord. Not a key like that. I mean to say, my dear child,
the key . . . the interpretation as it were . . . the er—er—
explanation of all I've seen.

Franc. O, indeed ! Just so ! Well, good-bye, Mr. Landlord.
Shall we have lunch soon, Mr. Landlord ?

Landlord. My good child, not to forget what I specially wanted
to say.

Franc. Well? only be quick about it. . . .

Landlord. Her Ladyship still has my ring ; I call it mine. . . .

Franc. You shan't lose it.

Landlord. I'm not anxious about it in the least : only wanted
to remind you. See you, I don't want it any more. I can
quite well reckon on my fingers why she knew the ring and
why it was so like her own. In her hands it is in the best of
keeping. I don't want it, and meantime will put down to
her Ladyship's account the hundred pistoles I gave for it.
That's right, is it not, my child ?

Scene IV

Paul Werner. Landlord. Francisca

Werner. Here we are again !

Franc. One hundred pistoles ? *only eighty*, I thought.

Landlord. True, true, *only ninety, only ninety*. I'll do that, my
child, I'll do that.

Franc. That will be all right, Mr. Landlord.

Werner. [*Coming up closer behind them and suddenly clapping
Francisca on the shoulder.*] Little woman ! Little woman !

Franc. [*Startled.*] Hey !

Werner. Don't be frightened ! Little woman, I know you're
pretty and quite a stranger.—And pretty strangers must
have warning. Little woman, beware of the man here.
                                         [*Pointing to landlord.*

Landlord. Ha! an unexpected pleasure! Mr. Paul Werner! Welcome to my house, sir! Ah, it is still the same jolly old Werner: honest and merry as the daylight! You are to beware of me, my pretty one! Ha, ha, ha!

Werner. Keep out of *his* way, I tell you!

Landlord. Me, me! Am I so dangerous, then? Ha, ha, ha! Listen, my pretty child! How does the joke please you?

Werner. The likes of him always call it a joke when one speaks the truth.

Landlord. The truth! Ha, ha, ha! Better still, my pretty one, isn't it? The man can joke! Me dangerous? Me? Maybe twenty years ago there was something in it. Yes, yes, my pretty one, I was dangerous then—many a one could tell you that—but now . . .

Werner. O, away with all old fools!

Landlord. There it is, you see! When we get old it's all over with our dangerousness. It will turn out the same with you, Mr. Werner.

Werner. Put the snaffle on your foolery! Little woman, you will credit me with sense enough not to talk about that sort of dangerousness. The one devil has left him in order that seven others may enter into him. . . .

Landlord. O, hear now, hear now! How he turns the thing about! Joke after joke; and always something new! Oh, he is a magnificent fellow, Mr. Paul Werner! [*To Francisca, whispering.*] A well-to-do man, and still unmarried. Three miles away he has a freehold farm. Heavens! the booty that man made in the war! And became sergeant under our honourable Major. Such a friend, too, of our Major, such a friend, he would be struck dead for him any day!

Werner. Yes, and *he* too [*pointing to landlord*] is a friend of my Major! Such a friend that the Major should have him struck dead.

Landlord. How? What? No, Mr. Werner; that is not a good joke. I no friend of the honourable Major? No, I don't understand the joke.

Werner. Just has told me pretty things.

Landlord. Just? I thought as much. Just is a malicious dirty fellow. But here is a pretty child on the spot; she can speak: she will say whether I am not the Major's friend, whether I have done him no service. And why should I not be his friend? Is he not a deserving man? It is true he has had the misfortune to be retired. What does that matter? The

King cannot know all deserving men, and if he did, he still could not reward them all.

Werner. Hear his conscience talk ! But Just—of course Just is nothing very particular, but a liar Just *is* not. And if that was true which he told me . . .

Landlord. I will not hear anything of Just ! As I said, let the dear child here speak ! [*To her, in her ear.*] You know, my child, the ring ! Tell Mr. Werner about it, and then he will know me better. And so that it shan't look as if you spoke to please me, I won't be present : I won't be present—I will go. But you shall repeat my words, Mr. Werner, you shall repeat my words—that Just is a dirty slanderer.

SCENE V

Paul Werner. Francisca

Werner. Little woman, do you, too, know my Major ?

Franc. Major von Tellheim ? Certainly I know the brave man well.

Werner. Is not he a brave man ? Do you admire him ?

Franc. From the bottom of my heart.

Werner. Really ? Look you, little woman ; that makes you as pretty again in my eyes. But what kind of services, then, are those the landlord is supposed to have done him ?

Franc. I can't very well imagine. Maybe he appropriates to himself the good that has fortunately arisen from his rascally behaviour.

Werner. O, then it was true what Just told me ? [*Turning to the side where the landlord has just gone off.*] Lucky for you that you've disappeared ! He has really cleared out his rooms ? To play such a trick on such a gentleman because his ass's-head imagined him to have no money left ? The Major no money ?

Franc. Well, has the Major money ?

Werner. Like hay ! He doesn't know how much he has. He does not know who are his debtors. I myself am one, and am bringing an old balance. Look you, little woman. In this satchel here [*drawing it from his pocket*] are one hundred louis-d'or ; and in this rouleau [*drawing it from another pocket*] one hundred ducats. *His* money, every stiver !

Franc. Really ? But why then is the Major pawning things ? I know he has pledged a ring.

Werner. Pledged ! Don't you believe it ! He probably wanted to be rid of the trumpery.

Franc. No trumpery, I assure you ! It is a very costly ring, which, besides, he had from hands he loved.

Werner. That's it, then. From hands he loved ! Yes, yes ! such a ring often puts us in mind of what we don't want to be put in mind of. So we put it out of sight.

Franc. How so ?

Werner. Funny things happen to a soldier in winter quarters. There he has nothing to do, and pampers himself, and in no long while makes acquaintanceships he only intends to last the winter, and which the good creature he makes them with accepts for life. Then all of a sudden a little ring is shoved on his finger ; he doesn't know himself how it came there. And not seldom he would gladly give the finger with it to be rid of it if he only could.

Franc. Eh ! And could that have happened to the Major ?

Werner. O, certainly. Particularly in Saxony. If he had had ten fingers on each hand, he might have got rings for the whole twenty.

Franc. [*Aside.*] That sounds rather queer, and should be enquired into, Mr. Sergeant-Major, or Mr. Freeholder. . . .

Werner. Little woman, if it's all the same to you, Mr. Sergeant-Major, I prefer.

Franc. Well, Mr. Sergeant-Major, I have here a note from the gallant gentleman to my Lady. I'll just run in with it and be here in a second. Will you be so good as to wait here so long ? I should like to have some more talk with you.

Werner. You like talking, little woman ? All right for me. Run in. I like talking too : I will wait.

Franc. Wait then, do ; just a moment.   [*Exit.*

SCENE VI

Werner. That's not a bad little woman ! But I shouldn't have promised to wait. For surely the most important thing is to find the Major. He doesn't want my money, and goes pawning instead ? I recognise him there. An idea strikes me. When I was in the town a fortnight ago I called on Captain Marloff's widow. The poor woman lay ill, and lamented that her man had died owing four hundred Thalers to the Major, and she didn't know how she was going to pay them. This morning I went to visit her again. I wanted to tell her, if I got the money paid down for my little property, I could lend her five hundred Thalers. For I must put something by in security in case things fall out badly in Persia. But she was over the hills and far away! And quite certainly she can't have paid the Major.—Yes, that's what I'll do; and the sooner, the better.—The little woman must not take it ill of me; I can't wait. [*Exit, thinking, and nearly stumbles against the Major, who comes in.*]

SCENE VII

Tellheim. Paul Werner

Tellheim. So absorbed, Werner?

Werner. O, there you are! I was just on the point of looking you up in your new quarters, Major.

Tellheim. I suppose to fill my ears with curses on my other landlord. Think no more of it.

Werner. That I should have done by the way, certainly. But really I wanted only to thank you for being so kind as to have taken care of my hundred louis-d'or. Just has given them back to me. I should have been very glad if you could have kept them yet awhile. But you have gone into new quarters, which neither you nor I am acquainted with. Who knows how things go there? They might be stolen from you, and you would be obliged to restore them; there would be no help for it. So I can't really expect it of you.

Tellheim. Since when have you been so careful, Werner?

Werner. It comes by degrees. Nowadays one can't be careful enough of one's money. After that I had another matter to arrange with you, Major: about Marloff's widow. I've just come from her this moment. Her man died owing you four hundred Thalers; she sends you here one hundred ducats. She will send the rest next week. Perhaps I myself was the reason why she did not send the sum complete. For she owed me too a trifle, and because she thought I had come to remind her—which was true, as a matter of fact—she gave it to me and took it from the rouleaux that she had put aside for you. You can better miss your hundred Thalers for a fortnight than I my few groschen.—There, catch hold!

[*Hands him the rouleau of ducats.*

Tellheim. Werner!
  S

Werner. Well! Why do you stare at me like that? Catch hold of them, Major!

Tellheim. Werner!

Werner. What's wrong? What has put you out?

Tellheim. [*Bitterly, striking his forehead, and stamping with his foot.*] That the four hundred Thalers are not complete!

Werner. Now, now, Major! Have you not understood me?

Tellheim. Just because I do understand you! That to-day my best friends plague me most!

Werner. What do you say?

Tellheim. It's only half to do with you! Go, Werner! [*Pushing back the hand with which Werner is holding out the ducats.*]

Werner. As soon as I'm rid of this!

Tellheim. Werner, what if I tell you that Marloff's widow called on me early this morning?

Werner. Indeed?

Tellheim. That she is no longer in my debt?

Werner. Really?

Tellheim. That she has paid me every stiver. What will you say now?

Werner. [*Thinking for a moment.*] I would say that I have lied, and that it is the devilish thing about lying that you may possibly be found out.

Tellheim. And you will be ashamed of yourself?

Werner. But what should he be who forces me to lie? Shouldn't he, too, be ashamed of himself? Look here, Major, if I were to say that your goings-on didn't vex me, I should be lying again; and I won't lie any more.

Tellheim. Don't be vexed, Werner! I know your good heart and your attachment to me. But I can't take your money. I don't need it.

Werner. Don't need it? You will rather sell and pawn things and set people talking about you?

Tellheim. People may know as soon as they like that I have nothing more. We mustn't try to seem richer than we are.

Werner. But why poorer? So long as our friend has, we have.

Tellheim. It would be unbecoming for me to be your debtor.

Werner. Unbecoming? When one hot day, which the sun and the enemy made hot for us, your groom with the canteen went astray; and you came to me and said, " Werner, have you anything to drink?" and I handed you my water-flask. You took it and drank, didn't you? Was that becoming? My soul and body! if a drink of stale water wasn't then worth many times over all this rubbish ! [*While he takes out of his pocket the purse of louis-d'or and holds out both.*] Take them, my dear Major ! Imagine it is water. God made that too for us all.

Tellheim. You torture me. Hear now ! I won't be your debtor.

Werner. First it was unbecoming; now you will not? That's rather different. [*Somewhat angrily.*] You *won't* be my debtor. But if you're that already, Major? Or do you owe nothing to the man who intercepted the stroke that would have split your head, and another day struck off the arm that was pointing the pistol at your breast? What more could you owe this man? Or is my neck of less value than my purse? If that is thought very noble, body and soul o' me ! it's in frightful bad taste !

Tellheim. To whom are you talking, Werner? We are alone, and I can say to you, if a third were present, this would be the idlest brag. I acknowledge with pleasure that twice you saved my life. But, my friend, would not I any day have done as much for you? Eh?

Werner. Only the opportunity was wanting. Who doubts that? Have I not a hundred times seen you venture your life for the commonest soldier in danger?

Tellheim. Just so !

Werner. But . . .

Tellheim. Why won't you understand me? I say, it is unbecoming for me to be your debtor; I *will* not be your debtor. That is to say, not in the circumstances in which I find myself.

Werner. So, so ! You will put it off to better times; you will borrow money of me some other time, when you don't require it, when you have some yourself, and I perhaps none?

Tellheim. One must not borrow if one does not see the way to repayment.

Werner. To a man like you means can't always be wanting.

Tellheim. You know the world !—Least of all must one borrow of a man who needs his money himself.

Werner. O yes, such a man am I? What do I want it for? Where they have need of a sergeant they give him sómething to live on.

Tellheim. You want it to become something better than sergeant: to get on farther in a course where without money even the most deserving will get left behind.

Werner. To become more than a sergeant? That I don't think

of. I am a good sergeant, and might easily turn out a bad
cavalry-captain, and more certainly a bad general. We've
seen that sort of thing.

Tellheim. Don't make me think anything unjust of you, Werner!
I did not like to hear what Just told me. You have sold your
farm, and want to knock about again. Let me not believe
of you that it is not so much the profession you love as the
wild and dissolute way of living that is unfortunately connected with it. One must be a soldier for his country's sake,
or from love to the cause for which he fights. To serve here
to-day and there to-morrow, without object, is to be no better
than a travelling butcher-boy.

Werner. What I want, Major, is to follow you. You know best
what is right. I will remain with you.—But, meanwhile, my
dear Major, take this money of mine. To-day or to-morrow
your affairs must be settled. You will get money in heaps.
Then you can repay me with interest. I only do it for the
sake of the interest.

Tellheim. Speak no more of it!

Werner. By my soul, I do it only for the interest! Often when
I thought, "How will it be with you in old age, or if you are
completely knocked out, if you have nothing? If you must
go begging?" Then I thought: "No, you will not have to
go begging; you will go to Major Tellheim. He will share
his last penny with you; he will look after you till you die.
With him you will be able to die an honest man."

Tellheim. [*Grasping Werner's hand.*] And, comrade, don't you
think so still?

Werner. No, I don't think that any longer. He who will take
nothing of me when he needs it and I have it, neither will he
give anything to me when he has it and I need it.—All right!
[*Is going.*]

Tellheim. Man, do not make me wild! Where are you going?
[*Holds him back.*] If I assure you now on my honour that I
still have money; if I promise you on my honour that I will
tell you when I have no more; that you shall be the first and
only man of whom I will borrow—will that content you?

Werner. Must it not? Give me your hand upon it, Major.

Tellheim. There, Paul!—And now enough of this. I came here
to speak to a certain young lady—

SCENE VIII

Francisca (from the room of Mademoiselle).   Tellheim.   Paul Werner

Franc. [*Entering.*] Are you still there, Sergeant? [*Observing Tellheim.*] And you too, Major? At your service in one moment. [*Goes back quickly into the room.*]

SCENE IX

Tellheim.   Paul Werner

Tellheim. That was she! But I gather you know her, Werner?
Werner. Yes, I know the little girl.
Tellheim. And yet, if I remember right, you were not with me when I had my winter quarters in Thüringen?
Werner. No, I was guarding stores in Leipzig at that time.
Tellheim. How is it you know her, then?
Werner. Our acquaintance is new-born. It is of to-day. But young acquaintance is warm.
Tellheim. So perhaps you have also seen Mademoiselle?
Werner. Is her Ladyship a Mademoiselle? She told me you were acquainted with her Ladyship.
Tellheim. Yes, don't you know? She's from Thüringen.
Werner. Is Mademoiselle young?
Tellheim. Yes.
Werner. Beautiful?
Tellheim. Very beautiful.
Werner. Rich?
Tellheim. Very rich.
Werner. Does the lady like you as much as the maid? That would be splendid!
Tellheim. How do you mean?

SCENE X

Francisca (coming out once more, with a letter in her hand.)

Tellheim.   Paul Werner

Francisca. My dear Major . . .
Tellheim. My dear Francisca, I have not yet been able to bid you welcome.

Franc. I dare say you have done it in thought. I know you like
  me. And I you. But it is not very nice that you should
  plague so much people you are fond of.

Werner. [*Aside.*] Ah ! I see now. It is true !

Tellheim. My fate, Francisca ! Have you handed her the letter ?

Franc. Yes, and here I hand you [*Handing him the letter.*]

Tellheim. A reply ?

Franc. No, your own letter back again.

Tellheim. What ! She will not read it ?

Franc. She would indeed ; but—we can't read manuscript very
  well.

Tellheim. You little wag !

Franc. And we think letter-writing has not been invented for
  people who can speak to one another face to face whenever
  they like.

Tellheim. What an excuse ! She *must* read it. It contains
  my justification—all the grounds and reasons. . . .

Franc. Which Mademoiselle will hear from you personally, not
  by letter.

Tellheim. From me personally ? So that every word, every
  look of hers, may embarrass me ? So that I may feel in
  every glance of hers all the greatness of my loss ?

Franc. Without mercy !—Take it ! [*Gives him the letter.*] She
  expects you at three o'clock. She wishes to drive out and
  see the town. You are to accompany her.

Tellheim. Drive out with her ?

Franc. And what are you giving me, to let you two drive and
  quite alone ? I will stop at home.

Tellheim. Quite alone ?

Franc. In a lovely closed carriage.

Tellheim. Impossible !

Franc. Yes, yes ; in the carriage the Major must stand fire !
  There he can't give us the slip. That's why !—In short,
  you're to come, my dear Major ; and sharp at three.—Well ?
  You wanted to see me alone too. Well, what have you to say
  to me ? Ah ! but we are not alone. [*Looking towards Werner.*]

Tellheim. Yes, Francisca, we should be alone. But as Mademoiselle has not read the letter, I have nothing to say to you.

Franc. But now we can suppose ourselves alone ? You have no
  secrets from the Sergeant-Major ?

Tellheim. No, none.

Franc. All the same, I think you ought to have some even from
  him.

Tellheim. How so?

Werner. Why so, little woman?

Franc. Particularly secrets of a certain kind—all twenty, Mr. Sergeant-Major? [*Holding up both hands, with fingers outspread.*]

Werner. Hist! hist! little woman.

Tellheim. What does she mean?

Franc. Presto! a little ring is on the finger. [*Pretending to slip a ring smartly on her finger.*]

Tellheim. What's all this about?

Werner. Little woman, I fancy you can understand a joke?

Tellheim. Werner, you have I hope not forgotten what I used to say to you—that one must not carry a joke beyond a certain point with a young woman.

Werner. Upon my soul, I may have forgotten it.   Little woman, I beg . . .

Franc. All right!   If it was a joke, for this time I'll forgive it.

Tellheim. If I positively must come, Francisca, then do you see to it that Mademoiselle reads the letter beforehand.   That will spare me the agony of thinking yet once more, of saying yet once more, things I would so gladly forget. There, give it her! [*As he turns the letter over and is about to hand it to her, he notices that the seal is broken.*]   But what do I see, Francisca?   The letter is unsealed.

Franc. That may quite well be. [*Looking at it.*] It is certainly unsealed.   But who can have unsealed it?   Read it we have not, Major; really, really not.   Nor do we want to read it, for the writer is coming himself.   Do come!   And do you know, Major, don't come as you are now—in boots, and your hair out of order.   We excuse you : you did not expect us. Come in shoes and have your hair trimmed.—At present you look to me a good deal too military, a good deal too Prussian !

Tellheim. I thank you, Francisca.

Franc. You look as if you had bivouacked last night.

Tellheim. You are not far wrong.

Franc. We too will have a brush-up, and then lunch.   We should be delighted to keep you to lunch, but your company would perhaps disturb us too much.   And look you, we are not so far gone in love as not to be hungry.

Tellheim. I go, Francisca.   Meanwhile prepare her somewhat beforehand; so that I may not become despicable either in her eyes or my own.—Come, Werner, you shall eat with me.

Werner. At the public table, here in the house? I couldn't relish a morsel.

Tellheim. With me at my rooms.

Werner. Then I follow you directly. Only one word with the maid here.

Tellheim. That will suit me quite well. [*Exit.*]

SCENE XI

Paul Werner. Francisca

Franc. Well, Mr. Sergeant-Major?

Werner. Little woman, when I come again shall I too come trimmed up?

Franc. Come as you will, Mr. Sergeant-Major, my eyes won't criticise you. But my ears must be all the more on their guard against you. Twenty fingers, all covered with rings! Oh, oh, Mr. Sergeant-Major!

Werner. No, little woman! Just that I wanted to say to you; the tale led me on a bit there! There is nothing in that. In fact, a man has quite enough with one ring. And a hundred times over, and a hundred again, I've heard the Major say, He must be a scamp of a soldier who can lead a girl on! So think I, little woman. Rely on that! I must hurry up and follow him. Enjoy your lunch, little woman! [*Exit.*]

Franc. Same to you, Mr. Sergeant-Major. I fancy I rather like the gentleman! [*As she is going in Mademoiselle comes out and meets her.*]

SCENE XII

Mademoiselle. Francisca

Mademoiselle. Is the Major already gone again? Francisca, I think I should have been now quiet enough to keep him with us for luncheon.

Franc. And I will make you still quieter.

Mad. So much the better! His letter, O his letter! Every line bespoke the gentleman, the noble, honest-hearted man. Every hesitation to accept me made his love more dear to me. —He will have seen that we had read the letter. Let him; if he only comes. Does he come, then, for certain? Just a trifle too much pride, Francisca, appears to me in his conduct. For not to be willing to owe his good fortune to his beloved is pride, unpardonable pride! If he shows this to me too strongly, Francisca . . .

Franc. Then you will renounce him, I suppose?

Mad. Eh? See now. Don't you commiserate him any longer? No, you dear little fool, for a single fault one doesn't renounce any man. No. But a little plan has occurred to me by which we may tease him about this pride by showing a little of our own.

Franc. Now indeed you must be very quiet, my Lady, if you can plan pranks on him already.

Mad. So I am, truly. Come only. You will have your part to play in it. [*They go in.*]

ACT IV—SCENE I

SCENE : *Mademoiselle's room. Mademoiselle (richly but taste-fully drest). Francisca. (They are rising from table which a servant is clearing.)*

Franc. You have eaten hardly anything, your Ladyship.

Mad. Do you think so, Francisca? Perhaps I didn't sit down very hungry.

Franc. We had arranged not to mention his dining. But we ought to have decided not even to think of him.

Mad. And in fact I have thought of nothing else.

Franc. I saw that quite well. I began talking of a hundred things, but you answered me from the point every time. [*Another waiter brings in coffee.*] Here comes a drink that goes well with low spirits. The dear, melancholy coffee!

Mad. Low spirits? No such thing. I am only thinking of the lesson I will give him. Do you understand, Francisca?

Franc. O yes; but the best would be that he should spare us one.

Mad. You will see that I know him through and through. The man who now refuses me with all my wealth will face the whole world for me as soon as he hears that I am unfortunate and forsaken.

Franc. [*Very seriously.*] Something to gratify the most delicate self-love.

Mad. My dear moraliser! Look now! Only yesterday you detected me in vanity; to-day it is self-love. Will you let me be, my dear Francisca. You shall do as you like with your Sergeant-Major.

Franc. With my Sergeant-Major?

Mad. Yes, however much you deny it, I know it's true.—I have never seen him, but by every word you have spoken about him I prophesy you a husband.

Scene II

Riccaut de la Marlinière.   Mademoiselle.   Francisca

Riccaut. [*Before coming in.*] *Est-il permis, Monsieur le Major ?*

Franc. What is that? Can that be for us? [*Going towards the door.*]

Riccaut. Parbleu ! I am not right.—*Mais non*—I am not wrong—*C'est la chambre* . . .

Franc. Quite certainly, your Ladyship, this gentleman thinks to find Major von Tellheim still here.

Riccaut. Oui, certainement—Le Major de Tellheim ; juste, ma belle enfant, c'est lui que je cherche. Où est-il ?

Franc. He does not live here now.

Riccaut. Comment ? steel dwenty-four hour ago he lodge here? And lodge he no more here? Where zen?

Mad. [*Coming forward.*] *Monsieur* . . .

Riccaut. Ah, madame—mademoiselle—your Grace forgive . . .

Mad. Monsieur, your mistake is quite easy to forgive, and your surprise is very natural. The gallant Major has done the kindness to me, as a stranger who could not find a lodging, to vacate his room.

Riccaut. Ah voilà de ses politesses ! C'est un très-galant homme que ce Major !

Mad. Where meantime he has withdrawn, really I am ashamed to confess, I do not know.

Riccaut. Your Ladyship not know? *C'est dommage ; j'en suis fâché.*

Mad. I ought certainly to have made enquiry. Of course, his friends will seek him here.

Riccaut. I am most of his friend, your Ladyship . . .

Mad. Francisca, don't you know it?

Franc. No, your Ladyship.

Riccaut. I haf to say to him, ver' important. I come bring a news of which he will be ver' glad.

Mad. I regret it all the more. But I am in hopes perhaps very soon to speak with him. If it is all the same from whose mouth he learns these good news, then I beg you, Monsieur . . .

Riccaut. I onderstant. *Mademoiselle parle français? Mais sans doute; telle que je la vois! La demande était bien impolie. Vous me pardonnerez, Mademoiselle.*

Mad. Monsieur . . .

Riccaut. Non? You speak not French, your Grace?

Mad. Monsieur, in France I would try to speak it. But why here? I can see that you understand me, Monsieur. And I, Monsieur, will certainly also understand you. Speak as you like best.

Riccaut. Good! good! I vill try to make me understood. *Sachez donc, Mademoiselle*—Your Ladyship must know, zen, zat I come from the office of the Minister—Minister of— Minister of—how you call the Minister out zere—in the long street, on ze broad square?

Mad. I am quite a stranger in the place.

Riccaut. Well, ze Minister of ze War Department. I dined with him midday—I dine mostly at his house—and there one is come to talk of Major de Tellheim; *et le Ministre m'a dit en confidence, car son Excellence est de mes amis, et il n'y a point de mystères entre nous*—His Excellency, will I say, haf confide me zat ze affair of the Major is about to end, and to end favourably. He had made Report to His Majesty the King, and the King have resolve thereupon, *tout-à-fait en faveur du Major.*—*Monsieur, m'a dit Son Excellence, vous comprenez bien, que tout dépend de la manière dont on fait envisager les choses au Roi, et vous me connaissez. Cela fait un très-joli garçon que ce Tellheim, et ne sais-je pas que vous l'aimez? Les amis de mes amis sont aussi les miens. Il coûte un peu cher au Roi, ce Tellheim, mais est-ce que l'on sert les Rois pour rien? Il faut l'entr'aider en ce monde; et quand il s'agit de pertes, que ce soit le Roi qui en fasse, et non pas un honnête-homme de nous autres. Voilà le principe, dont je ne me dépars jamais.*— What does your Ladyship say to it? Isn't he indeed a gallant man? *Ah, que Son Excellence a le cœur bien placé!* He has assure me last of all that if ze Major has not already receive a letter from ze King's hand, he must infallibly receive one to-day.

Mad. Certainly, Monsieur, this news will be highly agreeable to Major von Tellheim. I could only wish to be able to name to him the friend who takes so much interest in his welfare.

Riccaut. Your Ladyship wish to know my name? *Vous voyez en moi*—Your Ladyship see in me *le Chevalier Riccaut de la Marlinière, Seigneur de Prêt-au-vol, de la Branche de Preux d'or.*

Your ladyship is astonished to hear that I am connected with
such a ver' great family, which is undoubtedly of Royal blood.
But there's zis to be said : *je suis sans doute le cadet le plus
aventurant que la maison a jamais eu.* I was in the army at
eleven years of age. For an *affaire d'honneur* I had to run.
Since then I have served His Holiness the Pope, ze Republic
of St. Marino, ze Polish Crown and ze States-General, till at
last I find myself in zese parts. *Ah, Mademoiselle, que je
voudrois n'avoir jamais vu ce pays-là!* Had they but left me
in the service of ze States-General. I had been by now
Colonel at least. But have here remained captain for ever
and ever, and now indeed a half-pay captain——

Mad. That's very bad luck.

*Riccaut. Oui, Mademoiselle, me voilà réformé, et par-là mis sur le
pavé.*

Mad. I am grieved to hear it.

Riccaut. Vous êtes bien bonne, Mademoiselle. No, zere is no
relying upon merit here. A man like me, *en réformer!* A
man, too, who has ruined himself in zes service !—More
zan zat, I have sacrificed more than twenty thousand livres.
What have I now? *Tranchons le mot; je n'ai pas le sou, et me
voilà exactement vis-à-vis du rien.*

Mad. I am very sorry indeed.

Riccaut. Vous êtes bien bonne, Mademoiselle. But as people say,
every misfortune drags his brother after him : *qu'un malheur
ne vient jamais seul;* so it has happened with me. What
resource can an honest man of my extraction have other zan
play? Well, I have always been lucky in play, so long as I
had no need of luck. Now that I need it more than ever,
Mademoiselle, *je joue avec un quignon, qui surpasse toute
croyance.* For a whole fortnight not a day has passed that
ill-luck has not broken me. Even yesterday she broke me
three times over. *Je sais bien qu'il y avoit quelque chose de
plus que le jeu. Car parmi mes pontes se trouvoient certaines
dames.* I will say no more. One must be gallant towards
the ladies. They have invited me to-day, too, to give me my
revenge, *mais vous m'entendez, Mademoiselle.* One must
first have something to live on, before one can have something
for play.

Mad. I do hope, Monsieur . . .

Riccaut. Vous êtes bien bonne, Mademoiselle—

Mad. [*Takes Francisca aside.*] Francisca, the man really moves
me. Would he take it ill if I were to offer him something?

Franc. He doesn't look to me like that.

Mad. Good! Monsieur, I hear—that you play: that you keep bank; no doubt in places where something can be won. I must confess to you that I—that I, too—am rather fond of play . . .

Riccaut. Tant mieux, Mademoiselle, tant mieux! Tous les gens d'esprit aiment le jeu à la fureur.

Mad. That I'm very fond of winning, and willingly venture my money with a man who knows how to play. Would you be willing, Monsieur, to take me into partnership and grant me a share in your bank?

Riccaut. Comment, Mademoiselle? Vous voulez être de moitié avec moi? De tout mon cœur.

Mad. First of all, only with a trifle. [*Goes and fetches money from her purse.*]

Riccaut. Ah, Mademoiselle, que vous êtes charmante!

Mad. I have here something I won recently; only the pistoles— I am quite ashamed, so little . . .

Riccaut. Donnez toujours, Mademoiselle, donnez. [*Takes it*].

Mad. Of course, Monsieur, your bank is very respectable.

Riccaut. Certainly, certainly! Quite respectable. Ten pistoles! Your Ladyship shall have for them a third share in my bank, *pour le tiers.* For a third share, certainly it should be—rather more. Still with a pretty woman one must not cut it so fine. I congratulate myself thus to come into connection with your Ladyship, and from this moment I begin again to augur well of my fortune.

Mad. But I cannot be there when you play, Monsieur.

Riccaut. What need is there for your Ladyship? We other players are honourable people with one another.

Mad. If we are lucky, Monsieur, you will bring me my share? If, however, we are unlucky . . .

Riccaut. Then I shall come to fetch up recruits. Shall I not, your Ladyship?

Mad. By and by the recruits might run short. So defend our money bravely, Monsieur.

Riccaut. What does your Ladyship take me for? A simpleton, a silly devil?

Mad. Excuse me.

Riccaut. Je suis des Bones, Mademoiselle. Savez-vous ce que cela veut dire? I am out of my apprenticeship.

Mad. But still you know, Monsieur . . .

Riccaut. Je sais monter un coup . . .

Mad. [*Surprised*]. Ought you to?

Riccaut. Je file la carte avec une adresse . . .

Mad. Never !

Riccaut. Je sais sauter la coupe avec une dextérité . . .

Mad. But you will not all the same, Monsieur?

Riccaut. Not what, your Ladyship, not what? *Donnez-moi un pigeonneau à plumer, et* . . .

Mad. Play false? Cheat?

Riccaut. Comment, Mademoiselle? Vous appelez cela cheating? *Corriger la fortune, l'enchaîner sous ses doits, être sur de son fait.* Do the Germans call that *cheating*? Cheating! O what a poverty-stricken language is German! What a clumsy language!

Mad. No, Monsieur, if you think that . . .

Riccaut. Laissez-moi faire, Mademoiselle, and do you rest in quiet! What matters it to you how I play? Enough: to-morrow either you will see again with a hundred pistoles or see never again—your very humble servant, Mademoiselle, your very humble . . . [*Hastening off.*]

Mad. [*Looking after him, with surprise and vexation.*] I hope it will be the latter, Monsieur!

SCENE III

Mademoiselle. Francisca

Franc. [*Bitterly.*] Am I permitted to speak? Here's a pretty thing !

Mad. Yes, mock me; I deserve it. [*After a few moments' reflection, more calmly.*] No, do not mock me, Francisca; I don't deserve it.

Franc. Splendid! Now you've done something lovely—helped a swindler on his legs again.

Mad. It was meant for a man out of luck.

Franc. And the best of it is—the fellow takes you for one of his own kind.—O, I must after him and take the money from him again. [*Is going.*]

Mad. Francisca, don't let the coffee get quite cold; pour out.

Franc. He must return it to you : you've thought better of it ; you won't be partner in play with him. Ten pistoles ! Didn't you gather, Mademoiselle, that he was a beggar? [*Mademoiselle meantime herself pours out the coffee.*] Who would give so much to a beggar? And, besides, spare him the humiliation to have got it by begging? The charitable, who from magnanimity will not recognise the beggar, the beggar himself will also forget. Mademoiselle, it will serve you right if he misunderstands your gift. [*Mademoiselle hands a cup to Francisca.*] Would you make my blood boil still hotter? I cannot drink it. [*Mademoiselle sets the cup aside.*]—" *Parbleu*, Your Grace, *vous* rely nozing here on merit." [*Imitating the tone of the Frenchman.*] No, indeed, if one lets villains run around unhanged.

Mad. [*Coolly and thoughtfully while she sips her coffee.*] My girl, you understand good men so excellently well; but when will you learn to put up with the wicked?—And yet they are men, too.—And often not such bad fellows as they seem, by a long way.—We must look for their good side.—I fancy this Frenchman is only vain. From sheer vanity he makes himself out a cheat; he won't appear obliged to me; he will spare himself gratitude. Quite likely he will now go, pay off his little debts, live quietly and sparingly on the balance so far as it goes, and think no more of play. If so, my dear Francisca, let him come back for recruits when he will. [*Gives her the cup.*] There, clear away!—But, tell me, should not Tellheim be here by now?

Franc. No, your Ladyship; I can't do either the one or the other; neither look for the good side in a bad man, nor for the bad side in a good.

Mad. But he's coming for certain, is he not?

Franc. He should stop away! You perceive in him, in him, the best of men, a little pride, and for that would you tease him so cruelly?

Mad. Coming back to that, are you? Be still! I'm going to do it just once. If you spoil this game for me; if you don't say everything and do everything as we agreed!—I am to leave you alone with him; and then. . . . But here he comes. . . .

SCENE IV.

Paul Werner (*enters in a stiff attitude, as on duty*). *Mademoiselle. Francisca.*

Franc. No, it is only his dear Sergeant-Major.

Mad. Dear Sergeant-Major? Whom is this " dear " meant for?

Franc. Your Ladyship, please don't embarrass the gentleman. Your servant, Mr. Sergeant-Major. What is your message?

Werner. [*Without regarding Francisca, addresses Mademoiselle.*] Major von Tellheim commands me, Sergeant-Major Werner, to give your Ladyship his humble respects, and to say that he will be here without delay.

Mad. What is detaining him?

Werner. Your Ladyship will pardon me. We left our quarters before three o'clock struck; but then the Army Paymaster addressed him on the way; and as with that sort of gentleman talking has no end, he gave me a hint to report the case to your Ladyship.

Mad. Very good, Mr. Sergeant-Major. I hope only the Army Paymaster may have something agreeable to say to him.

Werner. That sort of gentleman very seldom has for the officers. Has your Ladyship any commands? [*Is about to go.*]

Franc. Now then, Mr. Sergeant-Major. Whither away so fast? Had we not something to talk over together?

Werner. [*Softly to Francisca and seriously.*] Not here, little woman! It is contrary to discipline, to subordination.— Your Ladyship.

Mad. I thank you for your trouble, Mr. Sergeant-Major. I am very pleased to have made your acquaintance. Francisca has spoken to me very highly about you. [*Werner makes a formal obeisance, and exit.*]

Scene V

Mademoiselle. Francisca

Mad. So that is your Sergeant-Major, Francisca?

Franc. I haven't time now to meet your mockery with more of the same.—Yes, my Lady, that is my Sergeant-Major.— You find him, no doubt, rather stiff and wooden. This time I almost thought so, too. But I know why: he thought in your Ladyship's presence he must put on his parade manners. And when soldiers are on parade they do indeed seem more puppets than men. You ought to see him, though, and hear him, when he is left to himself.

Mad. I should much like to, of course.

Franc. He will still be in the salon. May I not go and chat with him a bit?

Mad. So sorry! I must deny you that pleasure. You must

remain here, Francisca. You must be present at our inter-
view—I have an idea. [*Draws her ring from her finger.*]
There, take my ring, take care of it, and give me the Major's
in place of it.

Franc. Why so?

Mad. [*While Francisca fetches the other ring.*] That I don't,
myself, quite know yet; but I fancy I see something coming in
which it might be useful.—Some one knocks—Give it me
quick! It is he!

SCENE VI

Tellheim (*in same dress, but otherwise just as Francisca had
requested*). *Mademoiselle. Francisca.*

Tellheim. Your Ladyship, pray forgive my delay.

Mad. O, my dear Major, not quite so military, if you please.
You are really here. And expecting a pleasure is itself a
pleasure.—Well? [*Looking him laughingly in the face.*] My
dear Tellheim, haven't we been children?

Tellheim. Yes, children indeed, your Ladyship; children who
resist and struggle when they should quickly submit.

Mad. We will drive out, my dear Major, to look about the town;
and afterwards to meet my uncle.

Tellheim. How?

Mad. You see, the really important things we've not had a
chance yet of talking over. Yes, he is arriving to-day. It is
owing to an accident that I arrived a day earlier than he.

Tellheim. Count Bruchsall? Is he back?

Mad. The war troubles exiled him in Italy; the Peace has
restored him to us. Don't be uneasy, Tellheim. If at one
time we expected the strongest opposition to our union to
come from him . . .

Tellheim. Our union?

Mad. He is your friend. He has heard too much good of you
from too many people to be anything else. He is burning
to know face to face the man whom his heiress has chosen.
He comes as uncle, as guardian, as father, to give me up to you.

Tellheim. Ah, Mademoiselle, why did you not read my letter?
Why did you refuse to read it?

Mad. Your letter? Yes, I remember, you sent me one. How
was it then with this letter, Francisca? Did we read it or
did we not read it? What did you write to me, my dear
Tellheim?

T

Tellheim. Nothing but what honour commanded.

Mad. Which is, not to leave an honourable girl, who loves you, in the lurch. Certainly that is what honour commands. Of course I ought to have read the letter. But what I haven't read you can tell me now.

Tellheim. Yes, you shall hear it.

Mad. No, I don't need to hear it again. It is a matter of course. You could not possibly be capable of so foul a blow; to tell me you no longer want me. Do you not know that I should be insulted all the rest of my life? My country-women would point their fingers at me. " That's she "—so it would run, " that's the Lady of Barnhelm, who imagined, because she was rich, she could marry the gallant Tellheim. As if gallant men were to be had for money ! " So it would run; for my country-women are all envious of me. That I am rich, they cannot deny; but that I am also a fairly good girl who is worthy of her husband, they won't hear anything about that. Is it not so, Tellheim?

Tellheim. Yes, yes, my Lady; I quite recognise your country-women there. They will most wisely envy you a half-pay officer, dishonoured, a beggar and a cripple.

Mad. And all that are you? Something of the kind I heard indeed, if I'm not mistaken, this very morning. Truly, a mixture of good and ill. Let us look into it a little more closely. Cashiered, are you? So you tell me. I fancied your regiment was merely disbanded. How comes it that they have not retained a man of your merit?

Tellheim. It has come as come it must. The big people have convinced themselves that a soldier will do very little out of attachment to them; for duty's sake not much more; but anything and everything for his own honour. How, then, should they consider themselves in debt to him? The Peace has enabled them to dispense with many of my kind; and in the end they find nobody indispensable.

Mad. You speak as a man must speak, to whom the big people for his part are such as can quite well be dispensed with. And never were they more so than now. I am extremely grateful to the big people : they have renounced their claims on a man whom I only most unwillingly would have shared with them.—I am your commander, Tellheim; you need no other lord.—To find you discharged is luck I had hardly dreamed of ! But you are not only dismissed, you are still more. What are you still more? A cripple, did you say?

Well [*surveying him from head to foot*], the cripple is pretty complete and straight as yet; seems still pretty strong and sound.—My dear Tellheim, if you are thinking to go a-begging because of the loss of your sound limbs, I prophesy that you will get pity at very few doors, except the doors of kind-hearted girls like me.

Tellheim. I hear now only the saucy girl, dear Minna.

Mad. And in the whole of your lecture I only hear the " dear Minna."—I won't be saucy any more. For I reflect that, after all, you are a bit of a cripple. A shot has slightly lamed your right arm. But, all things considered, that's not altogether bad. I am all the more secure from your blows.

Tellheim. Mademoiselle !

Mad. You want to say, But you so much less so from mine. Well, well, my dear Tellheim, I hope you won't let it come to that.

Tellheim. You are determined to laugh, Mademoiselle. I'm only very sorry that I can't laugh with you.

Mad. Why not? What ails you against laughing? Cannot one be in earnest and laugh at the same time? My dear Major, good sense goes more often with laughing than with lamenting. We have the proof of it now. Your laughing friend judges your circumstances more correctly than you do. Because you have been retired, you say you are wounded in your honour. Because you have been shot in the arm, you make yourself out a cripple. Is that quite right? Is that no exaggeration? And is it an arrangement of mine that all exaggerations are apt to be laughable? I wager, if I come to an understanding with your " beggar," this too will fail to stand the test. You will have lost your kit once, twice, or even three times; some deposits with one banker or another have vanished; some advances you have made in service you will have no hope left of recovering. But are you on that account a beggar? Even if nothing is left you save what my uncle brings for you. . . .

Tellheim. Your uncle, my Lady, will bring nothing for me.

Mad. Nothing but the two thousand pistoles which you advanced so generously to our State-Council.

Tellheim. If you had only read my letter, your Ladyship !

Mad. Well, then, I have read it. But what it told me on that point is to me the merest riddle. Surely it is impossible for people to make a crime of a noble action. Do explain to me, my dear Major . . .

Tellheim. You recollect, my Lady, that I had orders to collect
the war contribution in your district in ready cash with the
utmost strictness. I wished to spare this strictness, and
myself advanced the deficiency.

Mad. Indeed, I do remember that.—For that very deed I loved
you, ere ever I had seen you.

Tellheim. The State-Council gave me their bill, and this I wished,
when Peace was signed, to register among the debts to be
settled. The bill was recognised as valid, but my property
in it was contested. People sneered ironically when I assured
them that I had provided the value in ready money. They
called it a bribe, a donation from the State-Council, because I
had agreed with them upon the lowest sum with which I had
authority to be satisfied. So the bill came out of my keeping,
and if it is paid it will certainly not be paid to me. By this
it is, my Lady, I hold my honour wounded; not by the dis-
charge; which I should have demanded, if I had not received
it. You are serious, Mademoiselle? Why don't you laugh?
Ha, ha, ha! I laugh, you see.

Mad. O, smother this laughter, Tellheim! I entreat you! It
is the horrible laughter of human hatred! No, you are not
the man to regret a good action because it has ill consequences
for himself. No, these ill consequences cannot possibly last!
The truth must come to light. The testimony of my uncle,
of all our council . . .

Tellheim. Of your uncle, of your council! Ha, ha, ha!

Mad. Your laughter will kill me, Tellheim! If you have any
faith in virtue and Providence, Tellheim, don't laugh like that!
I have never heard more terrible cursing than your laughter.
And let us suppose the very worst! If they are determined to
misrepresent you here, they can't misrepresent you to us. No,
we cannot, we shall not misunderstand you. And if our
Council have the slightest feeling of honour, I know what
they must do. But I am silly. What matters what they do?
Think to yourself, Tellheim, that you lost the two thousand
pistoles on some wild night. The King was an unlucky card
for you; the Queen [*pointing to herself*] will be all the kinder
to you.—Providence, believe me, keeps the honest man from
harm; and often earlier than he hopes. The act which once
was to have cost you two thousand pistoles won me for you.
Without this act I should never have desired to make your
acquaintance. You know that I came uninvited into the
first company where I thought to find you. I came entirely

on your account. I came with the firm intention of loving
you—I loved you already!—with the firm intention of making
you mine, even if I were to find you as black and ill-favoured
as the Moor of Venice. You are not so black and ill-favoured;
neither will you be as jealous. But Tellheim, Tellheim, you
resemble him in many ways! O, these savage, inflexible men,
who fix their staring eye for ever only on the spectre of honour,
and steel themselves against all other feelings! Turn your
eyes this way: to me, Tellheim! [*Who meanwhile, absorbed
and immovable, looks with fixed eyes upon one spot.*] What
are you thinking of? You do not hear me?

Tellheim. [*Distractedly.*] O yes! But tell me now, Mademoiselle, how came the Moor into the Venetian service? Had the
Moor no country of his own? Why did he hire out his arm
and his blood to a foreign State?

Mad. [*Terrified.*] Where are you, Tellheim?—It is high time
we broke off this talk.—Come [*Seizing his hand.*]—Francisca,
let the carriage be called.

Tellheim. No, Francisca. I cannot have the honour to accompany Mademoiselle.—My dear Lady, leave me still for to-day
my right mind, and permit me to withdraw. You are going
the right way to deprive me of my good sense. I control myself as much as I can.—But while I am still in my senses;
listen, my dear Lady, to what I have firmly resolved, from which
nothing in the world shall move me. If no lucky throw remains
in the game for me, if fortune does not entirely change, if . . .

Mad. My dear Major, I must interrupt you.—We should not
have told him of that at once, Francisca. How is it you do
not remind me of things?—Our talk, Tellheim, would have
taken quite another turn if I had begun with the good news,
which the Chevalier de la Marlinière only a moment ago came
to bring you.

Tellheim. The Chevalier de la Marlinière? Who is that?

Franc. He may be quite a good man, Major, barring that . . .

Mad. Hush! Francisca!—Likewise a discharged officer, of the
Dutch service.

Tellheim. Ha! Lieutenant Riccaut!

Mad. He assured us he was a friend of yours.

Tellheim. I assure you I am no friend of his.

Mad. And that one of the Ministers—I don't know which—
had confided to him that your affair was approaching a most
happy issue, and that a letter from the royal hand must now
be on its way to you . . .

Tellheim. How should Riccaut and a Minister come together?
Something indeed must have happened in my affair. For
just now the Army Paymaster declared to me that the King
has quashed everything that was alleged against me, and that
I might again take back my word of honour, given in writing
not to leave this place until I had been fully exonerated.—
But then that will be all. They will permit me to run away.
Only they will be mistaken; I shall not run away. Rather
shall the uttermost misery consume me before the eyes of my
slanderers . . .

Mad. Stiff-necked man!

Tellheim. I want no favour: I want justice. My honour . . .

Mad. The honour of a man like you . . .

Tellheim. [*Hotly*]. No, my lady, you can judge right well in all
things, only not in this. Honour is not the voice of our own
conscience, not the testimony of a few right-minded . . .

Mad. No, no; I know exactly. Honour is—honour.

Tellheim. In a word, Mademoiselle—you did not let me finish.—
I wanted to say, if they withhold from me so disgracefully what
is rightly my own, if the fullest satisfaction is not done to my
honour, then, Mademoiselle, I cannot be yours. For in the
eyes of the world I am not worthy to be. The Lady of Barnhelm merits a husband beyond reproach. It is an unworthy
love that thinks nothing of exposing its object to scorn. And
he is an unworthy man who is not ashamed to owe his whole
fortune to a woman whose blind tenderness—

Mad. You mean that in earnest, Major? [*Turning her back
suddenly on him.*] Francisca!

Tellheim. Do not be angry, my dear Lady . . .

Mad. [*Aside, to Francisca.*] Now would be the time! What do
you advise me, Francisca?

Franc. I can't advise you. But certainly he goes a little too far.

Tellheim. [*Coming to interrupt them.*] You are angry, Mademoiselle . . .

Mad. [*Scornfully.*] I? not in the least.

Tellheim. If I loved you less, Mademoiselle . . .

Mad. [*Still in same tone.*] O, to be sure, it would be my misfortune! Look you, my dear Major, I will not be your
misfortune either. People must be unselfish in their love.
Just as well that I have not been more open-hearted. Perhaps
your pity would have granted me what your love denies me.
[*Drawing the ring slowly from her finger.*]

Tellheim. What is your meaning, Mademoiselle?

Mad. No, nobody must make the other either more fortunate or more unfortunate. That's what true love demands. I believe you, Major; and you have too much honour to misjudge love.

Tellheim. I think you speak in mockery, Mademoiselle.

Mad. Here. Take back the ring with which you plighted your troth to me. [*Hands him the ring.*] Let it be so! We will be as if we had never known each other.

Tellheim. What do I hear?

Mad. And that surprises you? Take it, sir. You have not, after all, stood upon ceremony.

Tellheim. God! Can Minna say such things?

Mad. In one case you cannot be mine. I cannot be yours in any case. Your misfortune is probable; mine is certain. Fare you well. [*Will go.*]

Tellheim. Whither, my dearest Minna?

Mad. Sir, you offend me now with these familiar terms.

Tellheim. What's come over you, my Lady? Whither?

Mad. Allow me. To hide my tears from you, traitor! [*Exit.*]

Scene VII

Tellheim. Francisca

Tellheim. Her tears? And I am to leave her? [*Will follow her.*]

Franc. [*Detaining him.*] Not yet, my good Major! You will surely not follow her into her bedchamber.

Tellheim. Her unhappiness? Did she speak of unhappiness?

Franc. Why, certainly: the unhappiness of losing you after . . .

Tellheim. After? After what? There's something behind this. What is it, Francisca? Speak, tell me . . .

Franc. After she, I meant to say, had sacrificed so much for you.

Tellheim. Sacrificed for me?

Franc. Let me just say one word. It is, for you, a good thing, Major, that you are rid of her in this way.—Why should not I tell you? It cannot remain a secret much longer.—We ran away! Count Bruchsall has disinherited her because she would not accept the husband he had chosen for her. She left all, she disdained all, immediately. What were we to do? We decided to fly to him whom we . . .

Tellheim. Enough, enough! Come, I must throw myself at her feet.

Franc. What? What? Much better go; and thank your stars
   that . . .
Tellheim. Wretched woman! What do you take me for?—
   No, my dear Francisca, that suggestion did not come from
   your heart. Forgive my anger!
Franc. Do not keep me any longer. I must see what she is
   doing. How easily something might happen to her.—Go now!
   Rather come again, if you wish to come again. [*Follows
   Mademoiselle.*]

Scene VIII

Tellheim. But, Francisca! I *must* wait for you here. No, this
   is dreadful! If she considers it seriously, she cannot refuse her
   forgiveness. Now I need you, honest Werner! No, Minna, I
   am no traitor! [*Exit in haste.*]

ACT V—Scene I

Scene : *the salon ; enter Tellheim from one side and Werner the
   other*

Tellheim. Ha, Werner! I've been seeking for you everywhere.
   Where have you been hiding?
Werner. And I have been seeking for you, my dear Major; that's
   how it goes with seeking. I've brought you some real good
   news.
Tellheim. Ah! at this moment I don't want your news : I want
   your money. Quick, Werner, give me as much as you have,
   and then go gather as much more as you can.
Werner. Major?—Well, by my soul, that's exactly what I said :
   he will borrow of me when he himself has something to lend.
Tellheim. You're surely not looking for excuses.
Werner. So that I mayn't reproach him, he takes from me with
   the right hand, and gives again with the left.
Tellheim. Don't hinder me, Werner! With good-will I shall
   return it; but when and how, God knows!
Werner. You evidently are not aware that the State Treasury
   has orders to pay you your moneys? I heard it this moment
   from . . .
Tellheim. What are you chattering about? Is this how you
   clear yourself? Don't you understand that, if it were true,

I must certainly be the first to hear it? Quick, Werner,
money! money!

Werner. Why, of course, with pleasure! Here is some! This
is the hundred louis-d'or, and this the hundred ducats. [*Gives
him both.*]

Tellheim. The hundred louis-d'or, Werner, go and take to
Just. He is immediately to take the ring out of pledge which
he pawned for me this morning.—But where will you get more,
Werner? I need much more.

Werner. That let me see to. The man who has bought my
estate lives in the town. The date of payment is a fortnight
off, indeed, but the money lies ready, and a half per cent.
discount . . .

Tellheim. Why, yes, my dear Werner! You see that I make my
appeal only to you? I must tell you everything. Mademoiselle here—you have seen her—is unfortunate . . .

Werner. O misery!

Tellheim. But to-morrow she will be my wife . . .

Werner. O, joy!

Tellheim. And the day after I leave here with her. I *may* leave,
and I *will*. Things here may go as they please! Who
knows? Perhaps fortune awaits me somewhere. Come
along with me, Werner, if you wish. Let's take service again.

Werner. Really? But, then, where is there a war on?

Tellheim. O, somewhere or other: my dear Werner, we can
talk of that by and by.

Werner. Oh, my own Major! The day after to-morrow? Why
not rather to-morrow. I could get everything together by
then.—In Persia, my dear Major, there's a capital war on.
What think you?

Tellheim. We'll consider that; but go, Werner!

Werner. Hurrah! long live Prince Heraclius! [*Exit.*]

SCENE II

Tellheim. How is it with me? My whole soul has got new
pinions. My own ill-fortune struck me down, made me
peevish, short-sighted, timid, lazy; her ill-fortune lifts me up
again. I can look around in freedom, and feel myself ready
and strong to undertake anything for her—why do I delay?
[*Steps towards the room of Mademoiselle, from which Francisca
comes out.*]

SCENE III

Francisca.   Tellheim.

Franc. O, it is you, then?   I fancied I heard your voice.   What is your wish, my dear Major?

Tellheim. What do I wish?   What is her Ladyship doing?   Come!

Franc. She is driving out presently.

Tellheim. And alone—without me?   Where to?

Franc. Have you forgotten, my dear Major?

Tellheim. Have you not understood, Francisca?   I have offended her and she was sensible of it; I shall beg her forgiveness and she will grant it.

Franc. How?   After you have taken back the ring, Major?

Tellheim. Ha!   I did that in the confusion.   I haven't thought of it since.   Where have I put it?   [*Searches.*] Here it is.

Franc. Is that it?   [*Whilst he pockets it again, aside.*] If he would only look at it closer!

Tellheim. She pressed it upon me with a bitterness—a bitterness I have already forgotten.   A full heart cannot weigh words.— But she will not hesitate a moment to put the ring on again. And have I not still got hers?

Franc. That she expects back in exchange.   Where have you got it, Major?   Show it me, please.

Tellheim. [*In some confusion.*] I have—forgotten—to put it on.—Just—Just will bring it me presently.

Franc. I know it is one exactly like the other, but let me see this one; I have such a fancy for these things.

Tellheim. Another time, Francisca.   Now, come . . .

Franc. [*Aside.*] He will not anyhow be got out of this mistake.

Tellheim. What do you say?   Mistake?

Franc. It is a mistake, say I, if you imagine Mademoiselle to be still a good match.   Her own fortune is small; a little careless handling by her guardians might bring it almost to nothing. All her expectations were from her uncle, but this terrible uncle . . .

Tellheim. Let him be!   Am I not man enough some day to indemnify her for everything?

Franc. Listen!   Her bell.   I must in.

Tellheim. I'll go with you.

Franc. Don't, for heaven's sake ! She has expressly forbidden me to speak with you. At least only come a bit after me. [*Goes in.*]

SCENE IV

Tellheim. [*Calling after her.*] Announce me to her ! Speak for me, Francisca ! I follow you immediately.—What shall I say to her?—Where the heart may speak no preparation is wanted.—One thing only takes some thinking about : her reserve, her hesitation to throw herself in her misfortune into my arms. Why still represent herself in a happy position, when through me she has lost it? This mistrust of my honour and of her own value, how justify it to herself? To me it is already justified ! Ha ! here she comes.

SCENE V

Mademoiselle. Francisca. Tellheim

Mad. [*Stepping out as if she did not see the Major.*] The carriage is at the door, Francisca ? My fan !

Tellheim. Where to, Mademoiselle ?

Mad. [*With assumed coolness.*] Out, Major.—I guess why you have troubled yourself again : it is to return my ring to me.— All right, Major; be good enough to hand it to Francisca. Take the ring, Francisca.—I have no time to lose.

Tellheim. [*Stepping before her.*] My Lady, my Lady ! Ah, what have I heard ! I was not worthy of so much love.

Mad. What, Francisca ? You have told the Major . . .

Francisca. Everything.

Tellheim. Do not be angry with me, dear Lady. I am no traitor. You have in the eyes of the world lost much on my account, but not in mine. In my eyes you have won infinitely by this loss. It was too new to you ; you were afraid it would make a terribly unpleasant impression upon me ; you wanted to hide it at first. I don't complain of this mistrust. It sprang from the desire to retain my affection. This desire is my pride ! You found me unfortunate, and wished not to heap up misfortune on misfortune. You could not guess how your unhappiness would make my own as nothing.

Mad. All very well, Major ! But it is done now. I have released you from your promise. By taking back your ring you have . . .

Tellheim. Consented to nothing ! Much rather do I hold myself now more bound than ever.—You are mine, Minna, for ever mine. [*Draws out the ring.*] Here, receive it for the second time, the pledge of my fidelity . . .

Mad. I receive again this ring ? *This* ring ?

Tellheim. Yes, dearest Minna, yes !

Mad. What are you asking of me ? *This* ring ?

Tellheim. This ring you took from my hand the first time, when the circumstances of us both were alike and were happy. They are no longer happy, but again they are alike. Equality is always the firmest bond of love.—Permit me, dearest Minna ! [*Seizes her hand, to put the ring on her finger.*]

Mad. How ? By force, Major ? No, there is no force in the world that can compel me to put on this ring again !—Do you perhaps think I'm in need of a ring ? O, you can see quite well [*pointing to her ring*] that I still have one here, not a whit inferior to yours.

Franc. Goodness ! If even now he doesn't notice it !

Tellheim. [*Letting go her hand.*] What is that ? I see Mademoiselle of Barnhelm, but I do not hear her voice. You disguise yourself, Mademoiselle. Forgive me that I repeat this word after you . . .

Mad. [*In her own tone.*] Has this word offended you, Major ?

Tellheim. It has hurt me.

Mad. [*Touched.*] That it ought not, Tellheim.—Forgive me, Tellheim.

Tellheim. Ha ! this familiar tone tells me that you are coming to yourself, my dear Lady ; that you still love me, Minna.

Franc. [*Blurts out.*] The joke would soon go too far.

Mad. [*Imperiously.*] No meddling in our game, Francisca, if I may beg you !

Franc. [*Aside and taken aback.*] Not enough yet ?

Mad. Yes, my dear sir ; it would be womanish vanity to pretend to be cold and scornful. That be far from me ! You deserve to find me just as true as you yourself are.—I love you still, Tellheim, I love you still ; but nevertheless . . .

Tellheim. Say no more, dearest Minna, say no more ! [*Grasps her hand once more, to put on the ring.*]

Mad. [*Drawing her hand away.*] Nevertheless, all the more am I resolved this shall never happen—never ! Where would you, my dear Major ?—I should think you had enough in your own ill-fortune.—You must remain here ; you must exact the fullest satisfaction—defiantly. I know at the moment no

other word. *Defiantly*—even if the extremest destitution
consume you before the eyes of your calumniators !

Tellheim. So thought I, and so said when I did not know what I
thought and said.   Anger and suppressed rage had clouded my
whole soul; love itself, in the fullest brightness of success,
could not make daylight in the fog.   But she sends her
daughter, Pity, who, knowing better what gloom and pain
can be, disperses the mist and opens again all the inlets of my
spirit to the impressions of tenderness.   The instinct of self-
preservation awakes, since I have something more precious
than myself to preserve, and to preserve by my own strength.
Do not let the word " pity " offend you, dear Lady.   When we
are innocent of our own misfortunes, we can hear it without
humiliation.   I am the cause here; it is through me, Minna,
that you lose friends and kindred, property and country.
Through me, in me you must find them all again, or else I
have on my soul the destruction of the most lovable of her
sex.   Let me not forecast a future in which I must hate
myself.—No, nothing shall keep me in this place any longer.
From this very moment on I will oppose to the injustice that
oppresses me here nothing but contempt.   Is this country the
world ?   Is it here only the sun rises ?   Where may I not go ?
What employment will be refused me ?   And if I had to seek
it under the most distant sky, only follow me in confidence,
dearest Minna.   We shall want for nothing.   I have a friend
who will be proud to help me.—

SCENE VI

A King's Messenger.   Tellheim.   Mademoiselle.   Francisca

Franc. [*Noticing the King's Messenger.*] Hist ! Major . . .

Tellheim. [*To the King's Messenger.*] Whom do you want ?

K.'s M. I'm looking for Major Tellheim.   Ah ! it is yourself, sir.
I have to deliver to you, sir, this royal letter. [*Taking it from a
letter case.*]

Tellheim. To me ?

K.'s M. According to the address.

Mad. Francisca, do you hear that ?   The Chevalier, after all,
was right !

K.'s M. [*Tellheim meantime taking the letter.*] I beg pardon,
Major Tellheim; you ought to have received it before
this ; but it was not possible for me to find you.   Only to-day

at the parade I learnt of your lodging from Lieutenant
Riccaut.

Franc. Do you hear that, your Ladyship? That is the
Chevalier's " Minister." " Vat is he called, ze Minister, down
zere at ze Square ? "

Tellheim. I am much obliged to you for your trouble.

K.'s M. My duty, Major ! [*Exit.*]

Scene VII

Tellheim.   Mademoiselle.   Francisca

Tellheim. Ah ! my dear Lady, what have I here ? What does
this letter contain ?

Mad. I am not entitled to carry my curiosity so far.

Tellheim. What ? you still part my fate from your own ? But
why do I hesitate to open it ? It cannot make me more unfortunate than I am ; no, dearest Minna, it cannot make us
more unfortunate ; but maybe more fortunate ! Permit me,
your Ladyship. [*Opens and reads the letter, whilst meantime
the Landlord has slipped upon the scene.*]

Scene VIII

Landlord.   The Same.

Landlord. [*Approaching Francisca.*] Hist ! pretty one ! One
word !

Franc. You, landlord ?—Indeed, we don't ourselves know what's
in the letter.

Landlord. Who wants to know about the letter ? I come about
the ring. Her Ladyship must return it at once. Just is
here, he is to redeem it.

Mad. [*Who meanwhile has come towards the landlord.*] Will you
tell Just, please, that it already is redeemed, and tell him, too,
by whom ; by me.

Landlord. But . . .

Mad. I take it all upon myself. You need not wait !

[*Landlord exit.*]

SCENE IX

Tellheim. Mademoiselle. Francisca

Franc. And now, my Lady, make it all right with the poor Major.

Mad. My dear intercessor ! As if the knot must not presently unloose itself.

Tellheim. [*After reading, in great excitement.*] Ha ! here too he has not belied himself ! O, my dear Lady, what justice ! what kindness ! This is more than I expected ! more than I deserve ! My fortune, my honour, everything restored ! Surely I do not dream it ? [*Looking once more in the letter, to convince himself.*] No, it is no illusion of my desires ! Read for yourself, my dear Lady ; read for yourself !

Mad. I am not so immodest, my dear Major.

Tellheim. Immodest ? The letter is to me—your Tellheim, Minna. It contains—what your uncle cannot take from us. You must read it. Do read it.

Mad. If it will do you a favour, my dear Major. [*Takes the letter and reads.*] " My dear Major Tellheim, I desire to inform you that the affair which made me solicitous as to your honour has been cleared up entirely in your favour. My brother has learned all particulars of the case, and his evidence has proved you more than innocent. The State Treasury has orders to deliver to you again the bill in question, and to repay the advances made ; and I have further commanded that everything which the Army Treasurers urge against your accounts shall be quashed. Report to me, whether your health will allow you to take service again. I should be sorry to part with a man of your valour and character. I am your well-affectioned King, &c."

Tellheim. Well, what say you to that, my Lady ?

Mad. [*Closing and returning the letter.*] I ? nothing !

Tellheim. Nothing ?

Mad. Well, yes : that your King, who is a great man, is surely also a good man. But how does that concern me ? He is not my King.

Tellheim. And do you say nothing else ? Nothing about ourselves ?

Mad. You enter his service again ; the Major will be Lieutenant-Colonel ; perhaps Colonel. I congratulate you most sincerely.

Tellheim. And you know me no better than that ? No, as fortune

gives me back what is sufficient to satisfy the wishes of a
sensible man, it will depend simply on my Minna whether in
future I shall belong to anyone but her. To her service alone
be my whole life dedicated ! The service of the great is a
dangerous one, and does not repay the trouble, the servitude,
the humiliation which it costs. Minna is not one of the vain
creatures who value in their husband's love only their titles
and their honours. She will love me for myself; and for her
I will forget the whole world. I became a soldier for pure
partisanship, I don't know myself for what political principles,
and from the notion that it was a good thing for every honourable man, for a time to endeavour in this condition to make
himself acquainted with all that is called danger and to learn
coolness and resoluteness. Only utter necessity could ever
have forced me to make a vocation of this experiment, a handicraft of this casual employment. And now, when nothing
any longer compels me, I have only one ambition, and that is,
to be a quiet and contented man. This, my dearest Minna,
with you I shall infallibly become, and continue so, un-
changeably, in your society. To-morrow we shall be united
by the holiest of ties, and then we will look about us and find
of the whole habitable earth the peacefullest, cheerfullest,
brightest corner, that wants nothing for a paradise but a happy
pair. There we will live; there every one of our days. . . . What
is it, my dear Lady ? [*Who moves uneasily hither and thither,
seeking to hide her emotion.*]

Mad. [*Composing herself.*] O Tellheim, it is dreadful of you to
describe so charmingly a happiness which I must renounce.
My loss . . .

Tellheim. Your loss ?—What do you call your loss ? Whatever
Minna can lose is not Minna. You are still the sweetest,
loveliest, best, most adorable creature under the sun ; all
goodness and great-heartedness, all innocence and joy. Now
and then a little sauciness ; here and there a trifle of self-will.
So much the better ! so much the better ! Minna would
otherwise be an angel, whom I must worship with trembling,
whom I could not love. [*Seizes her hand to kiss it.*]

Mad. [*Withdrawing her hand.*] No, no, sir ! Why so changed all
at once ?—Is this flattering, ardent lover the reserved and
passionless Tellheim ? Could only his returning good-fortune
set him thus on fire ? He must allow me, in this transient
ardour of his, to take thought for both.—When he himself
could reflect, I heard him say it would be a worthless love that

could think nothing of exposing its object to contempt.—
True, but I aspire to just as pure and noble a love as he.—
And now, when honour calls him, when a great monarch
courts him, ought I to suffer him to give himself up to dreams
of love? the famous warrior to degenerate into the amorous
shepherd of a pastoral comedy?—No, my dear Major, follow
you the beckoning of your better fate. . . .

Tellheim. Then, be it so! If the great world, Minna, charms you
more, be it so: let the great world take us for its own! How
little, how poverty-stricken is this same great world! You
know it as yet only from its glittering side. But surely,
Minna, you will. . . . So be it! That be our destiny!
Enviers of my happiness will not be scarce, nor will your
perfections lack their worshippers.

Mad. No, Tellheim, that is not my meaning. I point you to
the great world, back to the path of honour, without wishing
to follow you there.—There Tellheim needs an irreproachable
wife! A runaway Saxon girl, who threw herself at his head . . .

Tellheim. [*Getting up and looking fiercely about him.*] Who dare
say such things?—Ah, Minna, I am afraid of myself when I
imagine anybody else saying this but you. My rage would
not allow of limits.

Mad. Yes, that is it! That is just what troubles me. You
would not suffer the slightest raillery about me, and yet every
day you would have to listen to bitter things. In one word,
Tellheim, let me tell you what I have firmly resolved, what
nothing in the world will move me from . . .

Tellheim. Before you finish, Mademoiselle, I entreat you, Minna!
consider a moment that it is a sentence of life or death for me
you are uttering! . . .

Mad. I need no further consideration! As surely as I have
returned the ring, with which you have plighted me your
troth, as surely as you have taken this same ring, so surely
shall the unhappy Barnhelm never become the wife of the more
happy Tellheim!

Tellheim. Is it so you condemn me to death, Mademoiselle?

Mad. Equality alone is the firm bond of love.—The fortunate
Barnhelm had no other wish than to live for the fortunate
Tellheim. And the unfortunate Minna would at last have
been persuaded to share the ill-fortune of her friend, whether
for better or for worse. He perceived that well, before this
letter arrived which once more removed all equality between
us, however much I may have seemed still to hesitate.

U

Tellheim. Is that the truth, my Lady? I thank you, Minna, that you have not yet sentenced me. It is only an unfortunate Tellheim you wish for? He is at your service. [*Coolly.*] I now realise that it does not become me to accept this belated justice; that it will be better if I entirely decline what has been robbed of honour by a disgraceful suspicion.—Yes; I will not have received the letter. Be this my only reply to it. [*Makes as if to tear it.*]

Mad. [*Seizing his hands.*] What would you do, Tellheim? What is your wish?

Tellheim. To have you for my own.

Mad. Stop!

Tellheim. Mademoiselle, it will certainly be torn in pieces if you do not soon change your purpose. And then we will see what you have still to object to in me!

Mad. How? in this tone?—Then I am to, I must, become despicable in my own eyes? Never! She is a worthless creature who is not ashamed to owe her entire fortune, her whole happiness, to the blind tenderness of a man!

Tellheim. False, utterly false!

Mad. Will you venture to condemn your own words in my mouth?

Tellheim. Sophistress! Then does the weaker sex dishonour itself by everything which is unbecoming to the stronger? Or is a man to allow himself all that is fitting enough for a woman? Which did Nature appoint to be the support of the other?

Mad. Compose yourself, Tellheim! I shall not be without protection even if I must decline the honour of yours. So much will at least be left me as necessity requires. I have had an introduction to-day to our Consul. I hope he will look after my interests. But, time flies. Permit me, Major . . .

Tellheim. I will accompany your Ladyship.

Mad. Please, not now, Major; leave me now . . .

Tellheim. Sooner shall your shadow forsake you! Come only, my Lady; wherever you will, to whom you will. Everywhere, to friend or stranger, I will relate: to their faces a hundred times a day relate what bonds unite you to me, and by what terrible self-will you wish to break these bonds. . . .

SCENE X

Just.   The Same

Just. [*Bursting in.*] Major ! Major !

Tellheim. Well?

Just. Come quick, quick !

Tellheim. What am I to do?   Here, to me ! Tell me, what's wrong ?

Just. Listen only. [*Whispers to him.*]

Mad. [*Aside to Francisca.*] Do you notice anything, Francisca?

Franc. O, you ruthless one !   I stood here as if on burning coals.

Tellheim. What do you tell me?   It is not possible !—She ! Say it aloud ; say it to her face ! Listen, your Ladyship.

Just. The Landlord says the Lady of Barnhelm has taken to herself the ring that I pledged with him ; she recognised it for her own, and would not give it back. . . .

Tellheim. Is that true, your Ladyship?   No, it cannot be true !

Mad. [*Smiling.*] And why not, Tellheim? Why can't it be true ?

Tellheim. [*Hotly*]. Well, then let it be true ! What a horrible light has in a moment risen before me ! Now I recognise her, the false and faithless one !

Mad. Who?   Who is this faithless one ?

Tellheim. She whom I will no longer name.

Mad. Tellheim !

Tellheim. Forget my name ! You came here to break with me. It is clear !—How willingly accident comes to the help of the faithless. It brought your ring into your hands. Your cunning knew how by stealth to procure mine.

Mad. Tellheim, what spectres you behold ! Be calm and hear me.

Franc. [*Sotto voce.*] Now let her have it !

SCENE XI

Werner (with a bag of gold).   Tellheim.   Mademoiselle.
Francisca.   Just

Werner. Here I am again, Major . . .

Tellheim. [*Without looking up.*] Who wants you ?

Werner. Here is the money ; one thousand pistoles !

Tellheim. I don't want them !

Werner. To-morrow, Major, you may command as much again.

Tellheim. Keep your money !

Werner. But it is *your* money, Major.—I believe you don't see to whom you are speaking !

Tellheim. Take it away, I say !

Werner. What's the matter with you ?   I am Werner.

Tellheim. All kindness is pretence, all service treachery.

Werner. Does that apply to me ?

Tellheim. As you like !

Werner. I have only carried out your orders, you know—

Tellheim. Then go on doing so, and get out !

Werner. Major ! [*angrily*] I am a fellow . . .

Tellheim. Then you are all right !

Werner. Who also has a temper . . .

Tellheim. Very good !   Temper is the best thing we have.

Werner. I beg you, Major . . .

Tellheim. How often must I tell you ?   I don't want your money !

Werner. [*In a rage.*] Well, want it who will ! [*Throws the bag at his feet and steps aside.*]

Mad. [*To Francisca.*] Ah, my dear Francisca, I should have listened to you. I have carried the joke too far. Still he might surely hear me . . . [*Approaching him.*]

Franc. [*Who, without answering her Ladyship, approaches Werner.*]   Mr. Sergeant-Major !

Werner. [*Sullenly.*] Go along !

Franc. Hu ! what sort of gentlemen are these !

Mad. Tellheim !—Tellheim ! [*Who bites his nails with rage, turns away his face and hears nothing.*] No, that is too bad ! Hear me only !   You deceive yourself !   A sheer misunderstanding—Tellheim !   Will you not hear your Minna ?   Can you entertain such a suspicion ?   I wish to break with you ? I come here for that ?   Tellheim !

SCENE XII

Two servants, running the one after the other from opposite sides into the salon. The Same.

1st *Servant.* Your Excellency, your Grace—the Count !—

2nd *Servant.* He comes, your Ladyship !

Francisca. [*Who has run to the window.*] It is he ! it is he !

Mad. Is it he ?—O now, one moment, Tellheim . . .

Tellheim. [*At once coming to himself.*] Who? who comes? Your Uncle, my Lady? this terrible Uncle? Let him come only, let him come! Don't be afraid! Let him dare only offend you with a look! It is with me he'll have to do.— You indeed do not deserve it at my hands—

Mad. Quickly embrace me, Tellheim, and forget all . . .

Tellheim. Ha, if I but knew that you could regret it!

Mad. I cannot regret having obtained this view of your whole heart! Ah! what a man you are! Embrace your Minna, your happy Minna! and in nothing happier than in you! [*Falls into his arms.*] And now, to meet him!

Tellheim. To meet whom?

Mad. The best of your unknown friends.

Tellheim. What? Whom?

Mad. The Count, my uncle, my father, your father. . . . My flight, his ill-will, my disinheritance—don't you see that was all imaginary? credulous knight!

Tellheim. Imaginary? But the ring? the ring?

Mad. Where have you got the ring I returned to you?

Tellheim. You will take it again? O, then I am happy. Here, Minna! [*Taking it out.*]

Mad. Well, look at it first! O blind men who will not see! Which ring is it? The one I had from you, or that you had from me? Isn't it the very one I would not leave in the landlord's hands?

Tellheim. Heavens! what do I see? what do I hear?

Mad. Say, shall I take it once more? shall I?—Give it me, give it me! [*Snatches it from his hand and herself puts it on her finger.*] Well, now, is everything right?

Tellheim. Where am I? [*Kissing her hand.*] O you wicked angel! to torture me so!

Mad. Just for a sign, my dear husband, that you shall never play me a trick but I shall straightway play you another?— Do you imagine that you had not tortured me too?

Tellheim. O you comediennes, I ought to have known you better.

Franc. No, really; I am spoilt for a comedienne. I trembled and quivered, and was obliged to hold my hand before my face.

Mad. Nor was my rôle quite an easy one.—But now, come!

Tellheim. I am not quite recovered yet. All right, but nervous to death! Just like a man waking suddenly out of a horrible dream!

Mad. We must not delay.—I hear his footstep.

Scene XIII

*Count Bruchsall (accompanied by various servants and the land-
lord). The Same.*

Count. [*Entering.*] She has safely arrived, then?

Mad. [*Running to him.*] Ah, my father!

Count. Here I am, my dear Minna! [*Embracing her.*] But what
is this, my girl? [*Noticing Tellheim.*] Only four-and-twenty
hours here, and already acquaintance, already company?

Mad. Guess who it is!

Count. Never your Tellheim?

Mad. Who else but he?—Come, Tellheim! [*Leading him to the
Count.*]

Count. My dear sir, we have never seen each other before; but
at the first glance I thought I recognised you. I wished that
it might be you.—Give me your hand.—You have my entire
good-will. I ask you for your friendship. My niece, my
daughter loves you.

Mad. That you know, father!—And is it blind, this love of
mine?

Count. No, Minna; your love is not blind, but your lover—is
dumb.

Tellheim. Let me come to myself, my father!

Count. Right, my son! I can hear that if your mouth cannot
talk, your heart is eloquent.—As a rule I am not very fond of
officers of this colour. [*Pointing to Tellheim's uniform.*] But
you are an honourable man, Tellheim; and an honourable
man may put on any dress he will, we must still love him.

Mad. Ah! if only you knew all.

Count. What is to prevent my hearing all? Where are my
rooms, landlord?

Landlord. Will your Excellency be good enough to step this
way?

Count. Come on, Minna! Come, our Major! [*Exit, with the
landlord and servants.*]

Mad. Come, Tellheim.

Tellheim. I follow you this moment, my dear Lady. But just
one word first with this man. [*Turning to Werner.*]

Mad. And a right good word, too; I think it is due. What do
you think, Francisca? [*Following the Count.*]

Scene XIV

Tellheim. Werner. Just. Francisca

Tellheim. [*Pointing to the bag which Werner has thrown away.*] Here, Just!—lift up the bag, and carry it home. Go!
[*Exit Just, with the bag.*

Werner. [*Who has been standing sullenly in the corner, and apparently taken no notice of anything : hearing this.*] Yes, I see!

Tellheim. [*In friendly manner approaching him.*] Werner, when can I have the other thousand pistoles?

Werner. [*At once resuming his good humour.*] To-morrow, Major, to-morrow.

Tellheim. I do not require to become your debtor; but I will be your treasurer. You good-hearted people should be put in charge of a guardian. You are a species of spendthrifts.— I moved you to anger just now, Werner!

Werner. Yes, by my soul! But I should not have been such a blockhead. I can understand it all now. I deserved a hundred lashes. Give orders for me to have them; only no more ill-will, my dear Major!

Tellheim. Ill-will. [*Pressing his hand.*] Read in my eyes all that I cannot speak. Ha! if there's a man who has a better girl and a trustier friend than I have, I should like to meet him.—Isn't that right, Francisca? [*Exit.*]

Scene XV

Werner. Francisca

Franc. [*Aside.*] Yes, indeed, he is a genuine good fellow.— I shall never come across such another—it must out! [*Shyly and bashfully approaching Werner.*] Mr. Sergeant-Major . . .

Werner. [*Who is wiping his eyes.*] Well?

Franc. Mr. Sergeant-Major . . .

Werner. What's your will, little woman?

Franc. Look at me, please, Mr. Sergeant-Major . . .

Werner. I can't just yet; I don't know what has got in my eyes.

Franc. Look at me, now, do!

Werner. I'm afraid I have already looked at you too often, little woman!—Well, I see you there! What's up?

Franc. Mr. Sergeant-Major . . . don't you want a *Mrs.* Sergeant-Major?

Werner. Are you in earnest, little woman?

Franc. Entirely!

Werner. And would you set off with me for Persia?

Franc. Wherever you will!

Werner. Truly? Hullo, Major! Isn't it capital? Here! I have just as good a girl as you, and as trusty a friend! Give me your hand, little woman! Done!—Let ten years go, and she will be either Lady General, or Widow!

PRINTED BY RICHARD CLAY & SONS, LTD., AT BUNGAY, SUFFOLK, IN GREAT BRITAIN.

EVERYMAN'S LIBRARY

A LIST OF THE 850 VOLUMES
ARRANGED UNDER AUTHORS

Anonymous works are given under titles.
Anthologies, Dictionaries, etc. are arranged at the end of the list.

NOTE—The following numbers are at present out of print:
110, 111, 146, 228, 244, 275, 390, 418, 565, 597, 664

LONDON: J. M. DENT & SONS LTD.
NEW YORK: E. P. DUTTON & CO. INC.

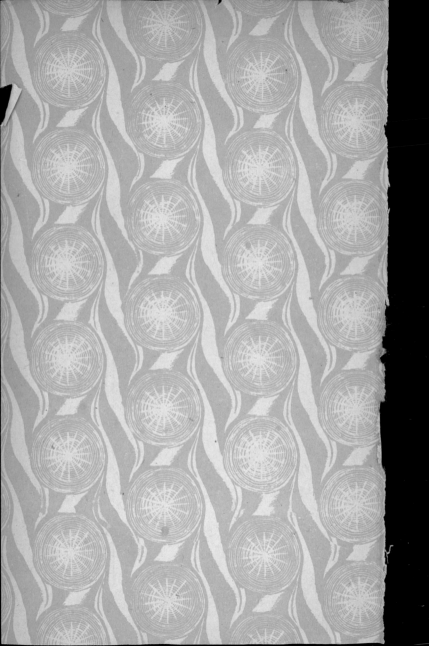